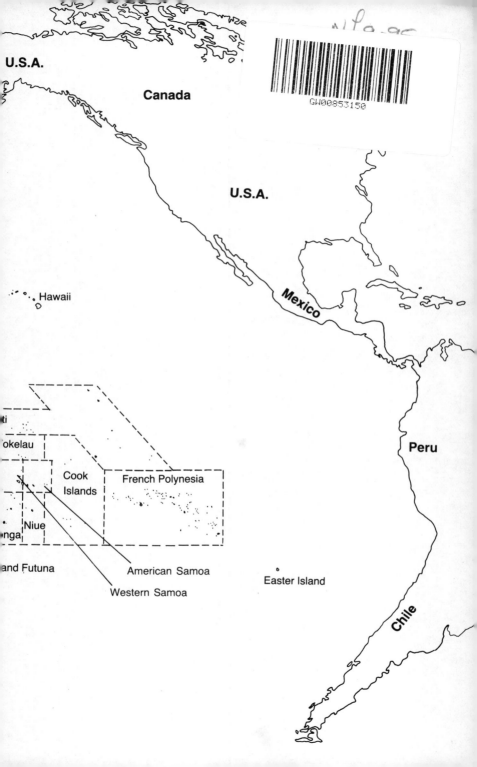

U.S.A.

Canada

U.S.A.

Hawaii

Mexico

Peru

ti

okelau

Cook
Islands

French Polynesia

Niue

nga

and Futuna

American Samoa

Western Samoa

Easter Island

Chile

THE SOUTH PACIFIC

THE SOUTH PACIFIC

AN INTRODUCTION

Ron Crocombe

Published in association with the
University of the South Pacific

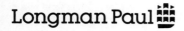

Longman Paul Limited
182–190 Wairau Road, Auckland 10,
New Zealand

Associated companies, branches, and
representatives throughout the world

The New South Pacific first published 1973
by Reed Education, revised and reprinted
1978. Published as *The South Pacific*, with
substantial additions and amendments, by
Longman Paul 1983, and further updated
for the 1987 edition.

ISBN 0 582 71813 9

All royalties from this book are used to
finance writing and research by Pacific
islands writers.

Produced by Longman Paul Limited
Typeset in 10/12 Palatino
Printed in Hong Kong

Contents

Preface

This small book aims to provide a brief and personal view of some major trends in the past, present, and possible future of the diverse and stimulating societies of the world's most widely scattered region. It was prepared as a set of talks in an extension series for a general audience at the University of the South Pacific. The New Zealand Broadcasting Commission then requested the series for use on radio, and the publishers asked for publication rights after the broadcasts.

The book is concerned mainly with the Pacific today, but emphasises that much of what happens today is conditioned, in varying degrees, by what happened yesterday, both within the Pacific and beyond. It also includes some exploratory projections into the future of the Pacific islands. No one can be definitive on such a topic, but it is a matter of such widespread concern that some discussion of issues and alternatives seems to be warranted.

The bibliography and notes on further readings, like the text, do not aim to be comprehensive, but rather to enable those with an interest in particular topics to follow them a stage further.

Ron Crocombe
University of the South Pacific

Acknowledgements

People who have kindly commented on particular sections of this book include Dr Gerald Arbuckle, Dr Terry Crowley, Mr Inoke Faletau, Dr John Garrett, Dr John Harré, Dr Geoffrey Hayes, Mr A. V. Hughes, Mr Joe Kamikamica, Dr Sione Latukefu, Dr Brian Lockwood, Masiofo Fetaui Mata'afa, Dr George Milner, Dr Rusiate Nayacakalou, Ms Anaseini Qionibaravi, Ms Susan Tarua, Hon Whetu Tirikatene-Sullivan, Mr Sione Tupouniua, Professor Albert Wendt, and Reverend Akuila Yabaki. Their views have been greatly appreciated.

For permission to use photographs grateful acknowledgement is made to Air New Zealand; *Kalonikali*, Tonga; Department of Information, Papua New Guinea; Volunteer Service Abroad; National Publicity Studios; *The Dominion*; Mr James Siers; *Auckland Star*; Dr John Garrett; *Fiji Times*; Mr Aloi Pilioko; TV News, New Zealand Broadcasting Corporation; *NZ Herald*; Mr Bruce Saunders; Mr Malcolm Botterill; *Pacific Islands Monthly* and Chris Plant.

PARAMETERS

1
People
A history of movement

Early migrations

Almost all the people, plants, and animals in the Pacific originated from Asia in the distant past. The first people probably
arrived about 50 000 years ago, moving from what is now
Indonesia into western New Guinea. At that time human technology was very simple, and canoe transport probably did not
yet exist. The water spaces between Indonesia and New
Guinea were then much narrower than today because the level
of the sea was considerably lower, so the crossings were probably made by raft or log, or even possibly by swimming.[1]
Though an earlier form of man had lived in the Indonesian
region for much longer, modern man (*homo sapiens*) seems to
have been there for a relatively short time (though still some
thousands of years) before spreading to New Guinea and
Australia.

The migrants presumably came in extremely small numbers,
at very long intervals of time, and probably in situations of
crisis — either escaping or being blown away. Most would
have died out, but on the few occasions when they had
females with them a new human community could develop.
These early settlers lived by hunting and gathering, which
necessitates a very large area of land to support an individual
— perhaps only one or two people per square kilometre. They
continued to filter into and spread over this huge and rugged
island but their technology did not enable them to get much
past Australia. The adjustment to the extremely diverse
climatic and biotic environments of that region must have
caused both acute suffering and its consequence — fast
learning for those who survived.

With the ending of the last Ice Age, sea levels throughout the world rose slowly over a period from 8000 to 10 000 years ago. This covered an extensive area of land with what we now call the Torres Straits and the Arafura Sea, and separated New Guinea from Australia. Thus a secondary migration to northern Australia about 7000 years ago (presumably direct from the Indonesia region) brought some cultural changes to Australia which did not affect New Guinea. Likewise, there is evidence of new migrants to New Guinea, and the evolution of agriculture and pig husbandry there over the past 8000 years or so, whereas neither reached Australia. Though Australians and New Guineans have common first ancestors, then, subsequent genetic and cultural infusions to each seem not to have had any significant impact on the other.

Agriculture, the domestication of animals and minor improvements in technology had been evolving slowly in Southeast Asia, and no doubt occasional migrants or castaways scattered elements of those new cultural systems along the northwestern coasts of New Guinea. Unlike hunting and gathering, efficient agriculture can support about one hundred people per square kilometre, so population multiplied.

Among other things, later immigrants from Asia who lived by fishing and agriculture, brought pottery, a new kind of stone technology, and the manufacture of bark cloth. The technology of bark cloth-making, and even the words for it in many Pacific languages, can be traced back to the South of China.[2] They also brought more efficient techniques of water transport. There is archaeological evidence of their being settled in the New Britain/New Ireland area more than 5000 years ago, and having consolidated there for more than a thousand years before, probably as a result of developments in canoe technology combined with population growth, they expanded slowly southeastwards in the only direction of reasonably close available land, through the long chain of Solomon Islands and Vanuatu, which seems to have become the next focal point of consolidation and then of further dispersal. Canoe transport was presumably being refined and developed with time and changing environmental conditions, and the growing population of these coastal fishermen would also have led to an increasing number of canoes on the water, irrespective of purpose.

The move south from Vanuatu to the Loyalty Islands and New Caledonia did not involve great distances, but from there south and east lie vast expanses of open water, and there is no evidence of these people having reached New Zealand or Australia. Some sailed from Vanuatu across the greatest stretches of ocean yet encountered (or yet crossed with evidence of survival), north to Micronesia and east to Fiji, where the earliest archaeological evidence shows their having arrived at least 3500 years ago.

These endless minor movements, over many thousands of years, involved very small numbers of diverse peoples. The diversity resulting from the small size and relative isolation of each group is reflected in the fact that the 5 000 000 people of Melanesia speak over 1100 languages. Linguistic fragmentation is greater in Melanesia than anywhere else in the world; so much so that nearly one-quarter of all the world's languages are in Melanesia.[3]

Fiji, which is isolated by considerable distances, became the next focus of consolidation. The diversity of human language and culture, like the number of species of plants, birds and animals, reduces sharply from Fiji eastward, and for the same reasons: the decreasing size and increasing isolation of the islands, and consequent difficulty of access and establishment. Only the ancestors of those people now known as Polynesian, all of whose languages and cultures are closely related, reached beyond Fiji.

The track of archaeological evidence, which is generally confirmed by linguistic and genetic research, traces the movement east from Fiji through the Lau Islands to its closest neighbour, Tonga, and thence to the next nearest lands: Niue and Samoa, where human settlement was established 2500 years ago.

The next expansion, with the possible exception of Tokelau (480 kilometres to the north) and the northern Cook Islands, where extensive archaeological research has not yet been undertaken, seems not to have taken place until some hundreds of years later. This is understandable given the vast distances that isolate Samoa, as well as the physical structure of those islands and the present wind and current patterns around them, which are not as conducive to the development of long-range voyaging as the scattered archipelagos of Tonga or Fiji for example. This makes it the more surprising that when the expansion did occur it was not to Samoa's closest neighbours (The Cook and Society Islands) but in an enormous leap of nearly 4000 kilometres to the Marquesas, about 1900 years ago. It could have been reached in a single voyage, as much more recent examples show that this would be possible though extremely difficult, and there is no indication of any intermediate population. From the Marquesas there is clear evidence of movement over enormous distances in every direction in which land existed (and probably also in every direction in which it did not — though those would not survive) — north to Hawaii, southeast to Easter Island and southwest to Mangareva, the Tuamotu and Society Islands. This last became the new consolidation and dispersal point from which were derived the main immigrants to the Austral and Cook Islands and ultimately New Zealand, which was probably first settled nine hundred to one thousand years ago.[4]

Thus Polynesia became the last part of the earth's surface (Antarctica excluded) to be settled by man. How many epic voyages were involved in this, one of the greatest sagas of human history, we have little conception. At each place the immigrants seem to have consolidated and expanded over a number of generations before migrating to neighbouring small islands and then undertaking long-range movements. In addition to the major trends, there has always been a great deal of movement in all directions throughout the Pacific. Even in recent years drift voyages occur. A few years ago a small boat sailing from Rakahanga in the northern Cook Islands to Manihiki about forty kilometres distant, was caught in a storm and landed 3000 kilometres away in Vanuatu, more than two months later. There were only a few survivors.[5] In December 1975, three men set sail to travel between two islands of Kiribati but the one survivor reached an island in Truk six months later.[6] Every year several such incidents are reported from various parts of the Pacific. This sort of haphazard, small group movement, sometimes through crisis and sometimes through design, sometimes by navigation and sometimes by drift, and in a great diversity of directions, has occurred throughout the Pacific for hundreds of years.[7]

People and ideas from South America also reached the Pacific Islands in eastern Polynesia. That contact however was late, small, and culturally not very significant. There was some contact between parts of Polynesia and parts of America (quite probably in both directions) but almost all the economic plants came from Asia or western Melanesia. The sweet potato (kumara) is the main plant of South American origin, but even that was propagated in the islands by techniques derived from Southeast Asia rather than the Americas (see Yen, 1963). The major linguistic affiliations are clearly with Southeast Asia, though some South American influence is probable in Easter Island and possibly other parts of eastern Polynesia (see Langdon and Tryon, 1983). Culturally too, the dominant linkages seem to be westward, though the probability of some contacts from the Americas and elsewhere in Asia needs to be kept in mind. Current research should make the details of the picture much clearer before the end of this century.

The coming of Europeans

The next major phase in the history of the Pacific began about 400 years ago with the expansion of European influence. For over 1000 years Polynesia probably had the most highly developed sea transport in the world, but its continued evolution was restricted by its very small population, limited resources, and lack of metals. Polynesian marine technology had probably reached its peak at the time that European technology was making the major advances which led to the movement of people from Europe into the Pacific.[8]

Like the whole process of expansion that has been going on in the Pacific for thousands of years, this expansion from Europe brought new peoples into contact, sometimes to mutual advantage and therefore harmoniously, sometimes to apparent disadvantage and therefore with hostility and conflict. The areas most suited to migrants from Europe, because of similar environments, were Australia and New Zealand, which soon became settled by Europeans whose population multiplied rapidly. The Maoris had not exploited New Zealand's resources intensively, for after more than 900 years of occupation the Maori population had only grown to about 250 000. The adaptation of the tropical Maori technology to the cold climate, like any human adaptation, was very slow and was interrupted by the arrival of migrants from Europe.[9]

People often explain the contrast between the impact of European migrants on Aboriginal society in Australia and on Maori society in New Zealand in terms of the better quality of the English migrants in New Zealand. But the different adjustments made by the competing human populations in Australia and in New Zealand were much more influenced by the differences in indigenous demography, technology, ecology, and social organisation.

European settlement in the Pacific was intensive in temperate areas like Australia and New Zealand, substantial in New Caledonia and Hawaii which are marginally temperate, sparse and scattered in the tropical islands like the Solomons and New Guinea, and negligible on the atolls. People from Europe still find it very difficult to adjust to the more extreme tropical environments, especially deserts and atolls, to which their indigenous inhabitants have adjusted well.[10]

New migrants from Asia

There seems to be much more awareness of the Europeans who came to the Pacific than of the Asians. But in fact more Asians have come to the islands in the last 100 years than Europeans. By the time of their arrival, however, the dominant roles in government, commerce, missions, and the military were already taken by Europeans, and the Asian people came mainly as unskilled workers or small traders. In Hawaii and Fiji, Asians came to outnumber the indigenous people, although not nearly to the same extent as the European populations of New Zealand and Australia.

Both Asian and European immigrants were divided by nationality and by religion. The Chinese,[11] like the Europeans, spread throughout the Pacific, but the other Asian peoples were more localised — Indians mainly in Fiji;[12] Vietnamese and Indonesians mainly in New Caledonia;[13] some Indonesians and Filipinos in New Guinea; Japanese in the Marshalls, Marianas, and Carolines between 1914 and 1944 when they came to outnumber the Micronesians;[14] and large numbers of Japanese, Koreans, and other Asians in Hawaii.[15]

One reason for some misunderstanding between Asian and Islands people may relate to the pattern of their cultures as influenced by the food crops on which they depended. Indian and Chinese people grew up in cultures which had long been conditioned to grain crops. These necessitate careful husbandry, conservation, storage between seasons, and first priority being given to one's immediate family. Pacific Islanders, on the the other hand, depended on root crops and fruit crops (like bread-fruit and bananas), few of which were storable, and therefore the greatest gain lay in the widest possible distribution, creating a social investment which required recipients to give equivalent help when others were in need. So while the one food production system engendered a narrow definition of self-interest, the other called for the widest possible distribution. This was probably a factor in the development of different value systems and cultural patterns which still cause mis-understanding between peoples of the respective cultures. The effects of that conditioning from so long ago constitute major political issues in some islands today.

The largest Asian community in the Pacific is in Fiji, where 360 000 Indians outnumber the indigenous Fijians. There are much smaller Indian communities almost throughout the Pacific. In Fiji many of them are farmers, particularly in sugar growing; but in other Pacific countries they are almost all in technical or professional roles.

The status of Indians in the Pacific has been constrained by various factors. Only in Fiji are they a significant proportion of the population, but even there, partly because most came as unskilled workers, they have not achieved significant political or military power. Residential separation, occupational specialisation, different religions (most are Hindu, and Moslem, and a tiny minority Christian), the use of Hindi and other Indian languages, and their generally conscious wish to isolate themselves socially from Islanders, have led to the Indian communities being probably the most socially isolated in the Pacific. Unlike the Chinese, marriage between Indians and Islanders is rare.

These conditions will change slowly, as Asians begin to integrate more fully into their countries of citizenship, as more of them move as professionals to other Pacific countries, and as those who feel uncomfortable in the Pacific emigrate. While tens of thousands of Indians and Chinese have left the islands, many of the Indians in Fiji have no choice but to remain, owing to their numbers. Most Indians and Chinese came as under-privileged labourers, but through hard work, careful invest-ment and education of their children, many have prospered.

Non-indigenous movement today

Since the Second World War there has been a new pattern of population movement in the islands. Asian and European populations are withdrawing from places where they are a minority. Where they are a clear majority, as in Australia, New Zealand and Hawaii, they appear firmly entrenched. Where they are not a majority, the withdrawal is selective. Particularly in government, and to a lesser extent in the churches, foreign staff are being localised. But localisation has been much faster in political and administrative posts than in technical fields, and is much less evident in business. Most Vietnamese and Indonesians left New Caledonia some years ago, and returned to their original homelands. About 1000 Indians are moving each year from Fiji to Canada, the United States, New Zealand, and Australia — very few want to go anywhere in Asia. This flow could well increase. And there is a major inflow of Javanese into West New Guinea (Irian Jaya) in a planned Indonesian resettlement programme.[16]

At the same time new people are coming in, as volunteers (with Volunteer Service Association, Peace Corps, and other organisations), as employees of international agencies and multinational corporations, as technical specialists. Most stay for only a few years. And large numbers are coming as tour-ists, as increasing levels of income make people more mobile.[17] All these categories have been mainly European, but the proportion of non-European — especially Japanese and over-seas Chinese — is increasing significantly and exceeds Euro-peans in Micronesia.

Ethnic mixture

This whole process of movement has involved ethnic mixture. Of course ethnic mixture has been going on since the first settlement in the islands, and Pacific Islanders, like the rest of us, are of diverse ancestry. With the arrival of Europeans and Asians, new ethnic mixing took place to such an extent that probably there is no person of Hawaii, Tahiti, Marquesas, Cook Islands, or New Zealand who does not have some European, Asian, or other non-Polynesian blood, even though many are not aware of it. After all, the average young person of today has over 500 direct ancestors, not just relations, dating from Captain Cook's time, and nobody of any race or nation knows all his ancestors, even though he may know that small fraction of them that constitute one particular line.[18] To look at it another way, a child of one of Cook' men could easily have traces of his blood spread by now through more than 10 000 people.[19]

By contrast with the extensive race mixture in Eastern Polynesia, the races in Fiji were sharply segregated during the colonial era as a matter of government policy, reinforced by differences in language, culture, religion, and interests. The Fiji case illustrates the most marked separation in the whole Pacific area, yet even there ethnic mixture has been considerable. At the opposite extreme is Hawaii, where the majority of marriages contracted today are between persons of different racial origins, and the majority of children being born are of racially mixed ancestry.[20] The 'native' people of Guam, according to recent studies, are now approximately, 36 per cent European and 17 per cent Filipino in genetic origin.[21]

Islanders on the move

For 50 000 years this process of movement and mixture has been going on in the Pacific, slowly in some periods and places, faster in others. It is not generally realised that Pacific Islanders were much more on the move in the mid-1800s, when sailing ships and new employment opportunities were introduced, than they were in the mid-1900s. This was because by 1900 movement was restricted by the establishment of centralised governments, both colonial and national. We do not know what will happen in the next 50 000 years, but at the moment there are three trends in the movement of Pacific Islanders.[22]

The first is the movement from the small islands to the large ones: from various islands of the Gilbert group into Tarawa, from the smaller Cook Islands into Rarotonga, from over a hundred small islands of Fiji into the main island of Viti Levu, from the whole Tongan Archipelago into Tongatapu, and so on. This has gone so far in French Polynesia that many atolls are now uninhabited. In addition, there is a movement within the large islands into their urban capitals: from the rest of Viti Levu into Suva, from all over Tongatapu into Nuku'alofa, from the rest of Guadalcanal into Honiara, and so on.

Many Pacific Islanders today live in towns. In places like Hawaii and Guam, almost everyone does, and if we include all people living by urban or governmental employment, the number is well over half the people in the Cook Islands, and about half in Fiji. Even in the more isolated and scattered places like the Solomon Islands, 10 per cent of the whole population lives in the largest town, Honiara, and about one-quarter depend on wage labour for a living.[23]

A second pattern of movement of Pacific Islanders is from those Pacific countries which have fewer employment opportunities to those which have more: for example, from the Mariana and Caroline Islands to military-linked employment in Guam; from Kiribati to the phosphate mines of Nauru; from Tahiti, Vanuatu, the Loyalty Islands, Wallis and Futuna to the nickel industry in New Caledonia; and from Western Samoa to heavily subsidised American Samoa. The immigrants generally have to take on the less attractive jobs.

The third and latest movement is that from the Pacific Islands to the Pacific border-lands. There are twice as many Cook Islanders in New Zealand as in the Cook Islands, more Wallisians off the island than on it, four times as many Niueans outside Niue as in it, and three times as many American Samoans in the U.S.A. as in American Samoa. Tens of thousands of Western Samoans live in New Zealand and the U.S.A. Many Tahitians live permanently in New Caledonia, France, and elsewhere. About 1000 young Kiribati men work on overseas ships, mostly based in Europe. These and other opportunities will attract more and more Polynesians out of their present environment, but overseas migration opportunities for Melanesians and Micronesians are very few. The U.S.A. is likely to accept a large proportion of Micronesians from the Trust Territory in future, and Australia may accept more migration from the Pacific.

Migration from island Polynesia is extensive. In the sixties these Tokelau migrants flew to New Zealand, where now over 100 000 Islanders live.

The outflow is mainly of unskilled workers, but there is also a serious flow of scarce trained and talented Islanders from Polynesia and Fiji. The rich countries on the Pacific rim tend more to select immigrants in terms of value to themselves — in other words, of greatest loss to the Pacific. The islands could offset this by similarly offering citizenship to selected highly skilled technical and professional people (the category in short supply) who would come if assured of permanent residence. But islands parochialism (which is partly a backlash against former colonialism) is at present too strong to allow the islands to benefit from the very process by which other countries get some of their best talents. Instead, the islands either go without or use very high priced, short-term foreigners, often under 'aid' programmes, which generally result in less effective manpower at higher cost. The consolation prize to the islands is a feeling of power over foreigners.

The Pan-Pacific person

A remarkable pattern is emerging in the staffing of Pacific regional organisations, of which there are now over two hundred (as described in chapter 13). Obviously, they need staff with a multi-cultural, multi-national orientation, aware of the region's diversity and responsive to the demands it creates and constraints it imposes. While these qualities no doubt increase as a result of working in regional organisations, it seems that a common broad pattern of preconditions leads to a special category of persons being attracted to, and selected by, regional organisations.

Islanders who staff the regional institutions are predominantly persons of multiple worlds: at least two and often three or more. Most of them are drawn from that very small minority of their home populations that fits most of the following criteria.

1 They have lived abroad for long periods *but* spent their early childhood in the islands. (About a quarter of a million Pacific Islanders live in New Zealand, Australia, U.S.A., Canada, and and Europe, but I am not aware of even one of the large number born in those countries who has returned to work in a regional organisation, though many born in other Pacific Islands have done so.)

2 A very high proportion are descended from two or more ethnic categories — and/or adopted or brought up by persons of cultures other than that of their parents. (And a disproportionate number have valued blood ties to more than one Pacific country.)

3 A remarkably high percentage are married to spouses of different ethnicity from their own.

4 Most have experienced some years of multi-cultural schooling.

The higher the post, the more marked these trends tend to be.

The above factors are readily measured. One that is not, but which seems equally important, is attitude. Many — but far from all — of the people who fit most of the four criteria identify strongly with the wider Pacific and may at times feel even better adapted to serve a Pacific regional body than their own countries alone. Their *primary* identification is in almost all cases with one country and usually with one ethnic or geographical category within it. They are perhaps the forerunners of people who might become primarily Pacific people and secondarily nationals of a particular country, rather than the reverse. (This trend seems to be less pronounced where people are employed by a regional organisation but in their own country.)

Nevertheless, legitimacy in the region requires a strong national base. As Lorini Tevi, then Secretary of the Pacific Conference of Churches, and herself of Fijian and Chinese ancestry and married to a Tongan, observed: 'I could only be one of the forerunners of taking regional solidarity and co-operation seriously because of my strong base as a Fiji citizen, and proud to be one. Both national and regional are important to me.' Probably all staff of the regional organisations would agree with her.[24]

The reality of the modern Pacific is one of indigenous cultures deeply involved in interaction with a variety of foreign influences — predominantly at this stage with countries of European origin with capitalist economies. In selecting the top political leadership at home, Islanders are electing men who have mastery of both these worlds, rather than persons typical of their own nation (in contrast, for example, with the United Kingdom, Japan, China, U.S.S.R., U.S.A., or Australia, whose leaders are much more typical of the populations that elect them). Some of the principles involved are similar to those in staffing regional organisations, but others are quite different. These people in leading positions, and particularly those in Pacific-wide organisations, constitute important models for others. They are one of the forces leading to an increasing feeling of homogeneity and common identification in an ocean of great diversity.

A new Asian connection

The Pacific people came originally from Southeast Asia, although during the last 200 years they have been greatly influenced from Europe. Direct European influence is now small, but American influence has greatly increased and other

pressures come from Australia and New Zealand. The main
future external influence is again likely to come from Asia
(Japan and China particularly) with possible subsidiary influences next century from South America.

2
Culture
Unity in diversity

Polynesia, Micronesia, and Melanesia

The boundaries between these three major culture areas, as
elsewhere, are not precise, and there is a great deal of overlap.[1]
They all contained relatively small-scale societies, deriving their
livelihood mainly from subsistence farming and organised
mainly on the basis of relationship by blood and marriage.

Melanesia is by far the largest, and contains 97 per cent of
the land and 75 per cent of the population of the Pacific
Islands. Diversity is the keynote in Melanesia: diversity of
terrain and diversity of people. The main components are New
Guinea (including Papua New Guinea and West New Guinea
or Irian Jaya) with about 4 900 000 people, Solomon Islands
(276 000), Vanuatu (147 000), and New Caledonia (151 000).

Micronesia is a series of small islands lying mainly north of
the equator, with only about 360 000 people in total in Kiribati,
Nauru, the Marshall Islands, the Federated States of Micronesia, Paulau (Belau), Guam, and the Mariana Islands. Most
people on Guam are directly or indirectly associated with the
American military or with tourism. Many of them are not
Micronesian.

Despite great distances, Polynesian cultures have much in
common. The points of the Polynesian triangle are New
Zealand at the bottom, Hawaii at the top, and Easter Island in
the far east. Within the triangle are Tonga, Samoa, Niue,
Tuvalu, Tokelau, Cook Islands, Tahiti, and other islands. The
Polynesian population today is about 1 000 000, which is a little
more than it was 200 years ago when Captain Cook arrived.
Last century the island populations fell drastically, mainly as
a result of epidemics, but this century they have regained their
former levels and are now increasing rapidly.

Fiji can be regarded as part of Melanesia or Polynesia or of both. The late Dr Nayacakalou, a Fijian anthropologist, once joked that the bodies of Fijians were Melanesian but their cultures Polynesian. There is some truth in this, for physically Fijians are similar to many other Melanesian peoples, but their culture has more in common with Polynesia. Fiji has for centuries been a region of contact and mixture between Pacific peoples. Indigenous Fijians now comprise only 46 per cent of the country's 714 000 people. Indians, mostly third and fourth generation Fiji-born, comprise 49 per cent. Family planning and emigration has led to their proportion of Fiji's population reducing slightly. Culturally, they are anxiously ambivalent about how far to identify with Indian language, religion, and culture, and how far to identify with the politically dominant Fijians. Small numbers of Europeans, Chinese and other Pacific Islanders make up the remaining 5 per cent of this culturally diverse and challenging nation.

Social contrasts

Both ascription and achievement are important in any human society, but there are marked differences of emphasis between Polynesia and Melanesia in this respect.[2] There was less social stratification in Melanesia, the emphasis being egalitarian. By contrast in Polynesia, Fiji, and most of Micronesia, social classes and hierarchical systems of chieftainship were very important. Many Polynesian and Micronesian societies, both past and present, are characterised by ascribed status, that is, determined at birth. One is born a chief or a commoner or whatever, and can do relatively little to change one's status. In such a system, the higher levels impose strict controls on marriage, as when King Taufa'ahau of Tonga recently annulled the marriage of his niece to a commoner. Parts of Polynesia and Fiji still have class structures of this general type today.

In achieved status systems, on the other hand, as in most of Melanesia, everyone's chances are ideally equal at birth, and whatever status one achieves as an adult is mostly a matter of one's own efforts. The man with ability and ambition could climb socially by successful economic activity, especially by trade, manufacture, or the accumulation and distribution of wealth. A person who thus gained economic power usually also gained political power, in principle rather like the modern American system. In Polynesia the relationship between political and economic power tended to be the reverse. A chief had political power because he was born a chief, and from this he derived power over the economy.

One classic distinction between Polynesia and Melanesia is that Polynesian social systems recognise what English speakers call cousins — that is, children of brothers and sisters are related to one another as cousins. But in parts of Melanesia, including Fiji, persons who are parallel cousins (the children of two brothers) are regarded as markedly different from those who are cross cousins (the children of a brother and sister). These two categories form the two basic divisions in many Melanesian societies. In a general way, parallel cousins are like brother and sister, but cross cousins are like husband and wife.[3] A stranger moving into this kind of system can be very confused if not aware of the rules.

Economic contrasts

Another interesting contrast is the much greater range of basic resources available to Melanesian people than to Polynesians. This was important in the pre-contact societies, as the more limited the technology, the greater the influence of environment on culture. In the stratified societies of Polynesia and Micronesia, the larger the island and the richer its resources, the more it was divided by social class, and the higher its hierarchy of chiefs extended. Leonard Mason once studied social class in seven atolls in Micronesia, ranging from the smallest to one of the largest. On the smallest atoll, where people lived barely at a survival level, there was almost no class differentiation. On the larger islands class differentiation and chiefly privilege increased. On the largest atolls special foods, places, and privileges were reserved for chiefs, who did not work in the gardens, and commoners had to show great deference to them.[4]

Trade too was affected by environment. On small isolated islands everybody had access to the same commodities: to interior hills for hunting and gathering, to lagoons for seafood, and to various kinds of garden land for particular crops. This situation was typical of much of Polynesia, so very little trade developed. In Melanesia, on the other hand, the great physical diversity fostered trade. Inland there were valuable resins, feathers, fats, and minerals that many coastal people did not have, while coastal peoples had surplus turtles, fish, sea-shells, salt, and pottery. Because of this uneven distribution of resources a mass of trade routes developed throughout Melanesia, even in the rugged New Guinea highlands, despite tribal warfare and other risks.[5]

Not only was the volume of trade much greater in Melanesia, it tended to be between equal trading partners. In Polynesia, on the other hand, goods passed up through the rank hierarchy according to the instructions or wishes of the chiefs. This still occurs on a large scale in places like Tonga and Fiji, particularly on occasions of marriage, death, accession to aristocratic titles, and other large-scale ceremonial exchanges. After the goods are accumulated by the tribal or other group, they are redistributed, but the people at the top of the structure — as all humans at the tops of structures do — 'milk it a bit' before redistributing the remainder to the lower levels.

Their different bases of traditional economic organisation have important implications for Melanesia and Polynesia today. In the early 1950s the New Caledonian agricultural economist, Jacques Barrau, observed that Polynesian people regarded themselves as generally superior to Melanesians. This may then have been so in terms of literacy, formal education, and degree of involvement in a money economy. Many Europeans also regarded Polynesians as in some way 'ahead' of Melanesians. Barrau said that, because of differences in social organisation, this situation would soon be reversed and that Melanesia would leave Polynesia far behind, economically, educationally, and culturally.

There may be some truth in this. Barrau attributed this mainly to differences in social organisation. Assuming that no major world war or changes in political systems occur, and therefore that the peoples of the Pacific will continue to be involved in a predominantly capitalist economy, the Melanesians will have a tremendous advantage. This is particularly so for New Guinea highlanders, who constitute nearly half the Melanesian people, and who have always traded, bargained, haggled, and struggled. Many characteristics of their cultures were not of the modern capitalistic kind, but nevertheless the adjustments that they need to make are much smaller than those of the Polynesian systems in which these features were anathema. Polynesian social and cultural systems contain tremendous obstacles to their members' exploitation of a capitalistic economic system. I am not advocating capitalism, but merely observing that it is the pattern at this moment.

The other resources which Melanesia has in quantity are minerals (nickel in New Caledonia, copper in Bougainville and mainland New Guinea, natural gas in Papua, gold in Fiji and Papua New Guinea), water suitable for enormous hydro-electric power in the New Guinea mainland, thermal heat in central Melanesia, a relative abundance of land, and significant numbers of people. Once these people acquire a high level of technical and political skill, they will have great advantages over the rest of the Pacific.

Cultures in conflict and contact

Contact with cultures from Europe and Asia brought some substantial changes to Pacific Islands cultures. One of the most important was the greater effectiveness of European military technology which enabled Europeans to dominate local people. This domination is related to the matter of confidence, which, though very difficult to measure, may have been one of the most important factors in the last 100 years of Pacific history. When one human group is, for whatever reason, dominant over another, they become not only very confident but often very arrogant. We share this behaviour with most other animals.

If the subordinate group cannot match that dominance, they may become embittered or resentful, but they must withdraw, and such a withdrawal has been manifest during the last century in the Pacific. It has not been an entirely happy withdrawal — human beings do not withdraw happily — and withdrawal is associated with people's confidence in themselves being diminished. We are now in a very exciting period when all this is changing, when the Pacific Islands people are regaining confidence in themselves. They will presumably gain more as the peoples of European origin lose confidence in themselves. The Europeans in the Pacific are now tending to be withdrawn and self-critical. There has been a reversal of roles.

This reduction in European confidence did not come about by military conquest, or through a loss of goods or better technology. It has come through Europeans' uncertainty of the legitimacy of their presence. The things Europeans now regard as bad have generally existed before in much the same ways, but were often previously regarded as good. This change of psychological orientation in Europeans is apparent throughout the Pacific. At the same time local people are asserting their new confidence. Some of them may become as arrogant as the Europeans were during their period of dominance, as any human group is likely to be when it wields power.

European cultures have been very important influences during the last 200 years, a short period relative to the 50 000 years of Pacific history. The waning of European influence will be followed by a resurgence of some aspects of Pacific Islands cultures, possibly followed later by a major cultural dominance from Asia, rather similar in kind, perhaps, to that from Europe.

People talk about the tremendous changes going on in the Pacific today, and there *are* tremendous changes. But they are much less than the changes that went on in most of the eastern Pacific last century, when the whole indigenous religion was overthrown, the indigenous economic system was destroyed, the native technology superseded, and new systems of government were imposed. Everything seemed to be changed.

Why then were these cultures not totally destroyed? Many people at that time understandably said that the Pacific cultures were finished. Some said so regretfully, some thankfully, but all felt that the forces of change were so great that the local cultures could not survive. Many still feel that way today and probably will for a long time to come. Yet Fijian, Tongan, and Samoan cultures, for example, are very much alive today; not the precontact cultures, but still very distinctively Fijian, Tongan, and Samoan.

The most extreme example in the Pacific of the persistence of aspects of indigenous culture is the island of Guam. Here an indigenous population of 50 000 was reduced in a few generations to 1500, most of whom had some Filipino, Spanish, or other non-Guamanian parentage.[6] Immigrants

from Spain, Japan, and the United States have totally dominated the indigenous culture there for centuries, and yet a
Guamanian culture and Chamorro language still exist.

The same principles apply throughout the Pacific. The
external influences have been so prolonged and so intense that
we should not be surprised if Pacific Islands cultures today
were like those of New Zealand or England or Australia. But
in fact they are not, and do not look like becoming so. There
will be substantial changes of various kinds, but the changes
that early observers had assumed these societies would experience did not come about. Pacific cultures today are very much
alive. Some have been bruised, all have been modified, but
they seem to be entering a new period of growth and development, each a unique adaptation within the common framework of world culture.

There is *assimilation*, especially of elements of culture by
smaller societies from larger more powerful societies. There is
some *integration*, particularly of related cultures, wherein their
differences diminish and they come to resemble one another
more. But for this generation at least the major reality will be
of *pluralism*: of different cultures maintaining much of their
uniqueness, but living in constant interaction with peoples of
other cultures. It was fashionable in the 1960s to dismiss
cultural differences as irrelevant, superficial or transient. World
realities of ethnic-based political and other action in the 1970s
and 1980s have shown the naiveté of that view. The fact that
individuals from diverse cultures, coming together in alien
environments, can enjoy and appreciate both their common
humanity and their ethnic differences (especially for short
periods and often superficial contacts) sometimes blurs the fact
that this is much more difficult at home, or in large numbers
abroad. Nevertheless, despite the tensions and difficulties, it
can also result in dynamism and creative adaptation. In future
the countries with only one culture may be looked back to as
deprived, those which had the benefit of plurality as having
been enriched.

One culture can be restrictive

The human animal is characterised more by intra-specific similarity than difference. All cultures always have had much in

common, and industrial technology and rapid communication are increasing the similarities. Nevertheless many differences are likely to remain.

Too much identification with one culture can lead to racism, religious persecution, or other negative and destructive feelings, but not enough can lead to insecurity and anomie.

Some Islanders who have little knowledge of European culture see its adoption as a solution to their problems. This is broadly how they came to accept Christianity, and then colonial government, but without quite the results expected. Some people expect that science and technology will solve their problems, but Sir Paul Hasluck, in opening the 1971 Pacific Science Congress, noted the growing 'disillusionment with science' and its overemphasis on material goals which have no necessary association with the achievement of human satisfaction. We have, he warned, come to confuse fatness with prosperity. Indeed in the United States of America, with more material things than any other country, the prevalence of crime, pollution, addiction, mental breakdown, and other indicators of lack of personal fulfilment is among the highest in the world. Unique identification provides a significant satisfaction for Pacific Islanders and elements of their value systems have continuing utility.

The need for diversity

Nothing would more quickly stultify human creativity or impoverish the richness of cultural diversity than a single world culture. Cultural uniformity is not likely to bring peace; it is much more likely to bring totalitarianism. A unitary system is easier for a privileged few to dominate. Cultural diversity is one of the world's potential sources of both sanity and fulfilment. 'A country without culture,' said the Fiji Education Commission in explaining its importance, 'is a country without soul.'[7]

In the 1980s each of us needs to be able to operate not only in more than one language, but also in more than one culture. This is no major problem — rather, perhaps, an enriching challenge. Te Rangi Hiroa (Sir Peter Buck), who had an intimate knowledge of both Polynesian and European cultures, emphasised that he belonged to both, appreciated both, and found the dual cultures much more rewarding than either one. Some people in a marginal position between two or more cultures find themselves at a loss to know which to belong to. They are not sufficiently aware that they have the much richer option of belonging to both. In Te Rangi Hiroa's day relatively few people successfully lived in two or more cultures — today it is both much more common and much more appreciated. We will soon reach the stage when a person who knows only one culture will be regarded as impoverished.

Most of the Maoris who have played outstanding roles in New Zealand, whether in Maori or Pakeha affairs, speak the Maori language and have a good knowledge of the culture. Yet only a small proportion of Maoris can do so. One might think that having to know and be able to function in two languages and cultures would be an obstacle to the emergence of such leaders. On the contrary, the facts in New Zealand and the islands suggest rather that it is an advantage.

Anyway, no Pacific Islander wants to be limited to one culture. Almost all use an international language and various features of other cultures. With the greatly increasing contact between peoples, there will be a growing tendency for all of us to learn relevant elements from many cultures rather than all aspects of one or two. As this stage approaches, it becomes less and less meaningful to speak of cultures as mutually exclusive packages. The uniqueness will not be in the components, but in particular combinations of them, with certain key features giving the stamp of identification to particular groups. The basic aim is to find oneself as an individual. Having achieved a satisfying identification with one's own culture group gives the confidence and strength to cope with others.

The tendency to form groups is neither good nor bad, it is an inevitable part of our innate heritage that needs to be accepted, like food and sex, as a fact of life. The main trends in human grouping are that there are more and more to choose from and that each individual belongs to more than ever before. Though almost all human activities are undertaken in groups, each of us belongs to a different set and each plays different roles in them. Nobody wants to be so unique as to be the only member of a culture, but each is increasingly able to adopt a personal style and occupy a personal niche.

At the University of the South Pacific one often hears students complain of insufficient integration, of too little cross-cultural communication, and too much segregation of ethnic groups. Those campaigning for office in the Students' Association use integration on the campus as a platform. None speaks against it. Yet in practice sports groups, lunch groups, dancing groups, talking groups, drinking groups, and most other groupings are substantially ethnically separate. Why the disparity between ideology and behaviour? Why is a desire that is so clearly expressed not more fully realised?

First, the ideology is currently international and is therefore popular. All mass media support it. But there is no necessary correlation between espousing a system of religion, politics, or behaviour, and behaving according to its tenets. Second, there is inhibition, restraining people from doing what they want to do because it is not yet usual. Third, there is a great difference between wanting to play a guitar and being able to play it. Any culture is very complex, and we each spend many years learning our own, largely informally and unconsciously. Learning another culture requires effort, concentration, and conscious learning over a considerable time. Language is just one of these aspects of culture which have to be learnt if a full involvement is to be achieved. Obviously there is a limit to the number of cultures one can learn deeply. I do not say totally, because we cannot ever know any culture totally, not even the one into which we are born.

Despite the limits on the learning of other cultures, there is scope for very much more than is undertaken in practice. The fastest way to learn a language or most other aspects of a culture is by intensive professional training reinforced by living within the culture concerned. Time, money, and other commitments limit the extent to which this can be done, but institutions can help greatly by providing readily obtainable courses. There is some inhibition and embarrassment to be overcome in the learner and in a few cases some resistance from the culture concerned. Generally, however, members of a culture are delighted to teach it to anyone who is genuinely interested.

The importance of legitimacy

What makes art or culture *authentic* (or *genuine* or *legitimate*)? And what period of history is to be regarded as traditional? The emphasis given to these terms by Islands leaders shows the value placed on and confidence derived from feelings of legitimacy and validity. They are also used so frequently (and often corruptly) in travel advertising because tourists want, or think they want, that which is 'authentic'.

What is described as authentic? Firstly, that which is considered unique to that culture. Secondly, it must have some traditional association. A pattern or practice is not considered authentic at the time of its creation. It only becomes so after people identify it as their own, and when they do, it usually gives confidence.

Which period of the past is not so important, so long as the feeling of identification is there? For example, Sir Arthur Gordon created a system of land tenure and local government in Fiji to suit the needs of a particular phase of colonial history. Over the years, however, the new system came to be accepted as Fijian, and as such acquired an aura of legitimacy. The concept of the 'Fijian way of life', like that of the 'American way of life', can be useful even though each culture is different for every individual.

Pacific cultures, like other human cultures, have always been changing. There is sometimes a tendency to accept selected parts of the culture from the time of first contact with Europe as in some way more authentic than earlier periods of history (and the earlier cultures are being increasingly revealed by archaeological research). It is like saying that Rolls-Royce is not English, or the stars and stripes not American, merely because they did not exist before Captain Cook sailed for the Pacific.

Importing the irrelevant

People often speak as though there was a naturally selective process which kept the best of one's own culture and borrowed the best of other people's. It does not usually work out that way, and needs more careful thought if it is to do so more often. The foreign can be deceptive and seductive, the local parochial and an easy way out.

Human groups in positions of dominance become so self-righteously arrogant that they impose the most unnecessary trivia on subordinate populations, who often accept it willingly (and even themselves demand it) as a sign of 'progress' or 'advancement'. Requiring cars in Kiribati to wear number plates (with six letters and numbers on them at that!) on islands with less than ten kilometres of road and numbers of vehicles you can count on the fingers and toes, is one of many illustrations of thoughtless introduction of irrelevant minutiae from a dominant culture. This small example was probably imposed by a colonial official with no sensitivity to the reality of a different situation, but after independence such things are often introduced by local officials who continue to be trained in the wrong things at the wrong places.

Rationalisations can always be built up to justify such actions, but the case for them is weak indeed. How one overcomes them is more difficult, as they become part of the all-pervasive intellectual dependency which is a characteristic of Islands cultures today, despite assertions to the contrary.

Is culture copyright?

Is tradition transmitted by blood or by learning? Most people would agree that culture is learned rather than innate, though practice does not always follow principle. Thus some who deny that foreigners can ever learn certain aspects of local culture, still believe that local people can learn any aspect of foreign cultures.

Quite apart from whether human beings *can* learn the culture of others (and all available evidence suggests that they can if they devote the necessary time, effort, and skill) the question is often implied whether they *should*. Is it proper for a Japanese to dance a *tamure*? Or an Australian to speak Nauruan, or a Fijian to speak English, or a Kiribati to sing a Solomons song? Or for a European to accept a Samoan chiefly title and participate in the associated ritual? Or for a Tongan to wear a Papuan tattoo? Or an Indian woman to wear a Fijian dress? Or ni-Vanuatu to wear the Tongan *ta'ovala*?

In practice there is an unstated sentiment that it is in varying degrees inappropriate for certain categories of person to engage in certain kinds of cultural activity. I have seen both Maoris and Europeans express displeasure at seeing Europeans publicly performing Maori action songs (even though action songs are a phenomenon of this century, not of precontact Maori culture), but most of the persons concerned would have welcomed such a performance in a private gathering. Likewise I have heard a distinguished Tongan speak very critically of a non-Tongan who wore a *ta'ovala* with the intention of showing respect.

Swamping by other cultures leads to both change and resistance. Cultures which are greatly affected by cultural dominance (for example the Maori) often make great efforts for selective regeneration and identification. People living in isolated, minimally influenced cultures often put much more effort into rejecting the old and reaching out to the new. But this differs for individuals according to personality, status, training, and interests. The creation of a new authenticity may, as John Kasaipwalova has pointed out, be a high priority for the creative intelligentsia.[8]

Foreign wolves in traditional sheep's clothing

Realising that customers are attracted by the package as well as (and sometimes more than) by the product, and that traditional precedents with favourable connotations are comforting to Islanders, some of the most foreign introductions get wrapped in some of the most traditional clothing. Many people with things to sell — whether goods, acceptance of a commercial enterprise, religion or political philosophies — realise the validity of Firth's comment that in a situation of rapid social and cultural change, people 'respond most easily to stimuli which have some continuity with, or analogy to, their traditional values and forms of organisation'.[9]

Theologians are seeking traditional symbols with which to present the Christian religion — a radically different belief system from those of the indigenous cultures. Many foreign corporations give their enterprises traditional names, traditional decor, and symbolic aspects of traditional imagery (including personnel of traditional status in visible 'front' roles) because they realise that the naked reality is unattractive.[10]

Selling artifacts to tourists.

Communists advocate their philosophy as being consistent with the 'natural' or 'communal' way of life of various Pacific cultures, even though the systems in fact have little in common.

The *Fiji Times*, probably the largest newspaper in the islands, daily reported proceedings of the Fiji Tourism Convention in November 1971. The majority of the photographs published were those of the tiny minority of indigenous people who took part, thus conveying the visual image, reinforced in the news columns, that this was a meeting substantially of Islanders concerned with indigenous interests, when in fact it was overwhelmingly a meeting of foreign businessmen concerned with foreign interests.

The tourist industry reflects this par excellence, and has tremendous potential to increase human understanding or to frustrate it. Sir John Guise, one of New Guinea's most prominent politicians, has pointed out that it invests vast sums on

the planned creation of largely spurious images of primitive-
ness, condescending notions of simplicity, and the exagger-
ation of differences. The foreign visitor is seduced into
participating in the myth so created. The reality is of sharing,
with other tourists of one's own culture, much the same
accommodation, food, and circumstances as are found back
home. But reality is made of little relevance. The artificial myth
of exotica which provides a validation for the purchase of the
status, receives a fallacious fulfilment in the presentation of
pseudo-traditional performances in the hotel lounge, the
purchase of evidence of 'cross-cultural' contact in the handicrafts from the Toorak lathes, and in the polychrome
postcards.

The Program of Tourist Development for French Polynesia
emphasises that the arriving tourist 'has a preconceived notion
of this tropical paradise and . . . is not so forgiving where he
is wrong in this image of the islands and their people'. If a
distinctive cultural pattern for visitor reception does not exist,
it states, one should be created to persuade the visitor 'that this
is indeed the vacation paradise of his dreams'. All employees
having contact with tourists are to be 'well indoctrinated in the
philosophy of hospitality' and the 'promotion and indoctrination' of a unique image is regarded as requiring immediate
priority, for 'the *product* must match the *image*'. (Their italics.)

American Samoa takes the process one step further. There,
the government-owned television service, beamed compul-
sorily into all classrooms as part of the school curriculum, indoctrinated children in the 'need' as well as the techniques for
them to behave in ways which tourists have been led to expect.
The Kingdom of Tonga's Visitors Bureau in 1972 published a
booklet for school children and adults, giving information on
Tongan culture and customs to tell to tourists.

Tourism is the fastest growing industry in the islands. It has
vast potentials, both positive and negative. It could be geared
to personal and cross-cultural enrichment as well as financial
gain, but unfortunately the trend is to turn the islands into a
giant Disneyland and the Islanders into well-trained puppets,
whose life and behaviour are fashioned to fulfil the dream
expectations of the travelling public from the richer nations. It
is not too late to change the pattern, but it is unlikely to be

changed in view of the tremendous effort needed to do so against the vested interests in keeping it as it is, for the quickest short-term profits come from a maximum flowthrough of preconditioned visitors, encouraged to consume the most expensive range of food, drinks, trips, and pampering.

At present the forces are so heavily loaded in favour of private investors that their short-term demands are the main determinants of the shape the industry will take. It suits investors best to assume that visitors only want to consume. Most tourists have more intelligence and more potential goodwill than they are given credit for or the opportunity to develop and express. What could become a bridge for cross-cultural understanding is becoming instead a monument to human greed and gullibility.[6]

3
Personality
Loading the dice

Personality and cultural change

Although all human beings share many attributes of personality in common, these are modified by our cultures. The
particular patterns of life that we have been brought up with,
the values we have learned to observe, the kinds of opportunities we have been taught to exploit or not to exploit, all greatly
condition our individual personalities. This is a field in which
much research remains to be done, in the Pacific as elsewhere,
but some findings to date are worth considering.

As cultures change personalities change, but personality
does not change at the same time or at the same speed, or
necessarily always in the same directions. It is now clear that
basic personality traits can withstand radical cultural change.
I am not suggesting that this is good or bad, but rather more
important, that it seems to be a fact. Psychological studies in
Hawaii, Tahiti, the Cook Islands, New Zealand, and elsewhere
in Polynesia and Micronesia, show that where people have
experienced extremely radical cultural change over a period of
100 years or more — radical change in technology, economy,
religion, and political organisation, in fact changes of almost
every type — nevertheless, some important aspects of basic
personality remain much less changed than most of us might
expect.[1]

For example, it was widely assumed by early Christian
missionaries that if Christianity were adopted by the islands
people they would develop the kinds of personalities and
adopt the kinds of behaviour patterns that were common
among middle-class Europeans at that time. This did not
happen. Similar assumptions were (and still are) made by
many European and Asian businessmen, government officials,

'development' experts and others. But none of these assumptions has proved valid, at least not to anything like the extent that was expected, even over a very long period.

Traditional child-rearing patterns

Some of the most significant influences on the formation of our personalities are the child-rearing practices by which we are conditioned. A number of studies show some broad similarities in the child-rearing patterns in the stratified or chiefly societies of the Pacific, especially those of Polynesia, Micronesia, and Fiji. The socialising influences in most of Melanesia, particularly in places like the New Guinea highlands, are very different, and are associated with different personality patterns. In most Polynesian societies the child receives, for its first year or two of life, a great deal of personal handling. It is indulged, passed from hand to hand, and given constant bodily contact and a great deal of affection. This must be a very comforting experience. All its needs tend to be immediately met. This is understandable and very sensible, particularly in communities where people live in close proximity. You cannot have screaming children if there are twenty people occupying a one-roomed dwelling.

Then, somewhere between two and four years of age, a child experiences what it perceives as rejection. This rejection is not seen or intended as such by the parents, although it is the parents whose behaviour causes this perception. The feeling of rejection is usually accentuated by the fact that another child comes along. Parents can only spare a certain amount of time to be with children and a new child must be given a lot of attention. The older child feels relatively neglected. Another factor is that the parents feel that because the two or three-year old can now walk, it is more psychologically mature than in fact it is. At first, children tend to react to this rejection by demanding reacceptance, but often feel punished for this by being laughed at, scolded, or pushed away.

Psychological studies so far indicate that this feeling of rejection has serious effects upon the individual's total personality structure, with these effects continuing, in many cases, for the rest of his or her life. The rejection response syndrome continues for the next fifteen years or so until young adults attempt to re-establish, through marriage or otherwise, the close personal relationships that were lost (or at least greatly reduced) in early childhood.

During childhood the individual continues to strive subconsciously for reacceptance, and finds that the only way he or she can gain it is by being passive. That is, the child is allowed to stay in the company of its parents or other elders provided it says little, does little, remains quiet, unobtrusive, and asks no awkward questions. It must not express itself freely in the presence of adults. If it wants to express itself, it must go well away from the adults and shout or perform with other children on the beach or elsewhere. Thus, much of its learning is unintentionally provided by other children. The main models to be copied or obeyed are older children and the child usually finds that if it does what they want, it will be reasonably well looked after; if it does not it will be beaten or made to conform by isolation or ridicule or some other negative method of conduct control. The older children will not support it, or play with it, or tolerate its company unless it does conform. Behaviour toward the father particularly is often characterised by subservience, obedience, holding oneself in, not expressing oneself, not developing oneself. Children of high-ranking parents who are being prepared for leadership may often be encouraged to develop and express themselves more than those of lower social rank. Generally, however, parents do not encourage their children to ask questions, to participate in conversations, to express ideas, or to undertake creative activity. The child finds that the best way to handle its environment is to put on a pleasant front, and face everybody with a friendly, accepting, agreeable image, without disclosing too much of its true feelings.

Adapting to changing circumstances

This pattern of docility was characteristic of, and rather well adapted to, the lower levels of stable, isolated, stratified (chiefly) societies. But in recent years the range of social and economic opportunities has greatly increased, there is scope for more kinds of achievement, and people move about much more. The traditional child-rearing practices which were well adapted for the former situation gradually lose their effectiveness.

Traditional child-rearing practices produce young people who tend to lack confidence in themselves as individuals, but who are relatively more confident as members of groups. Their early conditioning has taught them that if they act too much as individuals, or are creative, they are likely to be regarded as upstarts. Rewards, on the other hand, come from conformity. A young person serves, the older people reap the rewards. In a village situation with little social or economic change this system has many advantages. In a highly mobile commercial economy it has some drawbacks.

Aggression or hostility, which all human beings seem to have, has to be repressed or controlled in the interests of oneself and others, but some inevitably comes out. In the olden days, it could be expressed in warfare. Sometimes today it is associated with sports or the consumption of alcohol, which provides an opportunity to release some of the aggression that has been built in and bottled up. This is particularly noticeable when people from these traditional societies migrate to live in urban centres.

Where to be acquisitive and creative does not bring rewards, talented persons tend to use their skills in persuasion. Oratory, particularly the use of speech in persuasion or political manipulation, is highly valued. A skilled orator gives his listeners an aural massaging as it were, handling them verbally in a personal way.

This sense of the value in manipulating people is illustrated, for instance, in the choice of studies and occupations. For example, of the first 62 Marshall, Caroline, and Mariana Islanders who took university degrees, 28 majored in political science. There were more degrees in political science than in history, geography, economics, philosophy, and the other humanities together, and more than in all the physical sciences together. This is not an accident. People in these cultures greatly value the man who can persuade and manipulate others, and political science is the study of manipulation of people for political ends. Not one of the students was interested in commerce or industry. They aspired instead to jobs entailing the handling of people, especially political and, to a lesser extent, administrative roles. Many of the others moved into teaching and service roles, because these too are consistent with their personality training, that of being skilled in dealing with people rather than things. Few aimed to go into business, as the idea of making profit from transactions with one's own people, of innovation in an entrepreneurial sense, is contrary to the lessons of one's upbringing. It is perhaps significant that most of those who do go into business, apart from some who are culturally marginal by having been raised by Europeans or Asians or otherwise, prefer to deal with foreign tourists to whom these constraints are less applicable.

Some people feel that if they abandoned the chiefly system, the socialising and child-rearing patterns would change, and people would adapt to the new environment. But this is not necessarily so. Hawaii, for example, used to have a very powerful chiefly system, which was destroyed by the end of last century. Though the chiefly system has been as good as dead for three generations, recent studies demonstrate that a number of personality features that were present at the time of first European contact are still manifest in many Hawaiian people today.[2] This leads them not to want to achieve success in Hawaii's commercial culture. Those who are successful tend to be so mainly in service roles or in politics. In business there are extremely few.

A Fiji study

An interesting study was undertaken by Allan Howard of the comparative achievements of Rotumans and Fijians within Fiji.[3] Rotuma is a culturally distinct island 650 kilometres north of Fiji, but is politically part of the independent nation of Fiji. Many more people want jobs in the gold-mining industry than are available but, proportionate to population, there were nearly nine times as many Rotumans employed there as Fijians. More important still, there were about eighteen times more Rotumans, relative to population, in supervisory jobs there than Fijians. To take another example, there were over twice as many Rotumans in professional occupations other than teaching throughout Fiji, relative to population size, as

Fijians. Moreover, Rotumans saved several times more money per individual than Fijian people did, they were much more involved in business, and they had much greater success in business than Fijians.

What reasons can be given for such marked differences? Educational opportunities in Rotuma have been less than in Fiji. Opportunities for making money are much greater in most of Fiji than in Rotuma. Some have suggested that Rotumans have been favoured by Europeans but, even if this is so, it could not adequately explain the differences in many of these fields. Howard considered that much of the difference could be accounted for by differences between Rotuman and Fijian social systems.

The Fijian child (it is male children that these contrasts have been concerned with) tends to be dominated by his father. He is required to give total obedience, and not to express himself in front of his father.[4] The father is the authority figure and children become accustomed to a state of dependency, of remaining submissive and agreeable, of not developing the potential that they undoubtedly have. The conditioning process, except for persons of high hereditary rank, continues throughout life, teaching everyone to know his place.

But today, when all sorts of new opportunities are opening up, nothing holds people back more than 'knowing their place'. The Fijian system places great emphasis on teaching people to know their place. The Rotuman system is much more flexible.

The easy and popular answer to this problem is probably the wrong one. It is that if people want to achieve more in a commercially-oriented society, they should do away with the inhibiting aspects of their culture, including changing the child-rearing patterns, and diminishing the authoritarian aspects of the chief and the father. It is a difficult enough task to decide which are, let alone adapt, those aspects of society which are creating problems for people, or holding them back. Nobody in the world can say with confidence that theirs is the best child-rearing system. A serious vacuum is created if people do away with the old system but do not provide adequate substitutes. It leaves them worse off than they were, and helps create an unskilled, poorly motivated, generally unhappy, and often unemployed urban proletariat. You will find such people in most towns of the Pacific Islands, especially the larger and more distant ones like Honolulu and Auckland.[5]

Achievement among migrants

Once people leave their homeland culture and settle in a new environment, do they achieve much more? In some instances they do, but in many cases they do not. Of over 100 000 Pacific Islanders who live permanently in New Zealand, where educational and employment opportunities are generally considerably better than in the islands, few of the immigrants or their children go to university or into business or the higher professions. The same is true of the thousands of Samoans and Tongans in Hawaii. Rather paradoxically, a higher percentage of those brought up in their own cultures aspire to and reach university education, professional employment, and business enterprise. I think there are two main reasons for this.

One is that those who settle in New Zealand or Hawaii find that their aspirations for a higher income than they received in the islands are very quickly met, and can be satisfied by unskilled work. The difference between the wage of an unskilled worker and a skilled worker in New Zealand or Hawaii is not nearly as great as in the islands. A thrifty unskilled worker can have a motor car, a house, and other things which in his home island he may not have been able to own.

The second, and very important, reason may be that many of the immigrants acquire a feeling of inferiority. Many of them tend to lack confidence in their own abilities, or have been conditioned by their cultures not to 'push' themselves. The tendency is often reinforced by prejudice in the host society. They feel safe and accepted in the unskilled or semi-skilled categories where nobody is going to question them, where their ability is not going to be put to excessive tests, where they are not expected to innovate. Much of their cultural conditioning has taught them not to innovate, not to work out their own destiny, not to strive to improve their position. When people with this kind of conditioning move into an urban environment, especially if they come from the lower social orders, they tend to join the unskilled urban proletariat. Effective techniques for helping them to escape from that bind are not yet well developed.

4
Language
Will all 1200 survive?

Three language families

The languages of Oceania are of three main kinds. The more than 250 Australian Aboriginal languages, almost all of which seem to be in some degree related, are not related to any other languages in the Pacific or elsewhere.

The 740 or so 'Papuan' languages are spoken mainly on the island of New Guinea, but some are found as far west as Timor and others as far east as Santa Cruz in the Solomon Islands. The ancestral people who brought the languages from which today's Papuan languages are derived, seem to have replaced the earlier languages which were probably of the same origin as those of Aboriginal Australia (because the two populations exhibit genetic similarities). The Papuan languages originated from what is now Indonesia (but are very different from most languages spoken in Indonesia today which are more recent introductions) in three main 'waves' — the first probably more than 10 000 years ago and the latest about 5000 years ago.

All other languages in the Pacific, until the time of European contact, belonged to the Austronesian (or Malayo-Polynesian) family. This covered a wider area of the earth's surface than any other language — extending from Madagascar off the coast of Africa to Easter Island, not far from South America. In fact the bearers of Malayo-Polynesian languages quite possibly reached both Africa and South America. Of the more than 800 Austronesian languages, about 450 are found only in the Pacific Islands, and are known as the Oceanic group of Austronesian. The rest are found in Indonesia, Malaysia, Philippines, Southern Vietnam and among the Aboriginal people of Taiwan. The Austronesian languages are thought to have originated in Taiwan or Southern China[1] and to have moved south to the Philippines, thence Malaysia and Indonesia, from which some speakers of these languages moved west, reaching western New Guinea by 5500 years ago. Few Austronesian languages established on the island of New Guinea, but by 5000 years ago they seem to have reached New Britain and New Ireland where they flourished, but were also influenced in varying degrees by earlier Papuan languages.

From the New Britain/New Ireland region some Austronesian speakers moved back westward to establish on parts of coastal New Guinea, while they moved well over a thousand years later, southeast through the Solomon Islands and Vanuatu. Some people expanded south to New Caledonia, all of the thirty or so languages of which seem to have a common origin; others travelled north into Micronesia, coming into contact with speakers of languages which had entered that region from the southern Philippines. Others again reached Fiji, and, another period of consolidation preceded further expansion eastward to Tonga, thence Samoa, and thence to the rest of Polynesia (see Chapter 1).

Detailed linguistic reconstruction reveals a 'powerful set of comparisons indicating that Proto-Oceanic society had hereditary chiefs.'[2] Historical linguistics and archaeology provide such compatible evidence that it seems likely that the peoples who developed and carried Lapita pottery were that section of the people who spoke the Oceanic languages who evolved in the New Britain/New Ireland area and subsequently spread from there throughout island Melanesia, Polynesia and parts of Micronesia.

A complex problem

About 1200 languages, and many more dialects, are spoken in the Pacific Islands, which contains nearly one-quarter of all the world's languages, yet the Pacific Islands populations average less than 5000 speakers per language. That in itself creates a great problem. Moreover, few of the island nations are in the convenient position of Tonga and Western Samoa which have only one language each, and Samoan is the only language which is spoken in more than one country or territory except by small groups of migrants.[3]

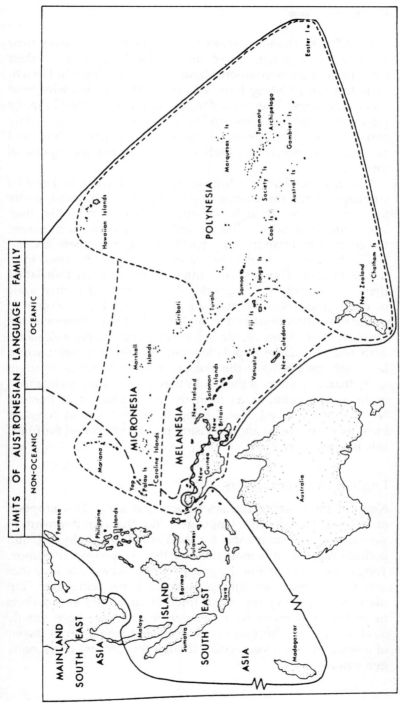

Reproduced, with permission, from "The Proto-Oceanic Language Community" by Andrew Pawley and Roger Green in *Out of Asia: Peopling the Americas and the Pacific*, published by The Journal of Pacific History, Canberra, 1985 (p. 163).

Most Pacific Islanders speak three languages — usually their home area language, the dominant local language of their country, and an international language (either English, French, or Indonesian).[4] Many have varying degrees of knowledge of other languages. There is a danger, and it is a reality in many places, that children grow up knowing several languages badly and *none* well. This greatly restricts their capacity to think and communicate effectively. Only a very small minority speak all three well.

It is natural that any human group will want to keep its language, partly for reasons of self-respect or sentiment, partly for convenience (though sometimes short-term rather than long-term convenience). But as world communication increases, the costs of maintaining very small languages increase greatly. The publishing of books and papers is only a tiny fraction of the extra cost. The cost of writing them, or even translating them, is not only vastly greater, but on any substantial scale is quite impossible because of the tremendous volume of publications produced and of highly skilled manpower needed for translation. Even countries like Australia and New Zealand, with relatively large populations and speaking a major world language, do not have the skills or finance to write or adapt more than a fraction of the books they use, so they make much more use of publications from the mass printers of Europe, North America, and Hong Kong than they would consider ideal. For most radio and television programmes, and for films, this is even more so.

English and vernaculars

None of the possible courses of action is ideal. The adoption of one or more world languages and the abandonment of vernaculars is unacceptable for valid social, psychological, and political reasons. It is most unlikely that the peoples of Samoa, Tonga, or other major language communities would either initiate or tolerate an attempt to replace their languages. But there is a tendency for minor internal languages and dialects to wither (and many have disappeared or have been greatly modified in the direction of the dominant language) in favour of a single national vernacular, though this process takes many generations.[5]

Moreover, neither English nor any other language can fully express all concepts. We are all constantly limited in our thoughts and expressions by the constraints of language. Anyone who has a good knowledge of two or more languages will know that although much can be expressed equally well in either, some things can be more meaningfully expressed in the one, and others in the other. World development may be hastened in the short-term if all people spoke one language, but it would almost certainly stultify development in the long-term. No existing language is adequate for the world of tomorrow, and the retention of multiple languages is likely to provide a stimulus to cross-fertilisation of different patterns of thought.

The cost of using multiple languages is high in money terms and allows less time for learning in other fields, but most Pacific peoples will be prepared to pay some costs for education, publication, and radio communication in one local language and one international language. In any case there are probably good reasons for everyone in the world today having to learn at least one language in addition to their mother tongue. Beyond two, there is more debate, and decisions in that field would be assisted by a detailed assessment for particular countries, of the financial, social, psychological, and political costs and benefits of various numbers of languages being supported or encouraged with varying degrees of intensity and for various purposes.[6]

There is a major problem too, in developing ways to increase the flexibility of languages that will remain in long-term use, to handle more quickly and effectively the wide range of additional things and concepts that mass communication and industrial technology have introduced to the cultures concerned.

The common argument that English is the only language suitable for the Pacific in the future is fallacious. Today it is the world's most widely used language (though second to Chinese in number of speakers) but that may not be so in the coming generations. English used to be as limited in vocabulary and concepts for dealing with modern science as any Pacific language. English was developed in a subsistence economy, but is has expanded greatly as a result of the expansion in knowledge, the great increase in communication, and in the number of speakers. No Pacific language will have as many speakers, but the expanded knowledge and communication is now *potentially* as available to Pacific languages as it has been to English. Moreover, English is a mess — unphonetic, irregular, and shattered into dozens of dialects. (Pacific Islands students have considerable difficulty with the respective dialects of English spoken by their various Australian, New Zealand, American, Indian, Scottish, French, Polynesian, and other teachers.) Like any language (or other trait of a culture which is temporarily in ascendance), English is likely to resist adaptation of spelling or otherwise, and could become increasingly cumbersome. If it does, substitutes will become more attractive.

French is the international language of New Caledonia, French Polynesia, Wallis and Futuna, and of about half the population of Vanuatu (though the proportion of French speakers in Vanuatu is probably declining relative to English). Since French is the international language of only about five per cent of Pacific Islanders, and since the main countries on the Pacific rim which impact on the islands are also English speaking, French is a somewhat embattled language in the Pacific. France is reacting to this by a vigorous campaign to strengthen and spread its language along with its political influence in the region. France did very little to encourage (and much to constrain) the tertiary education of islanders in its colonies and even the announcement by President Mitterand in 1986 that a French university would be established immediately in Tahiti was explained in terms of increasing French political influence in the region rather than in terms of upgrading the education of islanders.

Which Pacific languages?

To expand and adapt all the 1200 Pacific languages to the degree that English has been would be an impossible task in both time and effort. It is most unlikely to be attempted Expanding and adapting the major Pacific languages, however, has been proceeding as a result of increased communication, education, and range of experience. A major task of relevance to these areas is to determine the steps by which English,

Russian, and other languages developed in the last two hundred years (and, closer to home, Motu, Roviana, Kotte, and other Pacific languages which have been developed as languages of trade, administration, or Christian education) and to use this knowledge to make the expansion and adaption of the major Pacific languages faster and more effective. With radio and television, greater understanding of psychology, linguistics, and learning, and rising educational levels, the process should be achievable much more rapidly than it was for English. The great problem for Pacific leaders to solve is *which* languages are to be given the facilities in terms of use in formal education, radio and mass media time, publishing subsidies, translators and other skills, to encourage their development in this way.

The question of number of speakers applies not only to the language as a whole, but also to particular topics. The quarter million or so speakers of Samoan; living in a compact community with relatively few non-Samoans, are more than adequate for the perpetuation of that language. But the number of Samoans who will need to be expert in the details of aerospace technology, Eskimo ethnology, or Kantian philosophy is so few that attempts to provide a full range of terminology and concepts for them in Samoan would be both expensive and futile. But this is one of the dilemmas of the language issue. It seems almost certain that people will use one language for some aspects of life (particularly the intimate, domestic, and local issues) and one or more foreign languages for others (particularly scientific and philosophical esoterica).

If English or another foreign language is taught in schools, used by radio, worked and developed by hundreds of millions of people daily, it is going to develop further (though not necessarily in every direction) than languages with only a few thousand speakers. If the major Pacific languages are to be functional tools, kept reasonably effective for communicating the life of today, they too will need to be taught in schools, researched, and developed. Otherwise they may constrain the intellectual scope of those who speak them. An international language today is a universal necessity, but there is relatively little support for an international language (whether English or other) being the only language.

Many older Islanders speak of a decline in efficient use of their vernaculars by the younger generation. They refer to a reduction of precision, the loss of vocabulary, declining awareness of nuances of meaning, and diminishing skills in oratory. To the extent that the loss is in topics like stone technology, reef ecology, or traditional magic, the loss is a normal adjustment to changed realities of life. But those closely concerned with it assert that their concern is not with this sort of loss, but with the efficiency of the vernaculars as tools of communication for the circumstances of today. Almost all schooling is in foreign languages, but if certain vernaculars are to survive as effective instruments for communication and thought within the cultures concerned, many feel that they too will need to be taught in schools. This will necessitate the training of teachers as specialists in their own languages,[7] more detailed dictionaries, grammars, and other linguistic aids.

In a fascinating book on the future of Pacific languages, Benton (1982) quotes evidence from around the world to the effect that few languages with less than 50 000 speakers are likely to survive — perhaps less than twenty in the Pacific.

The future of Pidgin

Any discussion of language in Papua New Guinea, Solomon Islands or Vanuatu must consider the future of Pidgin (more commonly referred to in the countries concerned as Tok Pisin, Pijin, and Bislama respectively).[8] It is a new language, based on Melanesian grammatical principles and incorporating words from English and to a lesser extent Melanesian languages, Malay, German and other sources, and developing by the same process that English and other languages developed, but very much faster and under unusual circumstances. With the coming of formal education and mass media it is an open question whether Pidgin will continue to develop, or wither away. Many Melanesians are coming to accept it as a valid language expressing a Melanesian rather than European identity, but the controversy about its future continues. Percy Chatterton, after listening to Pidgin in Parliament for many years, described it as inadequate for the discussion of economic and political (and one might add legal) issues, though having a great future as a medium of social intercourse and for poetry, drama and creative expression.[9]

Pidgin has two great assets. First, it is easy to learn. Without being formally taught (and therefore at no cost to governments or other institutions) it has been acquired by over two million people in northern Melanesia. Second, Pidgin provides a verbal bridge between speakers of the 112 or so languages of Vanuatu, the 88 of the Solomon Islands, and the 720 of Papua New Guinea.

As many rural people in these countries still receive no formal education, and as much of what they do receive is not of high quality, the value of Pidgin as a lingua franca must not be underrated. Its long-term future is open to question, but even its opponents acknowledge its role and its value in this generation at least.

Barriers as well as bridges

It is also appropriate to look at some negative aspects of multiple languages. In the same way as separate national or linguistic identifications are cohesive for the group contained by them, they are divisive between groups. The use of more than one vernacular within a single country or territory (and this is the situation in most of the Pacific) inhibits national unity and probably increases costs.

Between Pacific countries as well as within them, multiple vernaculars can reduce effective communication. Everyone in the Pacific is familiar with the way in which people frequently use their vernacular language as a means to isolate, keep at a distance, or sometimes even reject, speakers of other languages. That is, the fact that multiple languages are sometimes used to segregate and to bolster prejudice needs to be weighed against their advantages. If people feel the need of a protective shield separate languages can indeed provide this defence, but it is well to be aware of their costs as well as their benefits.

PATTERNS

5
Tradition
Evolving a new synthesis

Leading Pacific Islands politicians, intellectuals, and writers give high priority to the preservation of the indigenous cultures.[1] There is widespread support for this principle, but much less action in practice, partly because few if any have spelled out in detail what they mean by indigenous culture. Some who strongly advocate it devote much of their own time and resources to acquiring specific goods, skills, arts, and institutions from other cultures. These are not necessarily incompatible with indigenous cultures, but more thought is needed about which aspects of existing cultures people wish to retain (and why, and how), which aspects of former cultures to revive, which aspects of other cultures to adopt, what amalgam of local and exotic cultures to develop, and what new cultural patterns to create. It is not a question of which one of these, but how much of each.

All human cultures are continually changing, sometimes slowly, sometimes fast. Culture is not a state but a process, in which some core themes are identifiable over a long period, while other, often less meaningful, facets change at varying speeds. The 1980s are a time of rapid change throughout the world and nobody, anywhere, wants to preserve the culture of today *exactly* in its present form. All cultures have considerable limitations. Moreover, when it comes to changing them, there is great difference of opinion as to what should be preserved, abandoned, or changed, and what should be adopted from other cultures. And anyway, cultures are not changed by laws or edicts, but by slow and complex processes which can be consciously modified only to a limited extent.

The debate on the advantages and drawbacks of different cultural forms is worldwide, and just as important for Western

Europe or the U.S.S.R., or the United States or China, as for any Pacific nation. This fact, however, is not always fully appreciated in the islands. Likewise, many are not aware of how diverse the cultures of the industrialised nations are. The existing cultural patterns that the industrialised nations have stumbled into in the 1980s are only in part derived from ancient patterns. The implied assumption that people in Europe today live a life just like that of their forefathers is false. The differences in the way of life between the 1780s and the 1980s are as great for many Europeans as they are for Pacific Islanders.

Nevertheless, the Pacific peoples are probably more conscious of their cultures than are most peoples of the industrialised nations, and because most societies in the Pacific are very small, they may be able to influence the future shape of their cultures more than individuals in the larger nations can. But their smallness also makes them vulnerable to being swamped by external forces.

Pacific peoples have a moral right to shape the cultures they wish to live in, though they will not be the only ones to determine what happens in practice, for mass media, military alliances, foreign travel, treaties, and trade will all influence the outcome.[2] Much of the influence of Pacific Islanders on their own cultures will be neither planned nor conscious, for a culture is the product of actual behaviour. As the advertising industry is well aware, behaviour can be manipulated and even exploited, but it can only to a limited extent be planned. This last point is fortunate, for if it were not so, those with power — whether commercial, governmental, religious, or other elites — would control personal behaviour even more than they do now. Nevertheless, unless Pacific leaders take positive and well-organised action to influence the pattern of their own cultures, they will be even more dominated by external forces than they have been in the past.

Culture can be broadly defined as a way of life — the way we think, believe, and behave, as well as the way we make, do, and use things. Culture is the way a people express themselves — not only verbally, but in dress, life style, beliefs, and practices. Again all culture can be seen as language, for all we do and the way we do it is communicated to others. Dance is clearly a language of movement and symbol, but so is religion a language, and customary behaviour and all aspects of living. It all has meaning for those using it and for those who see them using it.

Some of the aspects of culture which would need to be examined if one was to have a policy or set of priorities on cultural matters are listed below. The extent to which traditional precedents are adhered to tends to increase as we go down the scale from the technical and impersonal to the creative and personal.

Minimal traditional precedents:
Technology
Economy
Government

Moderate use of traditional precedents:
Politics
Religion, ethics, and philosophies of life
Social organisation

Major use of traditional precedents:
Customary behaviour
Creative arts
Language

Technology: if it works, use it!

Technology includes means of transport (vehicles, planes, roads, canoes, etc), other means of communication (radio, journals, books, letters, television, films, telephones, and so on), domestic technology (such as housing, cooking equipment, utensils, refrigeration, and furnishings) and the tools of production (industries, machinery, and equipment).

One aspect of technology which needs to be considered is its utility or efficiency. Pacific Islanders have generally adopted the products of industrial technology where these provide a quicker, easier, or otherwise apparently more advantageous way of achieving one's purpose. As with other peoples throughout the world, however, the decision to buy and use equipment is never made *only* on utilitarian grounds; prestige, status, personal expression, and other social and psychological values are also involved, as well as pressure from advertisers.

Thus, for example, it is common for small farmers throughout the world to want to buy tractors of their own even when their farms are so small that they would be much better served by hiring tractors on the few occasions they are needed. Much the same applies with motor vehicles, private boats, and rides on aeroplanes. Likewise with houses, refrigerators, and furniture it is extremely hard to determine to what extent these are purchased on criteria of utility (and these criteria are very arbitrary) and to what extent they are to fulfil social and psychological needs. Paradoxically some Pacific Islands farmers have abandoned relatively efficient features of traditional agricultural technology and replaced them by less efficient substitutes.

In any case, there seems to be a worldwide tendency not to be very nationalistic, or culture-bound about technology. That is, most people are not greatly influenced by traditional precedents in their choice of the main *things* they use. They may be more traditionally oriented in the *way* they use things, but even in use, most peoples are influenced more by convenience than tradition. The technology we use inevitably modifies the kind of life we live.

Symbols of identification

Traditional technology remains relevant in manual arts, which are discussed later, and in the preservation or reconstruction of outstanding features of the ancient cultural environment. Proposals for the development of a system of national parks throughout Micronesia 'by and for the Micronesian people' (see Wenkam's report) are of wider significance. Historical structures, such as the magnificent remains of the ancient stone city at Nan Madol in Ponape, have considerable psychological potential. They can be abandoned, weed-infested ruins which epitomise the collapse of one's ancestral culture and reinforce feelings of inadequacy or impotence. Or they can be well-maintained shrines to the memory of respected origins, a source of confidence and inspiration. It depends on how they are used and interpreted — and this is a field in which governments and particularly educational systems can play an important role. Such historic trusts can also be a source of income, although that is perhaps a secondary role which needs to be planned judiciously so as not to subvert their contribution to confidence and culture. The Pacific is full of such historic treasures, but few indeed of them have yet played a positive role in the development of cultural integrity.

This applies to natural features also, to some extent. The Swiss derive a range of satisfactions from 'possessing' the Alps, the Japanese from Mt Fuji, the Americans from the Grand Canyon, and New Zealanders from the 'thermal wonderland' — even though they did not make them! The Pacific-wide moves for national parks (including those under water where the Pacific's most exotic wild-life lives) make good sense both culturally and economically.

When people want to put technology into a museum, it is usually a sign that it is dead. Bad museums can become graveyards of culture, but good museums give the objects a new life as items of symbolic meaning and educational value when their utilitarian purpose has been superseded.

Traditional themes and designs may be of more relevance than the technology of their construction — in housing, for example. Professionally-built Samoan houses are works of art in themselves. Some New Guinean structures are quite magnificent. The materials used in contruction can in many cases be improved by manufactured substitutes, but some of the substitute designs are inferior in every respect. A few churches, hotels, public buildings, and private homes show the potential of marrying traditional and imported design concepts. The most spectacular example is the magnificent Parliament Building in Papua New Guinea, opened in 1984. Other attractive examples include the Catholic Cathedral in Port Moresby which is designed after a New Guinean cult house, the Pago Pago Intercontinental Hotel which expands the theme of the Samoan *fale tele*, Guam International Airport which draws on the Chamorro *latte*, Western Samoa's new House of Parliament based on the traditional meeting house, the Solomon Islands Museum, Ratu Sir Kamisese Mara's

The Port Moresby Cathedral, with the traditional Sepik *haus tambaran* of the kind on which it was modelled.

traditional *bure* in Suva and Lakeba, the Koror Council house in Palau, and Mr Jack Neale's home in Aitutaki.[3]. But there is still much scope for creative architecture in the islands. The emergence of a cadre of indigenous architects will probably be necessary before it is achieved.

Some customs are less useful than others

Europeans in the Pacific adhere to their traditional customs and beliefs rather more rigidly than most Islanders. This was even more pronounced during the colonial era, and understandably, any dominant group uses the symbolism of its customary behaviour as part of the means by which it continues its dominance. All power elites, whether foreign or indigenous, whether colonial, hereditary, military, or financial, appreciate this function of elite customary ritual. In time, the symbol comes to be valued for its own sake, and the costs and disadvantages or growing irrelevance of particular customs obscured.

Artificial cooling of artificial heating

The 'necktie syndrome' among Europeans in the Pacific is a minor example. The visible aspect of this customary complex of behaviour is a three-foot length of particular forms of cloth, cut in a very restricted range of shapes, adorned with a limited assortment of patterns and pins, and knotted at the throat by one of very few approved techniques. Once thus bound, one's whole pattern of dress is substantially determined. To wear the tie without a shirt would be unthinkable, or at least unactable. The shirt must be of a limited range of designs and styles, and must end about the genitals, though from the navel down it must be tucked out of sight between two, three or more other garments designed to cover the shame of the region between 'wind and water'. The tie carries an inbuilt compulsion to cover the legs, either by long trousers, a sulu, or long socks, and a leather shoe of a limited number of styles and colours. This customary wrapping evolved over many generations (though this does not give any custom the guarantee of suitability or validity that is often implied) in a different climate and culture.

In tropical climates the custom is so ludicrous that one would expect any human group to abandon it without further thought.

But traditional behaviour does not die easily. The pressures to conform to it are so great that, rather than adapt dress to climate, thousands of Europeans in the islands have willingly suffered great discomfort for many years. Those who can afford to spend large sums of money to redesign buildings and install machines to cool the air so that their skin temperature is similar to what it would be if they dressed, or rather undressed, in a way appropriate to the normal climate. In some down-town areas in the Pacific, these machines are so numerous that they increase the external temperature, thus necessitating more and larger machines to control the internal temperature. They add unnecessary noise and pollution, use resources which are scarce in these low-income countries, and exacerbate status differences between rich and poor. For of the factors which motivate people to install air-conditioning, archaic clothing is one, but social status is another.

Causes of continuity

Why are such apparently irrational customs adhered to so tenaciously? Partly, because they are common habits, they acquire an aura of respectability and people feel secure in conforming to them, and feel guilt and/or shame in not doing so. Partly, as they have been symbols of a dominant minority, they reaffirm the feeling of superiority and separateness of that minority. There has been an understandable weakening of the necktie custom with the closing of the colonial era, and it has persisted much more among the remaining agents of foreign power (especially businessmen and representatives of governments) than among those not competing for status recognition in this way (for example, volunteers, tourists, and academics).

But Europeans are not alone in their resistance to changing customary patterns. This is a human tendency which may have had survival value in the early phases of cultural evolution. Nevertheless, as the dodo and the bald eagle found at the cost of their extinction, behaviour should not be too far removed from the realities of life. Culture change in the Pacific has been

much faster than it was in Europe, but there is still considerable scope for a critical examination of particular customary
practices to determine their suitability to the context of today.
Unfortunately some of Europe's sillier customs have been
adopted rather readily. 'A tragedy occurs,' says Samoa's Albert
Wendt in a personal note, 'when the colonised ape the ways,
thoughts, attitudes, customs and values of the colonialists. We
develop an inferiority complex and consider all things foreign
superior to our own. The quest is then for the white-collar
miracle, with its symbols of dog-kennel houses, Mafia sunglasses, cocktails, thrift — and schizophrenia!'

Members of any culture want to be free from cumbersome
and awkward obligations and restrictions, but this freedom is
not always easy to achieve. In many cases everyone wants to
in theory, but no one is prepared to start in practice. The
conflict is between the vested interests of the individual and
the long-term interests of the society. Bride price is an
example.

Women's liberation?

Bride price is a term used to describe the various customary
payments made in many Melanesian societies from the
groom's relatives to the bride's relatives. There was usually a
series of transactions, beginning with engagement, and
repeated in a different form at the time of marriage, birth of
first child, and so on — sometimes continuing for longer than
the lifetime of the bride concerned. Customs varied, but it was
common for a wide range of relatives to contribute valuable
ornaments, shell money, pots, mats, wooden-ware, and food.
The amounts contributed were limited by relatively slow and
dangerous communication and the extensive time and energy
needed to make or buy shell money and other valuables. The
goods contributed were not retained by the bride and groom,
but were redistributed among their relatives in reciprocation
for like contributions from them for other birth, death,
marriage, and related ceremonies.

In recent years bride price has disappeared or declined in
some areas, but in many areas it has boomed on a larger scale
than ever before, and even been adopted by peoples who did

not practise it traditionally. Most of those who do practise it want to stop the custom, or at least reduce it. Local councils and committees have passed regulations forbidding or limiting it, but seldom with any effect. The public interest in limiting it is outweighed by those who stand to gain on any particular occasion. Everyone is ready to stop after he has recouped the payments due to him for his outlay — and that means never.

Moreover, whereas the traditional custom was to transfer goods for redistribution, the current practice is to include larger amounts of cash and capital goods. Even large new trucks have been given as bride price, and a truck cannot be cut up and shared to many dispersed relatives. In such circumstances the father of the bride can make a windfall if he manipulates the system to his own advantage.

Everyone sees the problem; the difficulty is how to get off the merry-go-round. Dr Latukefu's article on 'The Place of Tradition in Modernisation' highlights similar vicious circles in customary rituals and pig exchanges.

Women have been particularly bound by customary restrictions, but, as elsewhere in the world, these restrictions are slowly being modified. Taboos on contact between brothers and sisters, prohibitions on speaking to one's mother-in-law, restrictions on the use of names, and limitations on movement were all both customary and reasonable in a number of societies. Increased mobility and new patterns of living are making them cumbersome or unduly restrictive, but it usually takes considerable time and trouble to adjust to the new situation.

The status of women, as in subsistence communities generally, was very limited. Ever-improving access to higher education and to a slowly widening range of jobs is broadening the range of opportunities open to women. Though constrained by male prejudice and their own lack of confidence, the process is speeded up by active pressure from women's groups and even more from the inexorable developments of technology which constantly reduce the case for sexual distinctions in employment and make it more advantageous to use the potentials of all people irrespective of sex.

The University of the South Pacific in 1984 had 1042 male full-time internal students and 588 female, but there was considerable variation between countries: Kiribati and Tuvalu had more women than men, the Cook Islands about equal, Fiji almost fifty per cent more men than women, Vanuatu five times more men than women and Solomon Islands six times! The university's 3074 students taking credit courses by extension, and over 2000 undertaking non-credit courses, followed a broadly similar pattern. Only three Pacific parliaments (Western Samoa, Fiji, Papua New Guinea) have women members, but even in those the numbers are very small.

Women have had considerable success in many professions; not only as teachers, but increasingly as doctors or lawyers, and in some cases they have done very well in business. In Rarotonga, for example, most of the locally-owned businesses are owned and operated by women. The Pacific Theological College now accepts women candidates for theological degrees and some churches have begun to ordain them.

The quest for a unique, respected and functional identity

Many Pacific Islanders are seeking a revised identity. There are advantages in being part of a world community, but the scale of it is overwhelming. Most people need to belong to smaller units, to identify with groups which both cover a restricted area and have more interests in common. We also enjoy taking a part in the creative process, and the larger the population which uses a similar pattern, the fewer the numbers who effectively participate in its formation and adaptation.

Though the Pacific shares this problem with the world, there is a major difference. Most people in the Pacific (both Islanders and Europeans) confuse industrial technology with European people and the cultures of Europe. But technology is merely the tools; it is totally separate from race, and distinct from culture. More of the equipment used in the Pacific today comes from Japan than from Europe or America. Although technology influences a culture, to speak of industrial technology as European (or 'western') is as misleading as regarding all paper as Chinese, all cotton cloth as Indian, all glass as Egyptian, all rubber as Mexican, or Christianity as Palestinian, merely because the particular processes or thought patterns developed in those places. More than misleading, it is humiliating.[4]

Things that can more justifiably be classified as European (and/or American) include the English language, most of the newspapers, journals, books, and films available in the Pacific, much of the music and dance, and some rather trivial customs (like the wearing the neckties). Mass communication is likely to increase (though whether it will remain so overwhelmingly Euro-American remains to be seen), but this also generates a desire for a distinct identification, a haven from the over-whelming deluge of foreign words and images.

The people of small and isolated countries do not have the resources to excel in manufacture or science or military power. The task, as many islands leaders are aware, is to create ident-ities which are deeply meaningful but which do not obstruct their quest for other goals. There is at times an uneasy balance between the demand for the products of industrial culture and the welfare state on the one hand, and (perhaps as an uncon-scious reaction to the reduction of uniqueness as part of the process) the demand for one's own language and culture.

What is so good about the culture one happens to have been descended from? There are thousands of culture patterns in the world. They cannot all be the best. Why restrict oneself to the limited range of choices developed in communities where experience was governed by the distance one could walk or go by canoe, by the knowledge transmitted by word of mouth, and by the very restricted experience of an isolated, non-literate, stone-tool culture?

The short answer, of course, is don't. But also, don't throw out the baby with the bathwater. Cultural systems are easier to destroy than to create, and it is wise to consciously reject an aspect of culture only when a better substitute is offered. And cultural identification is vital to both individual and group confidence and integrity. It can be modified, but to totally and suddenly reject it is likely to lead to serious trauma.

A healthy mixture of cultures

The reasons given by Demas Nwoko for advocating the perpetuation of African artistic traditions were 'the *good health* of the New African and . . . our effective contribution to world civilisation'. In a similar vein Dr Karl Schmidt, a specialist in

New Guinea screen-printers with some of their creations.

mental health, wrote the following prescription for *mental health* for people of the South Pacific:

Live your own culture
Enrich it where possible
Incorporate the best from other technologies without
    identifying with the cultures from which they stem

Enrich and *incorporate* are the key concepts in this formula. The mix of the established and the exotic will vary greatly. Total reversion to traditional cultures is impossible. It denies the basic truth that any way of life is greatly influenced by the environment, by the number of people involved (e.g., village or city), the economic system (e.g., subsistence or market), the political system (e.g., isolated community or nation-state), religions and beliefs (e.g., unique local religion or international religion), and communication (e.g., over a few kilometres and seldom, or over much of the world and frequently).

How big a component should the traditionally-oriented be? All young Pacific Islanders want to know some language in addition to their own, to sing some songs of other origins (and sometimes only foreign songs to the exclusion of the indigenous), to dance some dances other than those of their forefathers, to see films and other non-traditional forms of entertainment and to take part in social relationships their ancestors never dreamed of.

A recent distinguished speaker urged fellow Melanesians to make their towns 'modern, but Melanesian in character'. It may be possible, depending on what is meant by 'Melanesian', which refers to the very diverse people of more than a thousand different language and culture groups. The speaker did not clarify the terms but they convey intense meaning and feeling to many who use them. The roads, basic structures, plumbing, lighting, fuel, shopping facilities, transport and communications aim to be essentially 'modern'. The people will remain physically Melanesian and they could retain distinctive styles of dress, creative arts, religion, and entertainment. Schools and churches, though introduced institutions, can take on distinctive characteristics both in the structures themselves and the activities undertaken within them. Another speaker at the same conference advocated more change 'while keeping intact the basic fabric of Samoan culture'. Which aspects of the fabric can be kept in a situation of rapid change? Language certainly, some features of social organisation, and distinctive styles of dress, creative arts, religion, and entertainment. There are limits, but the goal is legitimate if it is valued.

Speaking of the increased interest in local history and traditions which has arisen in the face of external pressures, Raymond Firth says:

> To maintain their social identity in a wider social universe, where so many pressures and attractions lead them to merge themselves in that universe completely, they want to call on any aids. Traditional tales are helpful here since they are relatively neutral from an action point of view . . . The tales can be maintained as true, they can be held to have a symbolic character or they can be regarded as . . . recreational or aesthetic products. In any case, as a property that is indubitably belonging to the group concerned, the traditions can serve as an identity badge, and a social rallying point.

Much the same applies to vernacular song, some forms of dance, and use of vernacular language. The recent post-independence surge of tattooing in Western Samoa likewise shows the value to the people of this form of identification and artistic expression, despite more than a century of mission efforts to stamp it out.

Emergence of national (rather than tribal or local) cultures is likely to increase as a result of the common 'enclosure'of many tribal cultures within a single nation-state. Thus, aspects of a distinct New Guinean culture are now appearing which transcends the hundreds of language and culture groups within that country, and draws elements from many of them into a new synthesis. The emergence of some pan-Pacific cultural features based on some common traits, is likely to increase with the increased awareness of common problems, vis-a-vis the wealthier industrialised cultures.[6] Common cultural heritage will be used to reinforce this, but the 'commonness' will be secondary — the unity will be derived from current circumstances. If circumstances change, societies can fairly readily adapt the content and emphasis of supporting historical and cultural information and belief to better secure the present need.

Culture and wealth

Traditional culture is sometimes glorified by privileged elites to make the poverty of the masses more bearable. Moreover, the extent of preservation of traditional culture and social cohesiveness in the Pacific does correlate inversely with income. Oversimplified, the more money, the less culture. To see the way in which money and the American emphasis on consumerism can erode a culture one need only compare the cultural richness and financial poverty of Western Samoa with the monetary richness and cultural poverty of American Samoa, where rates of crime, delinquency, alcoholism, addiction, emotional tension, and other indices of social stress are much higher. In Western Samoa, per capita income is vastly lower but social cohesion and cultural integrity greater.[7] Even within Western Samoa, nearly 70 per cent of the reported crime is said to be committed among the 18 per cent of the population which lives in the capital.

But it is a popular fallacy to think that higher income inevitably causes cultural deprivation. More money creates a potential for cultural enrichment, but the context in which the money is at present generated subverts much of the potential for human development into chromium plate, sugar coating, and stomach ulcers. It is the commercial ethic, the advertising, the media, and the thing-oriented planning that results in the over-valuation of goods and the under-valuation of personal growth and cultural development.

Culture and self-respect

If support for indigenous culture costs time and money in educational curricula, arts councils, subsidies, and organisation, why not simply take over American or other models? Ratu Sir Kamisese Mara, when he was asked what Fiji would gain by becoming independent, replied simply, 'Self-respect'. Language, the expressive arts, and certain forms of customary behaviour are symbols of identification, self-respect, and dignity which many people do not want to lose. As Ulli Beier has pointed out: 'Self-expression becomes the pre-condition for the attainment of the self-respect without which a nation cannot hope to succeed and grow'.[8] Moreover, these are not the kinds of issues that are decided by edict. The language a mother uses with her child and the way in which people express themselves are not determined by cost or efficiency.

There is an element of self-protection in the desire to retain a minor language or cultural form. But defence of this kind can be more readily justified at a fraction of the cost of conventional military-type 'defence'. We are unduly obsessed with measurement, and a consequent tendency to over-value things which can be measured. Today's economics (which can degenerate into a secular theology which overemphasises human greed and leads to everything being valued ultimately in material terms) does not adequately cope with concepts of dignity, expression, creavity, or self-realisation except in the very limited, and at times sordid, consumption aspects of these terms.

Most of us are inconsistent in our thought and action about culture, and express conflicting views, in different contexts and at different times. Leading exponents of traditional cultures generally live by them only to a limited extent themselves, but use key symbolic features of them to reinforce an identity which might otherwise be in doubt. The validity of a quest for identity may be reinforced by the fact that leaders advocating indigenous cultures include a high proportion who have lived for long periods in foreign cultures (and are thus aware of their limitations), or are themselves of part foreign ancestry. Such people are more aware of the relativity of cultural systems (which tend to be taken for granted by persons who are intimately familiar with only one). Marginal people are likely to be more aware of the losses sustained as well as gains derived in rejecting traditional values and practices, and tend to give greater emphasis to creating a firm identification in whatever model they choose to adopt.

The main spokesmen for encouraging traditional culture are urban-dwelling professionals, earning salaries in higher education, government, or politics. They follow a lifestyle which has more in common with, and keeps them in closer daily contact with, other professionals and overseas colleagues than with those living a more traditional lifestyle at home. This is probably to be expected, as it is among this section of any community that creative thought is most cleary expounded.

On the other hand, traditional identification is at times used to make a political leadership acceptable, by identifying it with goals and symbols which are valued, whether achievable or not. Politicians are aware that there are some goals which everyone favours verbally but no one acts (and in some cases no one wishes) to attain. This is because the *seeking* itself, the quest for identity, the acknowledgement of its significance, may be as important as (and is certainly separate from) its achievement.

In some instances, the feeling of being members of an economically underprivileged group may be compensated by (or defended with) assertions of strong pride in a distinct ethnic identity. There is at times an ambivalence about imported values, and a rejection of the identification that goes with them, which leads to a commitment to a vague intangible tradition but not to action for achievement of the goals implied (but seldom spelt out). Nevertheless, provisions to meet legitimate needs for personal identity do not necessarily achieve the social and economic goals which are sought at the same time. To some extent these distinct needs can be met by common or compatible action, but some action to meet the one may run counter to achievement of the other.

Cultural integration and integrity

Some islands leaders are anxious to avoid the depressing fate of creating degenerate sub-cultures, permanently dependent on the guilt, embarrassment, generosity, or self-interest of larger, richer neighbours. One has only to look at American Samoa to get a glimpse of the kind of process that could lead Pacific territories to a state of being permanent welfare cases, with the depressing psychological concomitants of permanently living on charity.[9] This is very different from interdependence in which each culture contributes the best its physical resources and skills can offer.

It is sad to see Tonga, historically one of the Pacific's greatest and proudest cultures, having to eke out a living today by contributing largely unskilled labour to Niue, Nauru, Hawaii,

American Samoa, New Zealand, Vanuatu, and elsewhere, doing jobs which are vacant because the citizens of those countries consider them the least acceptable forms of employment.[10] There is a vast difference between their former position as the Pacific's greatest navigators and present one as its most numerous deck-hands. In other words, a population which is allowed to greatly outstrip resources without developing alternative high-order skills is forced to humiliate itself by doing the menial tasks for, or begging handouts from, wealthier neighbours.[11] This reality is in direct contrast to the image which people want to create of themselves.

A unique identity is not enough; the Pacific peoples understandably want a respected identity. Dependency erodes respect and generates ambivalent feelings of gratitude and resentment. Whether economic or cultural, excessive dependency can have serious social and psychological consequences. The total dependency of the United States territories (Marshall Islands, Federated States of Micronesia, Palau, Northern Marianas etc) on the United States illustrates the impotent bitterness, the slackness, the gutlessness, the decadence that can be generated by extreme dependence. As a Micronesian told me: 'So long as you keep your mouth on the U.S. tit, you don't even have to suck, it just flows'. The short-term payoff is in vast amounts of money; the long-term cost a psychologically, economically, and culturally dependent and degenerate people. A self-respecting identity needs a considerable degree of self-reliance.

Finally, the integrated set of identifying symbols must be workable, they must provide an effective focus for unity and confidence, and for reasonable achievement of the goals of the society. A symbol system devised for isolated subsistence agriculturists will not be functional for the 1980s unless appropriately modified. Yet some key concepts from that culture of origin are an essential component of the new.

It is easy to explain the changes that have taken place in Pacific cultures in the last two hundred years. What is harder to explain is their extraordinary resilience; the extent to which they have retained so much in the face of such vast changes in technology, social organisation, communication, and belief.

Most culture change in the Pacific has not led to the total adoption of foreign models, but to a protective reaction, and a creative adaptation incorporating elements from both. Pacific cultures are not dead. Substantially modified and incorporating much that is old and much that is new (and more than is usually admitted of that which is simply human), the post-independence era in the Pacific may see a new surge of creativity and new adaptations of what may be one of our most sought-after needs — the human dignity that can be associated with unique and valued identity.

6
Belief
Religion, philosophy, values and ethics

Was the baby thrown out with the bathwater?

Polynesian religions were especially elaborate and contained elements of aesthetic beauty and philosophical genius. The traditional religions of the Pacific were nevertheless (like Christianity) the products of small, isolated societies. In their original form they have little relevance to life today, but some aspects of them may be very relevant, and research, thought, and action in this area of traditional culture may well be merited. Though much has been lost, much more than is generally realised was recorded, mainly last century, and is available as a source of some kind of precedent and identification.[1]

Christianity has during the past century been incorporated into, and modified by, local cultures to a considerable extent. More recently, some students at the Pacific Theological College have been seeking traditional precedents for inclusion in Christian ritual and teaching, and a recent meeting of indigenous Melanesian priests expressed 'an urgent need to reformulate Christian theology in accordance with Melanesian religious concepts and expressions'.[2] Other Islanders may look to the traditional philosophies for precedents concerning other aspects of life.

Cannibalism, the strangling of widows, the killing of certain categories of infants, and the launching of canoes over human bodies were all integral parts of some traditional belief systems. No one favours their reintroduction. But it is false to assert that because of these features, all other aspects of traditional belief systems are inappropriate. It is like saying that Christianity or Islam have no redeeming features just because both have been closely involved with massive warfare from the Crusades to the

Second World War; or that the cultures of Europe have nothing to contribute because it was once common to burn witches at the stake and to determine innocence or guilt by methods involving physical suffering of the most brutal kind.

Inherited outward forms

To look at more material aspects of religion today, we need to consider the costs of religious services. This is not to suggest that they merit more expense or less, which is a matter for the communities concerned. But in much of the rural Pacific, the total costs of religious services and structures (in terms of labour, food, and other costs as well as money) as against their utilisation (in terms of hours per week and number of persons etc) are the heaviest form of tax the community has to bear. In urban areas, on the other hand, one often hears requests for more religious facilities.

What is a reasonable volume or proportion of total resources to devote to these purposes? There are several common arguments. One is that a work of art transcends material value, and that a community is enriched by the creative act of making and using beautiful structures. I agree with this principle, and feel that few communities in the world devote enough of their talents and resources to things of beauty, creativity, and symbolic expression. The mural on the Catholic church at Naiserelangi in Fiji is of continuing value not only to that parish, but to the people of Fiji and beyond. There are many other examples of creative expression through religious structures, but let us be honest: many churches in the Pacific, as elsewhere, are deadly dull.

If people want to build churches to the glory of God, then why should they not make them longer, wider, higher, larger than is needed to seat the congregation? This argument would make more sense if the main motivation was the glory of God, but a much stronger motivation in building outsize churches has been the glory of the community which built them, and the humiliation of neighbours with smaller churches. And many such churches reflect the greed and conceit of their builders.

Another view is that if people choose to build churches larger than are needed to seat their congregations, that is their own business since the money and resources have been given freely. This is reasonable, but with a qualification: how free is one to give or withhold? Many feel obliged to give more for social and supernatural reasons based on fear — fear of what their neighbours and leaders might say, and of what God might do, if they do not (and corresponding favours if they do).

If a church is big enough to accommodate those who use it, how frequently is it used? The number of services per week and the proportion of people attending them have been declining in the Pacific in the past decade, as elsewhere in the world. This raises the question of alternative or additional uses of church buildings, staff, and other resources. Some consider it an insult to God to use a church building for art, music, education, health, or other community needs. Others consider it an insult to God not to. But even among those who accept the latter view little action has been taken.

If Christian ministers were to dress as Christ dressed, or like fishermen or carpenters dress today, I could accept the symbolism (for dress is an important symbolic system of communication in any culture). What do Christian ministers communicate by their dress? Those who wear a cross bear a symbol which makes their beliefs and role clear. Now that we all move about so much, it enables those who want to communicate with ministers, or avoid them, to do so more easily. But objective study of the garments worn by ministers of religion in the islands today would show that many who base their dress on foreign models seem to have done so in the pattern of foreign businessmen and colonial administrators, and many who pattern their dress on indigenous models tend to have done so in the style of chiefs. I wonder how consistent it is with the teachings of Christ that his spokesmen should dress in ways which identify them with the aura of certain attributes of foreign businessmen, colonial administrators, and hereditary chiefs? The 1970s, however, saw a significant shift in the dress of ministers towards that of the people they serve.

Contribution of Christian missions

The rigidity and association with privilege shown in the dress of many ministers should not lead us to overlook the major contributions which Christian missions have made to the Pacific. Almost all formal education was until recently provided by the churches, as were most medical and welfare services. Their religion too was more universalist than the traditional systems. Again, their concern for indigenous interests, exemplified by those who devoted their lives to the care of lepers when cure seemed impossible, stands to their eternal credit. The conflicts between denominations have reduced greatly in the last decade and the transition from foreign mission to indigenous church has been accomplished in most cases.

Most missionaries in the Pacific islands have been Pacific islanders — over 1000 Samoan, Cook Islander, Niuean, Fijian, Tongan, and Tuvaluan missionaries have served in New Caledonia, Vanuatu, Solomon Islands, Papua New Guinea, and elsewhere, as well as many more from island to island in their own countries.[3] These people also contributed to feelings of Pacific awareness and Pacific unity.

But Christians have not necessarily practised all they preached, and allegations of public exploitation by ultra-conservative churches in Samoa and Tonga, for example, contain elements of truth. The average stomach girth of religious ministers in those countries is sufficient indication.

Churches now make a significant contribution to political leadership. In Vanuatu the Prime Minister is Father Walter Lini, the first two Deputy Prime Ministers were Reverend Fred Timakata and Reverend Sethy Regenranu; and the first Leader of the Opposition was Father Gerard Leymang. In Bougainville the Premier and some other outstanding politicians have been priests or former priests. John Doom of Tahiti, Bishop Finau of Tonga, Iosia Taomia of Tuvalu, and many others play a less direct, but equally significant political role.

Churches of the people

People who study Christianity across the world observe that there are few places where such deeply rooted 'folk churches' bind the communities, including both leaders and led, so closely and effectively as in the Pacific islands. Partly it is a result of the communities being small and relatively isolated. While such churches facilitate cohesion, they also reinforce conservatism and delay adaptation.

Women of Lau welcome delegates to the Pacific Conference of Churches.

Increasing external pressure is leading to the erosion of the still dominant 'middle of the road' churches as the young people move either away from the religion or into more fundamentalist options. The fundamentalist groups come mainly from the U.S.A., especially the South. Their package-deal explanations, action-oriented living, and ample funds seem to make them attractive despite their being dominated by foreign staff and foreign concepts. Along with conservative Christianity some of them tend to advocate, or at least facili-tate, very conservative political philosophies and practices. Historically Christianity was closely, though often unintention-ally, allied with colonialism. The new fundamentalist churches are even more closely, but still usually unconsciously, inte-grated with neo-colonial forces.

The indigenous-run churches often communicate with the people more effectively than the new bureaucratic elite. As power concentrates increasingly within central governments, guided by both internal and external power groups which are motivated largely by expediency and self-interest, the churches seem to be becoming a welcome source of independent thought and integrity. The spreading 'liberation theology', focussing on the needs of the poor, is a helpful antidote to the growing stratification of wealth and privilege in the Pacific's towns.

Inter-church co-operation expanded greatly in the 1970s. The Pacific Conference of Churches provides linkage between denominations and sponsors a number of joint programmes in human development, media, justice, and other fields. In Fiji, New Caledonia, and Hawaii, tentative contacts are being made between Christian, Muslim, Hindu, Buddhist, and other faiths.

Religion in the future

Radical changes in the content and functions of religious beliefs and practices are already in progress. As many aspects of the traditional religions were not well adapted to the industrial culture which was accepted at the same time as Christianity, so many aspects of Christianity are ill adapted to the age of computer technology and mass communication. Yet nineteenth century Christianity has become a sheet-anchor for many, a fixed point in a sea of sometimes bewildering uncertainty. But the anchor is neither as fixed, nor as secure, nor as useful as it used to be, and the task of reshaping new philosophies, new ideologies, new beliefs and values, and new ethical principles, is now being faced by some of the most creative minds among young Pacific Islanders.

And they will not be dealing only with Christianity. The teachings of Muhammad, Baha'ullah, and Marx are among the other perspectives that are likely to have some impact on the next phase of belief in the region.

Guidelines for living

The easy alternative to shaping one's own way of life is to adopt an existing model, but the two major export models — of General Motors and Coca-Cola on the one hand, and of Marx and Mao on the other — seem equally sterile. The Pacific peoples may create some adaptations from which the rest of the world could learn.

Conflicting values

Great emphasis is often given to the importance of preserving the philosophy of life of particular island cultures. It is difficult to define precisely what this means, though it has intense meaning in many cases. Some values which are commonly discussed in this context are unlikely to survive because people are attracted more by other changes which are antithetical to these values.

A common example is people's lamenting the decline in co-operation among relatives, particularly in towns. Some co-operation between relatives is likely to continue throughout the world, but its extent will probably continue to diminish (though it will probably remain more important in the Pacific Islands than in Europe or America). The demand for more paid employment, for laws and police and courts to deal with persons who deviate too far from acceptable standards of behaviour, for governments to provide facilities which were formerly provided by the family or village, and for much more movement of things and people, all lead to a continuing reduction in co-operation among relatives. One cannot legislate for the preservation of co-operation among relatives, and indeed action to increase it would be so directly opposed to other things which people in practice value even more, that it would be futile. In other words some behaviour which is valued as 'traditional' may be more correctly described as universal behaviour of small groups in partially subsistence economies.

One often hears pleas for the preservation of this or that traditional philosophy of life and, almost in the same breath, pleas for equal success in business, education, or other pursuits with Asians, Europeans, or other Islanders whose lives are influenced by significantly different philosophies. In fact, the acceptance of the one is often related to non-achievement of the other. Seldom are we prepared to think through, let alone accept, the consequences of adopting a particular philosophy. This is understandable, because it is difficult to substantiate the precise connection between particular aspects of philosophy and particular degrees of success or otherwise. But detailed studies demonstrating the nature and scale of this relationship would be valuable indeed, for common assumptions about features of traditional philosophy being obstacles to other goals may be as false as those which deny or ignore any causal connection.[4]

One apparent difference of emphasis is in the relative value placed on goods as against personal relationships. Even though all cultures support reciprocity and generosity and all individuals want to accumulate things for themselves, cultures vary greatly in the relative emphasis they place on the one or the other, for they inevitably conflict. In a general sense, a higher value is placed on the *accumulation* of property in western, and particularly highlands Melanesia (and among Indians, Europeans, and Chinese) while the emphasis in most Polynesian and Micronesian societies is on *distribution*. This may facilitate the more ready adoption of capitalistic enterprise in western Melanesia than in Polynesia or Micronesia. One way in which traditional behaviour limits new opportunities is seen in the relatively few Fijians who sell at the Suva market (the biggest retail produce market in the Pacific) and their lack of salesmanship, as such behaviour is incongruent with Fijian values. Nevertheless, some Fijian sellers are now becoming assertive and skilled.

If all members of a society place a similar emphasis on accumulation and distribution, equilibrium is maintained. But if one group emphasises generosity and distribution (as do Fijians) and another emphasises hard bargaining and accumulation (as do Indian businessmen in Fiji) there is an inevitable flow of property from the 'distributors' to the 'accumulators'. As Indians do not reciprocate in the manner of Fijians, this causes strained relations between them. Other differences in wealth are caused by physical size and cultural values. The average Fijian is *much* larger than the average Indian and thus spends more on food. This is accentuated by the emphasis on plentiful food in Fijian culture and economy of food in Indian.

Traditional social commitments (births, deaths, marriages, festivals etc) formerly necessitated walking or paddling, consuming home-grown foods, exchanging bark-cloth and other domestic products, and contributing energy to carry out all tasks involved. The process was reciprocal, so that costs and benefits were reasonably balanced over time, and the economic resources remained within the community. Today, where the same values are retained, the effect is radically different. The obligation to attend is met by hiring buses, planes or taxis; the obligation to provide food is increasingly fulfilled with imported frozen meats, canned fish, Australian rice, bottled drinks and other consumables purchased largely through non-indigenous sources and from abroad. Home made bark-cloth is replaced by rolls of cotton cloth from Hong Kong or Taiwan, and energy in many places involves extensive use of electricity or gifts of drums of kerosene, hired expertise (e.g. for sound systems, photography, lighting and so on). Most of the goods and services involve the accumulation by Islanders of a significant proportion of their total income and contributing not in a closed reciprocal system, but through a process in which the reciprocal obligations remain, and costs escalate, but the economic benefits are almost totally drained out to non-indigenous people both within the country concerned and overseas.[5]

In the Cook Islands, for example, the obligation to honour the dead leads to many charters of aircraft to transport bodies and/or relatives, to the import of expensive headstones and chartering of aircraft to outer islands together with cartons of imported frozen chicken and other goods for the accompanying feast. The total cost of a death will often run to ten years or more of annual per capita income. To take another example, the ladies of the island of Atiu are expert at baking cakes, but it is now considered shameful to have a local wedding cake, and almost all are flown in by 767 jet from Auckland to Rarotonga, thence by commuter aircraft to Atiu — at enormous cost relative to income levels. For a wedding in Rarotonga early in 1986, involving people of modest income, 1500 guests were invited to a lavish ceremony which would have absorbed substantial costs to hundreds of contributors. In such a context, with constant drains to numerous social commitments, capital accumulation for productive purposes receives low priority, so the economic benefits flow out to those who provide the capital, the goods and services including — in the Cook Islands case the foreign-owned Banks, Japanese vehicles and equipment, American aircraft, New Zealand foods and service companies.

New forms of authority

Many island peoples feel respect and honour are diminishing. These values are hard to measure because the words are given many different meanings. Honouring is ideally the recognition of outstanding personal qualities or performance. Respect for authority partly reflects fear of the consequences of displeasing authority, but it is also an acceptance of a certain system of authority as right and proper. With authority being taken over increasingly by centralised governments (and the independent governments are at least as centralised as the colonial ones) it is inevitable that respect for persons in local authority will diminish.

There is a need to transfer at least some of the respect which attached to earlier forms of authority (e.g. community councils, chiefs, or churches) to the newer forms (e.g. central governments, new political institutions, and police). Otherwise, as respect for older forms disappears, the new forms are not treated with respect, and those in power may use crude force to get obedience, conformity, and even submission. This is a poor substitute for respect based on mutual understanding and an appreciation of the various roles in society. Unfortunately a few governments in the Pacific, like some in other parts of the world, are introducing a degree of intimidation and coercion that many citizens do not regard as a legitimate means of achieving social order. Increased coercion is likely to lead to a reduction in the legitimacy of government, and thus to further coercion. In brief, some governments are taking the course which is easiest in the short run but likely to create most difficulty in the long run. Gross coercion is self-defeating — it either fails and leads to anarchy, or it succeeds by breaking the spirit of people, and with it the creative potential of the society.

Attitudes to time

The value and use of time is another much-discussed aspect of philosophy. Again this is partly moulded by technology (especially industrial technology with its compulsion to man the machine), partly perhaps by climate and partly by tradition. Pacific Islanders are eager to have regular paid employment, and at present this is geared to a forty-hour week (give or take a few hours). Since urbanisation is a part of this process, few can live at work, and commuting takes time. When one then sets aside time to eat and sleep there is not a great deal left to allocate in either traditional or non-traditional ways, though shorter working hours in future may give more scope for people to handle time in their own way.

Most traditional social rituals took more time than can be spared today, both because there are many more things to do, and because each person is doing different things. There is thus a continuing trend to reduce the time spent on each funeral, marriage, birth, reception of guests, or celebration of achievement, as well as to divert these activities from day to night and week-day to week-end. But many Pacific people still find themselves in conflict with non-islander employers (and increasingly with islander employers too) for giving priority to the meeting of such social obligations over paid employment.

The religion of commerce

One of the greatest needs today is for a new ethical system or systems to be evolved in the islands. The traditional religions are largely gone and the associated philosophies greatly eroded. Christianity, Hinduism and Islam are less referred to as guidelines for behaviour. They are being supplanted by the much more effective preaching of the commercial advertisers who, over every radio, in every newspaper, on every package proclaim the ethic of selfishness and greed. The main commandments of the religion of commerce, imbedded in almost every one of its advertisements, are to value:

1 Yourself over others
2 Consumption over production
3 Waste over conservation
4 Immediate effects over long-term consequences.

The world contains many ethical systems, but this is one of the most barbaric. The great religious and ethical systems recognise the nature of the human animal as well as the advertisers do. That is, man's immediate, instinctive reaction is self, now, consume. Whereas commerce uses this knowledge to exploit, most ethical systems aim to provide a framework within which these basic needs are integrated with the less instinctive needs of wider groups, which are of relatively recent formation in human history. It is only with contemplation and cultural evolution that man sees the need for, and builds, ethical and other systems to modify primitive individual drives, to give higher priority to the needs of others and to longer term perspectives.

The religion of commerce is so powerfully represented through its influence in politics and the mass media that it will take great courage to challenge it. Fiji's Prime Minister, Ratu Sir Kamisese Mara, once warned commerce to think a little less of its legal rights and a little more of its obligations to society. It could have been a step on a long road to the evolution of more humane ethical systems for the Pacific of the future, but where even those who advocate it do not follow it, the prospects are limited.

The new evangelism

The competition between indigenous and foreign lifestyles, as with religious and political beliefs, is complicated by the carryover to the islands of competition between rival groups in the 'reference' societies — the industrialised power systems which influence the islands. The fundamental/liberal split in Christianity spills over from Europe and North America to the islands, white hippies do their best to introduce hippiedom, while white commercial staff and foreign aid personnel try to support and inculcate conservative European middle-class values. Pot smoking yachties and Peace Corps volunteers try to give islanders the 'benefits' of marijuana and other aspects of their subcultures with the same enthusiasm that Jehovah's Witnesses, Marxists, Maoists, and Playboy fans proselytise their respective tastes and values. Last century's competition for influence over islanders between Puritan missionaries, conservative merchants, starched officials, and transcultural beachcombers is as vigorous as ever.

7
Social organisation
Networks of commitment

Social organisation includes the ways that rights, obligations, and privileges are distributed, the ways the many groups to which we all belong are structured, and the ways groups form, regroup, or disintegrate. As technology, economy, and government change, so do social systems. Each influences the other. When one gets markedly out of alignment with the others (and they are never in perfect alignment) some tension or loss of satisfaction results. The need for adjustment is often not noticed for some time because so much of our behaviour is learned unconsciously that we tend to do things in the way we are accustomed, without thinking about the reasons or consequences.

Old and new elites

The present distribution of privilege is questioned most strongly in the remaining colonies, where the privileges of the colonial elite are challenged to such an extent that the system is no longer acceptable to many, except for a short transitional period. While attention is focussed on rejecting old-style colonialism, however, economic and cultural imperialism flourishes. The social and political consequences of this system of privilege have hardly begun to be understood, let alone dealt with. Consideration must also be given to the privileges accorded to senior civil servants, both national and international (including academics), in places where they are grossly disproportionate to those available to the public. Education is becoming a source of privilege and power, and some islanders have suggested that the gap between commoners and the local educated elite is becoming as great as it was between Islanders and the colonial elite.

The second area of contention is hereditary privilege, which is most marked in the central South Pacific (especially Fiji, Tonga, and Samoa). The religious and philosophical assumptions which formerly provided a legitimate basis for these privileges are now less accepted. Some who advocate the retention or strengthening of traditional practices emphasise those aspects which enhance the interests of a privileged elite. This creates a reaction among the young and the under-privileged, and particularly those of humble social origins with high formal educational or other qualifications of a non-traditional kind.

But there is a danger that the abandonment of traditional rank structures in the absence of equally effective substitutes will improve the lot of foreigners, not islanders. The indigenous commoners of Hawaii, French Polynesia, Easter Island, and New Zealand were accustomed to taking a subordinate role, and thus when the traditional polity was destroyed it was not skilled commoners who filled the power vacuum and took over, but foreigners.

This is not a case for the artificial propping up of effete and decadent aristocracies whose power will inevitably be eroded by both internal and external forces. But it is a case for hastening the preparation of a new leadership, for to the extent that one goes without the other being effectively present, foreign (and local) business interests, foreign governments, and other foreign interests tend to fill the gap — the pay-off for them can be considerable. Privileged elites can play an important role, but unless they adapt to the needs of the times, they fossilise and either wither into insignificance or are overthrown. The world is too full of examples to need quotations.

Shame inhibits people of any culture, and often for good reason, but in societies based on hereditary stratification (chiefly societies) shame restrains those high up the scale less than those below. When the young reject the values of traditional hierarchy, they become less constrained by shame. Done to a mature extent this can release creative talent, but overdone it can lead to the abandonment of all restraint and consideration for others. Those at the top of the scale are as much to blame as the deviants at the bottom. If the privileges of others seem unachievable, and inconsistent with what is felt to be

reasonable or proper, aggressive rejection of the system is a natural reaction.

The extent of social differentiation, whether on grounds of class, caste, income, occupation, race, intelligence, religion, or otherwise is a debated issue anywhere, but has special significance for Pacific cultures, in which there is more internal diversity than in most. The main lines of cleavage between the diverse tribes of New Guinea, the Solomon Islands, and Vanuatu are linguistic and cultural, and to a lesser extent, physical. In New Caledonia and Fiji the deep divisions are racial — between Asians, Europeans, and Melanesians — though there is also considerable division within each racial group. In Samoa, Tonga, and the Marshall Islands, the major divisions are in terms of rank.

There is now a general preference for reducing the boundaries between these various categories, despite a widening in practice in some cases. Narrowing the gaps necessitates positive change in the factors which led to the differentiation in the first place, and it inevitably takes considerable time — and even the most desirable adjustments are seldom painless.

Social classes

It is usual to speak of widening class distinctions, but hard to be sure to what extent and in what directions this is occurring. My superficial impression is that this process is moving fastest in some places (for example, Papua New Guinea) in relation to the growth of local and foreign capital, in others (like Tuvalu) it is mainly in relation to a rapidly widening bureaucracy and an increasing gap between the bureaucratic elite and the rural poor. In Tonga, aristocratic links to commercial interests and bureaucratic leverage, with control of police and army, are creating a more powerful and more broadly based elite. In Fiji, the widening gaps are between the higher levels of bureaucracy and business and the trade unions with strong

Last century a number of kingdoms existed in Polynesia. The only one left is the kingdom of Tonga. Above, King Taufaahau Tupou IV accedes to the throne. Below, in his capacity as the then Chancellor of the University of the South Pacific, he awards a degree.

leverage, on the one hand, and the rural and urban poor on the other. There are also growing gaps between Indians, Europeans, and Chinese on the one hand, and Fijians and other Pacific Islanders within Fiji on the other. And of course, especially with rapid communication, those with common interests have more contacts, so that networks of elite communication connect the islands as well as the neighbouring industrialised nations. Islands businessmen, bureaucrats, politicians, academics and church leaders have some (but far from all) interests which are more congruent with Australian or American counterparts than with their fellow citizens.

But it is too often implied that stratification is greater today than it used to be at various earlier phases of history. This is an important question on which one hears many loose generalisations but sees little detailed evidence. And it depends on how one defines stratification: whether in terms of material resources (including money); political, economic, religious or other powers; social privilege or otherwise. To take a minor example, chiefs in Rarotonga at the end of last century would require their followers to supply vast quantities of food for a feast, and to provide gifts and entertainment. When the chiefs had eaten they would walk over the remainder — the bulk of it — so that commoners could not eat it, and it was destroyed. Likewise, for years the people of Atiu were required by their chief not only to supply crew without payment for his ship, bearing his name — Ngamaru Ariki (though sometimes described as 'theirs' as they had been required to pay for it), but also to supply copra and other produce to fill it. He sold the produce, usually in Tahiti, and kept the proceeds. When he eventually died the people burnt the ship and danced for joy.

Even in Fiji or Tonga, when one looks at the powers, privileges and consumption levels of various categories of chiefs as against commoners last century as compared to now, the gaps are smaller in some cases, and in some aspects of life, larger in others. No longer can chiefs give away vasts lands and villages with the people on them as happened in Fiji, or use the kinds of extreme coercion then in vogue. On the other hand, new technologies and concentrations of money facilitate new potentials of differentiation. Some objective research is needed into precisely how these patterns are changing.

Family structures

With increasing urbanisation, mobility, and monetisation of transactions, there will be continuing changes in social organisation. Not all of them will be in expected directions. For example, Dr Adrian Mayer made a study of three rural Indian communities in Fiji in the 1950s. In a restudy twenty years later he found that there were *more* extended and joint families than previously. Dr John Harré's research in urban Suva likewise shows that a large majority of urban Fijian households, even those living in housing reserved for nuclear families, are in fact extended families. Urbanisation and monetisation do not necessarily result in nuclear family households as is often believed.

The disadvantages that can be associated with urban extended families are well known, for extra residents can consume the time, money, and energy of their hosts. But the system can also have some positive functions in the provision of accommodation and other services for aged, unemployed, and other disadvantaged persons. It is not necessarily to the disadvantage of the household head, for some additional members are wage-earners, or supply domestic help in the home.

Social needs and services

Pensions and insurance against unemployment, accident, sickness, and other risks are being introduced. Banks, savings societies, and related means of capital accumulation are spreading. Laws, police, and other bureaucratic means of social control are growing. All these facilities replace traditional systems. Although many of the new techniques are better suited to town living and a money economy, some do not serve their purposes as well as those they replaced.

The impersonal bureaucratic facilities not only require more money and more skilled personnel than many countries can afford, but governmental social services are unlikely to be able to adequately cope with growing social problems. Even the United States, spending more per head on governmental social services than any other country, has failed rather miserably to cope with the problems it set out to solve. Dr Margaret Mead once observed that those American towns with most voluntary and community (as opposed to governmental) social services had the fewest social problems. In other words, it will be both economically and socially wise to encourage such aspects of welfare and social cohesion as can reasonably be handled by existing social systems. Moreover, functional social systems save time and human dignity as well as money. The relatively small populations of the Pacific Islands provide a context for more extensive use of these facilities than in more populous countries.

No development plan that I have read makes any realistic assessment of the additional financial or social costs of extra police, welfare services, mental health services etc, which become necessary as a result of the implementation of the plans.

A small example lies in a contrast in social control between American Samoa and Western Samoa. The former uses nearly four times as many police, relative to population numbers, as the latter. The difference in density of police between Kiribati and their neighbouring Marshall Islands is even greater. To take an example of another kind, Polynesians in both New Zealand and Hawaii have much higher crime rates than the dominant populations (against whom most of the crime is committed), but had, until recently, much lower rates of mental breakdown. The greater emotional interdependence in *rural* Polynesian cultures seems to have provided greater psychological security, but this is limited in urban environments.

On the other hand, we must avoid overstating the extent to which traditional societies looked after their aged, infirm, and disadvantaged. Some romanticise that such people were fully cared for in the past. In parts of south coast Papua the aged were killed and eaten by their relatives, in the belief that they were thus re-incorporated into the clan; in Niue the aged were left to die in small houses in the bush (given the difficult terrain and meagre subsistence there was probably not much option); and in some other places there was evidence of occasional serious neglect. In contrast, much was done for the aged in many islands, more effectively than in industrialised societies. Irrespective of what might have been, neither introduced facilities for the care of the aged nor traditional procedures are adequate in many situations (e.g. when the active adults have left the village for urban work, leaving the aged ill-catered for). Cardinal Pio Taufinu'u, the first Samoan to take over the Catholic church in Samoa, established an excellent home for the aged and infirm, realising that the theory of loving care from extended families did not always work in practice. Between 1976 and 1985 the number of Pacific nations with compulsory pension schemes (usually only for some categories of worker) rose from two to seven. Both voluntary and governmental welfare facilities are expanding, but many people still have no adequate solution to pressing welfare problems.

The unintended effects on social organisation and social relations of the rapid expansion of tourism must also be considered. It has been demonstrated that the tourist industry in the islands of the Caribbean has actively worsened relations between local people and foreigners.[1] Though there is no research data available for the Pacific, I have the impression that this is also true here.

A brief look at the cultural degradation of the Caribbean islands, measured by almost any criterion, made me feel that almost any integrated culture is better than none. Barbed wire around private homes, steel bars over windows, overt personal aggression on a large scale, despondency, resentment, hostility, and despair among common people — all in societies which the tourist industry projects as being happy and carefree!

Drug consumption is a growing problem in some areas, where the volume consumed per person, and the proportion of income spent on them, vastly exceeds that in the industrialised world. As the advertising of alcohol and tobacco is restricted in the richer countries it tends to expand in the poorer, where controls are fewer — and some Pacific governments are heavily dependent on tax revenue from these sources. The Minister of Health in the Cook Islands (himself a doctor and a social drinker) told me in 1986 of the urgent need for a publicity campaign and other action as over 80 per cent of the patients in the Rarotonga hospital were there as a direct result of alcohol and tobacco — drunk driving being much the largest single cause. Marijuana is spreading in many rural communities while cocaine and heroin seem to be largely confined to certain urban centres, though the overall consumption of these drugs is as yet low by current standards in the Western world.

These small examples illustrate the need for much more detailed thinking about the social consequences of economic goals in the development plans. Careful social planning can be helpful, though comprehensive thinking about the forces of change and the degree to which certain adaptations can be encouraged or resisted has scarcely begun. Segments of it are being dealt with in educational policies, broadcasting, housing, migration, rural development, social legislation and so on, but it merits the kind of detailed analysis and comparison of alternatives that is now given to economic planning. In fact the priority now being given to economic planning in the Pacific, without equivalent resources, thought, or skills being devoted to social processes, is leading to a gross imbalance — an over-emphasis on money rather than people, on volume rather than quality, and at times on measured trivialities rather than deeper but presently unmeasured fundamentals.

8
Creative arts
The soul of a people

A need for selectivity

Traditional creations in stone, bone, and wood have been reasonably well preserved (though often in overseas museums from which at least some must be returned). The revival of most handicrafts or manual arts could only be for different purposes, such as for sale to tourists,[1] for use as patterns or styles on things which are currently used, or as aesthetic objects or identifying symbols. These are all legitimate, and the market for high quality artefacts is considerable in some islands. Traditional design precedents may give a stamp of uniqueness and of confidence, and are almost essential for many exotic craft objects.

Music, dance, drama, and decorative arts have not been well preserved. In fact, there are large gaps in the knowledge about these arts before contact with industrial technology. The total resuscitation of traditional fine arts would be artificial in the extreme. The life of which they were a meaningful part is no longer lived. Some of these art forms do have aesthetic appeal, and some may be an effective means of asserting one's identity or independence (though in some circumstances they may also unnecessarily isolate or divide communities). But too much insistence on adherence to 'true' forms can be sterile, even ludicrous. John Kasaipwalova has warned fellow Papua New Guineans against lamenting the present and overglorifying the past, and advocates instead a 'creative and continuous transformation of the present'. Or as Jack Golson recently observed, culture should be preserved 'as a living body, not an embalmed corpse'.

There is a much-quoted opinion in Fiji that the 'true' kava ceremony must be performed in full for tourists whether they

The kava 'ceremony' in modern life — kava being served to a helicopter team at a drillhead.

like it or not. As there was considerable variation traditionally, both in different parts of Fiji and according to the different purposes of the ritual, and as there was little traditional precedent for tourists, only an arbitrary decision could determine what ritual pattern and sequence should be regarded as the 'true' one. Fijians themselves modify kava ritual greatly in terms of the method of its preparation (sometimes ground by machine and plastic-packed, sometimes ground at home in a steel pipe end), the containers it is served in (wood, enamel, glass, china, or tin of various shapes and sizes), the social purposes it is to serve (the function of honouring seems to be diminishing and that of socialising to be increasing), and the concoctions that are mixed with it (including rum, methylated spirits, and shoe polish).

There is a danger that if kava rituals are performed in full for tourists, foreign dignitaries, and the local aristocracy, they could become archaic and artificial, losing their relevance to life as it is lived. If the formal ritual takes on a new role as an entertainment or dramatic performance (as it may be doing), this may be justifiable provided it is recognised that this is very different from its original function.

Traditional arts and tourist income

Herein lies a dilemma which actively concerns many islands people. Should their fine arts be an expression of their own culture, as part of themselves, as a vital aspect of their way of life? This can be psychologically very satisfying (though it is not necessarily so). Or should the fine arts be used as a marketable resource which may have little other meaning? For many aspects of art the two are compatible, but for some esoteric areas there is conflict. In other words, the more these aspects of culture become something to sell to tourists, the less they are uniquely your own. It is these aspects of culture that tourists most want to buy. Giving others access to one's secrets can reduce their value as secrets, for while we want to share some aspects of culture, we want to keep others as a refuge for ourselves.[2] We all fear the humiliation of being 'seen into' while we yearn the appreciation of being 'understood'.

All human groups use the mystique of unique features of

The tourist industry creates distorted images of the Pacific Islands. Above, an advertisement for Pacific Harbour is captioned 'Man's longing for a paradise where man and nature are in harmony and at peace comes true.' Below, a Qantas advertisement symbolises the new colonialism.

their culture to some extent as insulation or as a protective shield. Bringing others into our private world has the potential for either greater or less understanding, for creating respect or contempt, for generating admiration or derision. This dilemma about which result is likely to occur, makes the reaction to self-exposure (which tourism feeds on) very ambivalent.

It is not only the over-commercialisation of most travel, but also its present gross imbalance in favour of white peoples and industrialised nations, that creates a problem out of what could be a solution. Unless the visiting is two-way, a high density of visitor population becomes indigestible. What could lead to cross-cultural understanding can then lead instead to cultural pollution and mutual contempt.

In Tahiti, Rarotonga, and Hawaii many people earn their living by dressing in clothes they never wore traditionally and never wear today, *except* when performing for tourists. In fact, grass skirts were not traditional in Polynesia, but most tourists are prepared to pay to have the images that the travel industry has trained them to expect revealed to them and their cameras — even though double deception is necessary to artificially satisfy the artificial demand. Men taking off their trousers to put on grass skirts for tourists brings money, but it also brings cynicism and after a time, quite frequently, hostility.

If performers feel that what they are doing is a sham or a deception, they find it hard to maintain for long much respect for either those they are deceiving or themselves. Such a condition has adverse effects on the personality of the performer as well as on inter-group relations. Mr. Taura Eruera recently reminded us that it strips not only the performer, but his people, of their human dignity.[3] And what is dignity? Confidence, worth, esteem, faith in oneself — the basic needs of any healthy human personality. The travel industry is, alas, corrupt. Not in the sense of money bribes perhaps, but in the deeper sense of distorting, twisting, falsifying, cheapening, in order to increase its income. Though at present among the most reputable of businesses, aspects of it will probably come to be regarded as shameful, possibly as criminal. Successful pirates used to be among the most respected of businessmen too, and both blackbirding and the slave trade were, in their respective hey-days, rewarding both financially and socially.

Masiofo Fetaui Mata'afa, then Pro-Chancellor of the University of the South Pacific, told tourist industry representatives:

> The culture, the friendliness, the songs and dances, the handicrafts and customs of my people of the Pacific are your most valuable asset, an asset which you can use without having to invest one single cent. . . . Destroy it and you have destroyed your main asset which can never be created again . . . new business opportunities beckon. Let us safeguard these opportunities by safeguarding our customs and traditions in a way that will preserve both our profits and our heritage.[4]

There will be considerable support in principle for the views expressed. Detailed planning for their implementation is a major and vital task. Much more needs to be known of the very complex processes by which aspects of cultures are influenced, in beneficial ways as well as in deleterious, by tourism as well as by other aspects of large industrial, urban cultures.

Clearly one cannot have all the traditional culture as well as all the tourist income, and islanders do not insist on all of one or all of the other. Nevertheless, many travel industry investors are in practice adopting policies which are likely to be destructive of assets which can 'never be created again'. Investors will not suffer much — they can transfer their capital to more profitable alternatives, particularly as products that worsen human welfare are often more profitable than those which improve it. But what they have destroyed will be irreplaceable.

Development plans so far make little or no provision for encouragement of the creative arts. When the potential contribution of creative talents to the development of both the individual and the society is more fully realised, however, more is likely to be done. Even in the narrow field of employment and monetary growth, the potential is substantial. Tourists are unlikely to be greatly attracted by bands which play third-rate versions of the noises many of them are trying to escape from at home, nor be entertained by what a Solomon Islander once aptly described as a 'bastardised Tahitian hippie-hippie shake-shake'.

Above left: Tongan carver, Aleki Prescott, at work. Above right: Vanuatu artist, Aloi Pilioko, works on a tapestry. Below: Solomons women making shell ornaments for use in marriage, funeral, and other ceremonies.

Pacific Islanders have great talents for developing both the entertainment industry and the manual and fine arts for commercial markets. Both need the opportunities for their most skilled peoples to get together and study (but certainly *not* to be 'trained' by foreign 'experts'), preferably within the islands, to refine their arts, and to transmit them to others.

Sport goes Olympic

Some traditional sports, like *tika* (throwing long darts on an open pitch) were spread through much of the Pacific, but few of them have survived the competition of football, cricket, and other introduced games. One of the main motivations of sport is prestige, which necessitates recognition by others, and focusses effort inevitably on international games. The South Pacific Games includes traditional Pacific sports as a minor part of its programme, but there is little likelihood of them becoming of more than local significance.

The Festival of Pacific Arts

The first Festival of Pacific Arts (originally called the South Pacific Arts Festival) was held in Fiji in 1972. It attracted participants from throughout the Pacific and was a major breakthrough. At the same time, we need to heed the sentiments expressed by Francis Bugotu, a distinguished Solomon Islands creative artist, Secretary for Foreign Affairs then Secretary General of the South Pacific Commission from 1982 to 1986, who said of the first Arts Festival:

If we say that the Arts Festival will show the world 'the best of Pacific culture' (as Mr Carrell seems to believe), we are making a completely false statement, since all it will show are some technical aspects of some Pacific cultures — it will not show that we Melanesians are transforming our culture, quickly and painfully, to take over our own destinies, or that Tongan culture is strangling its people politically, or Gilbertese culture acting as a dead weight on economic progress, or Fijian culture giving the Indians a clear field in commercial enterprise. The Festival will show the trimmings, the pretty wrappings on our cultures, and that is all.

So let's be honest about it. The main benefit of the Arts Festival will be to the tourist trade. The tourists will love it, and so will the Suva hotel-keepers, shop-owners and brothel-minders . . . another $3 million in trade for Fiji. Very good; we're not saying it's bad; but let's be honest about why Fiji and the rest of us want an Arts Festival . . . Let's not pretend that we are 'preserving our culture' (whatever that means) through the Arts Festival.[5]

At the national level, the Fiji National Dance Theatre, Cook Islands National Theatre, Papua New Guinea National Arts Theatre, and others have emerged, as well as private commercial dance groups, working as far away as Japan, Europe, and the U.S.A.

The expression explosion

Literature too has blossomed, with the South Pacific Creative Arts Society alone having published over 1000 different stories, poems, dramas, and other items by over 400 Pacific Islands authors since it was founded in 1972. In most islands nations at least one journal for creative writing was established in the 1970s but Papua New Guinea began the process for the Pacific with the quality journal *Kovave* in 1968. Annual national cultural festivals are also becoming widespread, with the quality of Tahiti's 'Tiurai,' the Cook Islands 'Constitution Celebrations' and Vanuatu's 'Cultural Festival' being among the most outstanding.

In carving, music, dance, and drama there has been a visible surge of energy and creativity, and in painting, the annual Pacific Artists Workshop begun at the Michoutouchkine-Pilioko Foundation in Vaunatu in 1984 promises to make this relatively new art form a popular outlet for talented islanders.

PROPERTY

9
Land
Resource or obstacle?

Customary tenures

Emotional involvement in land is very strong in the Pacific. It is sometimes suggested that emotion should be ignored in planning, but this would be unwise for human beings make decisions much more on feelings than on facts. Emotional feelings become political realities, and feelings are among the most important factors in land matters in the Pacific today.

The very diverse tenure systems in the Pacific have several features in common.[1] They were devised for subsistence agriculture, in situations where people produced almost all their own food. About a tenth of a hectare of land per person was needed under crop at any time, although this varied with the crop and the soil. Because of high temperatures, heavy rainfall, and leaching of soil, the land was left fallow for some years after cropping, so half to two hectares of agricultural land per head, or up to eight hectares per family, was needed. In addition land was needed for hunting, foraging, and other purposes.

Rights to land were in all cases vested in groups. The groups varied in composition, and there were rights held by individuals, extended families, lineages, clans, tribes, and so on. That is, in any one piece of land there was a hierarchy of rights at several levels.

The sale of land was traditionally unknown in most of the Pacific Islands, and is still forbidden by law in many of them. The transfer of land in the customary systems was mainly by inheritance from parents, but a number of subsidiary provisions provided flexibility to accomodate the varying needs of very large or very small families, adoptees, illegitimate children, refugees, migrants and so on.

Warfare was another very important means of land transfer. When governments and missions stopped warfare, they did so without adequate assessment of the functions it served in land distribution. When warfare ceased there was a need for other means of land transfer. Unfortunately in most of the Pacific throughout the 100 years since local warfare ceased, no adequately flexible facilities for land transfer have been provided.

Whereas one could live off a tenth of a hectare of crop in the subsistence society, more was needed to earn an equivalent living from cash cropping. There was no shortage of land for the first few generations after contact, because the populations of the Pacific were drastically reduced by introduced diseases, by warfare with more lethal weapons, and by labour migration. The populations declined from the first half of last century until the turn of this century, and this created an apparent surplus of land. It was assumed that population decline would continue.

A second major effect of contact on traditional land rights concerned transport. Five kilometres had been about the limit within which one could effectively maintain land rights. But with improved shipping, motor transport, and no risk of attack, it became possible to hold land rights over a very much longer time and distance. This has led to a very acute problem in much of the Pacific — that of the absentee landowner. Registration of land aggravated the problem. In the traditional society land rights were retained not by inheritance alone, but also by residence and active participation in the community. If active participation ceased and was not renewed within a reasonable time, one's rights withered away.

This major difference between the land tenure systems of Europe and the Pacific Islands has led to a great deal of misunderstanding. In the islands societies land rights waxed and waned, they increased and they diminished, whereas in capitalistic societies they start and finish at a particular moment, that is, at the moment of sale the seller's rights are completely extinguished and the buyer takes them over in total. This was not so in any traditional Pacific Islands system, where rights were subject to the land-holder's continuing to be an acceptable member of the community. Rights were never absolute but were constantly strengthened or weakened or faded out for those absent too long. When the registration of land was introduced, it was at first assumed that it would provide stability, yet in practice registration introduced too much rigidity.

Problems of codification and registration

When land commissions were set up in most of the Pacific to demarcate and register land, people usually insisted that they register the traditional boundaries of the areas then recognised as theirs for subsistence purposes. But the small, fragmented lots into which they had traditionally marked their lands for subsistence gardening were very different in size, shape, and distribution from what is needed for commercial farming.

After registration land can usually be acquired only by accident of birth; that is, by inheritance from one's parents. By any principle of logic this is a poor basis for allocating what is in many cases the nation's most valuable resource. It leads to many people who never used land owning lots of it, to many who would like to use it having none, and to vast areas lying unused or under-used throughout much of the eastern Pacific. The only child of an only child is usually rich in land, but is also likely to be in regular paid employment and does not use it; whereas the fifth child of a fifth child, starting from the same original amount, has an uneconomic fragment, although he is probably dependent on it as he is likely to have fewer educational and other opportunities. Traditional mechanisms of gift, permissive occupancy, adoption, voluntary reallocation, and even warfare have not been adequately substituted for, and a mobile population in a modern economy needs much more flexibility of land transfer.

In the subsistence society the over-riding rights of the local community were recognised — the need of the society as a whole was greater than the need of one of its members. The community is now the nation, and land rights will increasingly become allocated in terms of national interest. But cultural change takes place at different speeds, and land is always an area of cultural lag. It may take some time for the system of land allocation to catch up with the current needs of the society.

Problems due to the persistence of aspects of the subsistence system include those associated with livestock. In the early stages of contact with Europeans cattle were in great demand because they contain a lot of meat, yet in more than a century they have not become significantly incorporated into any island's agricultural system. This is important — people want them and many people have tried to farm them, but most have either abandoned them or kept only a few. One of the reasons is that very few individuals have sufficiently exclusive rights over a sufficiently large area to allow them to farm cattle effectively.

Moreover, many islands people have a strong psychological resistance to fences. One's land should be accessible to neighbours and friends. People need to walk over it to get to their own land, and building a fence suggests to your neighbours that you do not trust them. One hears many instances of people getting their fences chopped down by others who are resentful of them. Putting up fences was not the done thing, and it is only slowly becoming acceptable. Problems of these kinds are being overcome, but a number of adjustments are necessary in the process.

Many governments have tried to codify custom, but this very process changes the custom. Introduced legal, judicial, and administrative structures all modify the custom very greatly because one of the keys of these customary systems was that they were not based on law, or formal administrative structures, or written records. This left them with a great deal of flexibility. The people who first codified the customary systems were not to blame, because at that time the populations were declining and it seemed that there was going to be plenty of land, and also because the problems did not arise until the generation after first registration. At that stage governments should have been on the alert for problems of multiple ownership and made appropriate provisions for freer transfer of land to meet the changing needs, but in no case did they do so.[2]

One of the major problems as a result is that everybody's

name, once on the register, stays on the register, and people
who by customary processes would have dropped out and no
longer have been regarded as land-owners, now retain their
legal title to the land. In most of eastern Polynesia people
inherited land either through their father *or* through their
mother, but not generally through both. But the governments
of Tahiti, the Cook Islands, Niue, and New Zealand all
misunderstood these systems. The people said in effect, 'We
inherit from our fathers and our mothers', which indeed was
true, but they did not normally or *continuously* inherit from
both. Where colonial governments legislated to give full rights
of inheritance to all children from both parents, they unintentionally created problems which are now of fantastic proportions. Many plots in Tahiti, the Cook Islands, and New
Zealand, with hundreds of legal owners each, are not big
enough to support a single farm. Many single house sites in
the Cook Islands have 100 or more legal owners. These problems are caused, not by the traditional systems, but by colonial
governments which misunderstood the customary ways in
which unused rights withered away, for custom does not
prescribe the obvious: it provides rules or principles for situations in which there would otherwise be doubt.

   If land is registered and not allowed to be sold (as in most
of the Pacific), and *all* offspring inherit equal rights to it, this
doubles the number of registered owners per plot each generation. This is now a major problem in much of the Pacific.[3] It
has gone on for so long that many islanders wrongly believe
it was their ancient inheritance system.

Land alienation

Between 1850 and 1900 Europeans alienated substantial areas
from islanders by purchase, fraud, confiscation and otherwise.
The most extreme cases of fraud and misrepresentation
occurred in Vanuatu,[4] and the worst examples of confiscation
in New Caledonia.[5] In Samoa there was extensive cheating by
Samoans and Europeans alike — so much so that Samoans
'sold' Europeans three times the total area of the country![6] But
even in the many cases where both sides dealt honestly there
was much scope for misunderstanding: Europeans familiar

with the concept of freehold purchase often thought they had bought land when the islanders from whom they acquired it thought equally genuinely that they had made the land available to immigrants in the customary way whereby ultimate title remained with the original owners, and that continued rights of the immigrants depended on occupation and use of the land as well as on periodic contributions of tribute to the landowners.

Many islanders sold willingly in the early stages in return for goods or money which they wanted, but the exhaustion of the money and goods was compounded by misunderstandings and the frustration of often unrealistic expectations. So it was understandable that at the beginning of the colonial era in the islands there was considerable opposition to further sale. The United Kingdom, having seen the disastrous wars over land between Maori and European in New Zealand — and other examples elsewhere — in most cases restricted further sales. Alienation of any land was generally greatly limited (except in the Solomon Islands) and was restricted to leasing. This was reasonably acceptable in the early stages — the original landowners received an annual income and would get their land back at the end of the lease. But increasing population this century, and inflation which reduced the real value of the generally fixed rental, meant that by the middle of this century conventional leasing was also unpopular.

Since 1950 the process has reversed (except in New Zealand and Hawaii) with land being returned to Pacific Islanders from alien settlers. When most of Micronesia was a Japanese mandate, Japanese settlers outnumbered Micronesians, and acquired most of the land. Since World War II most of it has gone back to Micronesians. In Kiribati the lands of foreign owners have been bought back. Nauru was Australian territory until 1968 when it was re-acquired by Nauruans. In Papua New Guinea changing political forces led the Australian government to hand back 50 000 hectares and the local government to take back much more; in Solomon Islands, Lever Brothers returned 30 000 hectares; and in New Caledonia the grant of Melanesian voting rights was associated with the return between 1958 and 1963 of 30 000 hectares to Melanesians, and much more since then. In Fiji, local co-operatives started to buy foreign-owned land in the 1960s, but a tourist boom then inflated land prices beyond the reach of local people. Though economic forces took it outside their range, political forces are bringing it back. As aliens lose political power, their rights to land also diminish. Almost all independent Pacific countries have taken back all land and do not allow foreigners to buy land. Fiji is at present an exception, although the government has set up a Land Purchase Commission to buy back — either for the government or for resale to local groups in need — modest areas of foreign-owned land.

Land distribution

Pacific people talk a lot about land shortage, but by world standards there is a surplus. Average density throughout the Pacific is only 8 persons per km^2 (square kilometre), but there is great variation between nations — about 6 per km^2 in Melanesia (ranging from 3 in Irian Jaya to 11 in Vanuatu) but 113 per km^2 in Micronesia (Nauru being highest with 433 per km^2, but little of it is used owing to the high phosphate income). Polynesia is more densely populated, with 54 per km^2 if Hawaii and Fiji are included, or 64 per km^2 if they are not.

Internal differences are much greater. Though most Pacific Islanders have some land they can call their own, few can use it fully and freely without fear of dispute, constraint, or drain on the crop or its proceeds by kin or community. Despite rapid population increase, much land is used less and less effectively. The immigrant populations contained some highly skilled agriculturists, particularly Indians in Fiji, Chinese in several countries, and a few Europeans. But the parochialism of indigenous landowners and other constraints lead to the immigrants leaving rural occupations.

The land rights of women

In most of the Pacific customary rights to land were predominantly a matter for men. Women's rights were in most cases secondary, and inheritance was most commonly from father to son. In Micronesia and parts of Central Melanesia, however, land rights were and still are transmitted through women. But the emphasis must be on *through*, for the main powers over land were still exercised by men.

The customary land rights of women have changed radically in some parts of the Pacific, though very little in others. In Tahiti, the Cook Islands, and Niue, where chiefly titles and the land rights that go with them used to be the prerogative of men, they are now just as commonly held by women. Whereas formerly women held significant land rights only in special cases, today they have the same rights as men and as many of them, for 'customary' land rights are now derived by bilateral inheritance, irrespective of the sex of transferee or heir. The same trend is now discernable in Kiribati and Niue, and is beginning in Samoa. However, there is little sign of it in Fiji or Tonga, and it is visible only in some parts of Western Melanesia. Almost none of the changes so far are the result of intentional government intervention.

Customary tenures and productivity

The most fertile and best located land is not under 'customary' tenure: most of it has been sold or leased and is occupied by immigrants. The lands under 'customary tenures' (most of those used by Pacific Islanders) are, on the whole, less fertile and less conveniently situated. The reality is often missed, because land is usually spoken of by *area* rather than by *value*, which is more important but more difficult to measure. Everyone in Fiji, for example, emphasises that Fijians have 83 per cent of the land. By area that is true, but it is also irrelevant, and leads to much misunderstanding. The important question is what share of Fiji's land do they have by value? No one seems to know but it is probably closer to 25 per cent. In Papua New Guinea, where by area only 2.8 per cent of land was alienated, it included perhaps as much as 30 per cent by value. Much of this has been taken back to indigenous ownership. We must not blame customary tenures for accidents of history which have little to do with tenure.

No land tenure system can be an incentive *to produce*, but tenure systems can be disincentives and inhibit production. The aim, then, is to have tenure systems which *facilitate* productivity, i.e. which do not impede the operation of other motives. Productivity should not be the sole (or necessarily the primary) criterion.

Socialisation is a vital factor in productivity. People with different values produce radically different outputs from the same tenure system, or even irrespective of tenure system. The way in which some New Guinean highlanders migrate to coastal towns and outproduce coastal neighbours — both local and immigrant — despite acute insecurity of tenure, is paralleled by the way Chinese with no land rights in Tahiti outproduced Tahitians with secure tenure. Socialisation and the value systems are crucial factors, in addition to tenure.

Converting subsistence farmers into factory or hotel workers is relatively easy — they are given a new motivational context with clear directions, guidance and goals (short-term ones at least, such as weekly pay). Converting pure subsistence farmers into fully commercialised farmers, on the other hand, is difficult, slow and expensive. I am not aware of any example, anywhere in the Pacific, of rapid or even successful conversion of whole communities of subsistence farmers into commercial farmers. Aporosa Rakoto has shown that a high proportion of highly productive Fijian farmers are those who are self-selected (which an established local community cannot be) and have moved a sufficient distance from their communities of origin to be able to avoid undue calls on their time and resources. The 'productive' farmers still meet their customary obligations, but with less loss of working time, and they avoid marginal obligations.

This implies that if increased productivity is a major goal, farmers must be able to get land away from that they were born on, and that those who are not highly motivated to farming (and the percentage who are seems to be small in any human community that has much choice) should be encouraged to leave the land for other occupations. Once they are established, the land needs to be made securely available to more productive, self-selected farmers. It may be expedient to keep some land for the small percentage of urban workers who ever do go back to the land. In the longer term, however, and for the larger areas of land and numbers of people, a permanent transfer is going to be necessary, and perhaps the sooner it commences the better. All traditional tenure systems had some mechanisms for permanent transfer of rights.

In the early colonial phase, with very limited administrative machinery and many disputes to resolve, it was reasonable to adopt a simple formula and tie land to social groups more firmly than any precontact tenure systems had done. But as the late Dr Rusiate Nayacakalou frequently pointed out, in most cases the disadvantages of tying land to social groups now greatly outweigh the advantages. It reduces flexibility when greater flexibility is needed. And this inhibits productivity.

Determination of the customary land rights of groups was done in most of the eastern Pacific around the turn of this century, when populations were at their lowest ebb. Most populations have trebled since then, but the number of groups has not, leaving large unwieldy dispersed populations, with less land, but with smaller undivided shares. Redistribution to individuals or smaller component groups who actually use the land would be more consistent with customary practice than is the present unintended result of colonial tenures.

The proud claim that every islander has customary rights to land is hollow when, in almost all Pacific countries, there is a rapidly increasing number whose rights are so fragmented, so small, so restricted, so badly located or shared with so many others, that they give no real benefits to their holders. This problem is now very widespread.

The tying of land to social groups is worsened when the only way one can become a member of the group is by accident of birth. In a situation of pure subsistence, minimal mobility and local government on the basis of kinship groupings, accidents of birth can be a useful principle on which to allocate land rights. Even so, it was always qualified in practice by a number of other criteria — use, need, number, adoption, marriage, acceptance of refugees and so on.

Allocating scarce resources on the basis of accidents of birth is neither very just, very economical, nor even very sensible. It inhibits the achievement of the goals of all Pacific governments for higher productivity, and it is not in accord with the increasing desire and practice of islanders to move more freely. Imagine if educational opportunities could go only to those whose fathers had had the same education, or if the only job one could be employed in was the one your father had (and many societies in Europe, Asia and Polynesia used to do just this). We would be much poorer and much less efficient than we are. Yet many Pacific countries still allocate land, their most valuable resource, on criteria which guarantee to reduce its productivity and thus keep the people poorer than they need to be. The common argument that 'this is the way we've always done it' is simply not true. In practice, most pre-colonial systems were more flexible.

It was common traditionally for major land rights to be held by local groups or kinship groups, but for use rights within them for cultivation to be held by individuals or households. For several decades, though, as a matter of administrative convenience, most colonial tenures gave primary emphasis to group rights. Only since the 1950s have we seen a significant extension of legal provisions for individuals to establish firm rights within their groups. The two main processes are leases (in which the individual pays his customary group an annual rental) and occupation rights (in which, once given group approval to occupy, the individual has secure title without payment for such time as he or his direct heirs occupy and use the land, plus five or so years thereafter).

Leases are widely used in Fiji, especially for facilitating the use of land owned by indigenous Fijians, by the larger Indian population. Occupation rights are widespread in French Polynesia, the Cook Islands and Niue. Occupation rights are cheaper to administer, longer term (perpetual if used), and tied to usage. They are also closer in principle to the pre-contact pattern, if this is felt desirable. The occupation rights concept can give individuals secure rights, thus meeting the social demand which is strong in many places, plus continuing group identity and reversionary rights. In French Polynesia and the Cook Islands, the lands held under occupation rights have been associated with much higher investment and productivity.

Land reform

A law will not be effective if it is too far from the realities of life in the society. Colonial governments which tried to change land tenure by legislation alone seldom succeeded. France introduced its metropolitan law to Tahiti 100 years ago, but despite four generations of pressure the actual system bears little relationship to the legal intentions. It has left French Polynesia (as in New Caledonia) with some of the worst land tenure problems and the lowest agricultural productivity in the Pacific. Similarly, few of the land reforms introduced elsewhere in the Pacific over the last century have achieved the hoped-for increases in productivity.

I once studied six land reforms in the islands and was amazed to find that in almost all cases productivity declined after the 'reform'.[7] Although much greater changes are necessary, they will have to be tailored much more closely than in the past to the specific needs of the islands concerned. In an extreme national emergency, or with a powerful military government like Taiwan or the Philippines, radical changes can be made. But if, like Indonesia, which adopted similar legislation, there is inadequate internal co-ordination or political will to carry the reform through, it remains a dead letter. Most land reform laws in the Pacific have not achieved their goals because planners have not assessed accurately enough what could be changed, and how far, by what forces, and at what speed.

One of the points that has been missed in most reforms programmes is that land rights provide psychological and social security, and unless you have old-age pensions, sickness benefits, building societies, and all the other things to provide for your time of vulnerability, then you need your land rights. In Kiribati several years ago I studied 214 pieces of land that had been individualised only fifteen years before. By the time of my visit, only 38 per cent of them were being worked individually by the owners. The people preferred to borrow from a relative here, lend to an in-law there, allow a friend to use a bit somewhere else and so on, partly because each arrangement implies a body of unspoken commitment to reciprocate in some way at some time. The people who introduced the reform did not give sufficient attention to the social security functions of this complex network of customary land rights, and thus did not make appropriate alternative provisions for social security.

Populations are rising rapidly, so it is desirable to make the fullest use of available land, but legal, cultural and administrative difficulties are almost certain to keep land under-used for a long-time. Part of the reason is that land reform is difficult to implement, expensive, and politically hot. No government likes to tackle these things unless real pressure is on, and independent governments, like their colonial predecessors, keep putting off the evil day.

The situations for which the traditional land tenure systems were devised are very different from today (and even more from tomorrow) and it would be wise to adapt them. But this does not mean copying the French or the English or the New Zealand system; it requires effective planning to suit local circumstances.

Despite these very real constraints, there is scope for specific, small changes which could lead to significant improvement in output of subsistence and commercial crops. The first is in the area of land transfer. Past fears are understandable, but outdated, and appropriate restrictions on size, value and retention of land for use by original landholders can be designed and implemented. The second relates to reducing the number of persons in any landholding group. The third concerns re-establishing a more effective organisational structure within groups of joint landholders. The fourth concerns making principles of land allocation more in accordance with economic efficiency, including freeing land increasingly from ties with social groups which came into being for quite different purposes, and to make access to land more a function of productive potential and need than of accident of birth.

Such changes would be more acceptable if it were more widely realised that they are all more in accord with the traditional customary practices of island societies than are the present systems, which are incorrectly thought to be traditional. In other words, people need to become more aware that their greatest current land problem is to overcome the legacy of colonial tenures.

The most recent trend in land management in the Pacific is in conservation — an awareness that industrialisation and population growth necessitate protective measures for the natural environment. Legislative preparation has begun, but it will probably be another decade at least before significant action programmes are implemented.

Returning to the sea

Islanders used to be uniquely linked to the sea. As Pardo (1982) noted: 'Micronesians and Polynesians were among the most skilled mariners, navigators and fishermen of their day. And the pre-European Pacific Islander had learned to manage the living resources of estuaries, reefs and lagoons in a manner far more rational than that prevailing in Europe at the time.' But the drastic population losses last century through epidemics, indentured labour, and migration, followed by the adoption of commercial agriculture, wage labour, and imported proteins, have progressively led them away from the sea.

During the 1970s, the Law of the Sea Convention, the declaration of 200 mile Exclusive Economic Zones by all Pacific Islands states, the increasing competition for fishing and mineral rights, and the filling up of the land with people, is leading to a return to the sea. Tuna and other fish are being caught in islands waters in vastly greater numbers than ever before, though mainly by Korean, Taiwanese and American fishermen. But Solomon Islanders, Fijians, Tuvaluans, I-Kiribati, and others are adopting the techniques.

It is with new perspectives and advanced technologies that islanders are beginning to reinterpret their maritime heritage and re-evaluate their marine resources. Certain seaweeds are being shown to have significant economic potential (in Tonga, Fiji and Kiribati, for example, commercial seaweed farming is developing fast), and the vast mineral deposits on the Pacific seabed are being located and measured in preparation for their harvesting, probably during the coming generation when the relevant technology is more developed. An experimental ocean thermal energy conversion plant has been established in Nauru, and wave energy possibilities are being explored. Institutes dedicated to the study of marine resources are becoming established in the islands, and a renewed awareness is permeating through schools and adult education.

The area of sea controlled by nations and territories within the various regions is in inverse proportion to the area of land controlled. Melanesian nations average only 2 km² of sea per person, in contrast to Micronesia's 32 km² per person, with Polynesia in a middle position with 20 km² per person. Marine rights close to the shore were often claimed by the village, clan or tribe which controlled the adjacent land. In many cases these rights have been taken over by government and all sea-water is in the public domain, but even where this is not so, the vast bulk of the water claimed under the Law of the Sea Convention belongs to governments. It remains to be seen whether U.S.A., one of the few countries which has not signed the Law of the Sea Convention and which has flagrantly abused Pacific Islands marine rights in relation to fish, will respect the claims of islands states to seabed minerals in their economic zones. And the relative benefits which will be derived by claimant islands nations as against companies with the massive capital and technology needed to exploit seabed minerals, also remains to be resolved.

Land and water are slowly being reintegrated in a new synthesis. Next century is likely to see vastly greater dependence of Pacific people on both — and if well managed this will help them reduce their dependence on the industrialised nations of the Pacific rim.

10
Economy
Not only what kind, but whose?

Many ways of doing it

The love of money may be the root of much evil, but cash is so convenient that it has developed from ancient origins in the Middle East, Asia, *and Melanesia*, into a universally used medium of exchange. Much of western Melanesia and western Micronesia had their own — in some cases quite complex — monetary systems centuries before European contact.[1]

There were probably two main reasons — one environmental and one social — for the absence of such economies in Polynesia and elsewhere in the Pacific. The first is the extreme environmental diversity of western Melanesia where a range of products (salt, resins, shells, stone for tool-making, bird of paradise feathers, and a number of other commodities) which were available only in certain localities was traded through a complex series of trade routes that criss-crossed New Guinea, the second largest island in the world. Most of Polynesia, by contrast, was comprised of small, relatively uniform islands where similar commodities were generally available in each district or accessible island.

The social reason for the difference in trade lies in the fact that western Melanesian societies were among the most egalitarian in the world, with strong emphasis on individual achievement: the ideal social context for trade. In Polynesia's highly stratified chiefly societies, on the other hand, redistribution was largely confined to ritualised contacts — particularly marriages, funerals, and accession to chiefly titles. Contributions were passed up the chiefly hierarchy and redistributed through the channels of blood and marriage relations.

A money economy greatly influences the life of any people,

but the ways in which money is used in Pacific cultures, as well as the priorities and purposes it is used for (at all levels from the personal to the national) differs in significant respects from, for example, Australia or China or Egypt. May it continue to do so — at least in some respects. For example, many indigenous Pacific economic systems emphasised public standards of living much more than private. Some of the world's most powerful nations are now beginning to appreciate this principle more fully than they have in the past, and to reorder their priorities accordingly.

No one wants to return to the fully subsistence economy of their ancestors (and everybody else's ancestors, incidentally). And Pacific peoples are well aware that industrialisation makes most things available to more people at lower cost, and that specialisation and international trade are generally to their advantage. Farmers in the Pacific generally earn more if their crops are sold on the other side of the world (for example vanilla, copra, sugar, coffee) than if they are sold locally.

But many want to modify the organisation, control, operations, and effects of the way the economies function at present — and with good reason. Some others want not so much to modify the forms of organisation as to take them over. This too can be a legitimate goal. Having power to determine policies and to control organisations is a major source of satisfaction in any culture.

Societies where the indigenous culture remains strong may also be productive economically. Lockwood's comparative study of Samoan villages showed that Poutasi people put in the highest working hours per villager, had the best housing and a relatively high income. Poutasi was also the most 'Samoan' in such things as not allowing non-Samoan houses to be erected in the main village, in the frequency and effectiveness of meetings of traditional institutions, and in the power of its chiefs. The Tolai of new Britain, the Mekeo of Papua, and the Aoba of Vanuatu, some of the most productive groups of farmers per head in the Pacific, are also among the most strongly attached to their own cultures. This is not to suggest that the present systems are ideal, but to note that it is incorrect to assume that those who value their indigenous cultures highly are therefore less successful in money terms.

Impact of colonisation

About this time last century Pacific Islanders were involved in shipping in quite a big way. Many sailing ships were captained by islanders, but they were owned by tribal groups (often in the name of the chief) because the chiefly hierarchy provided a clear, effective means of capital accumulation which fitted into the people's desire to be involved in ship owning. This was then the most prestigious form of business enterprise.

By the turn of this century or shortly thereafter, islanders withdrew from shipping. One of the causes was inadequate knowledge of book-keeping and business management. Another obstacle was that when motorised ships were introduced, tribal and other groups could raise money to buy them, but lacked the technical knowledge, and the opportunity to learn it, to keep them running. Soon the money was gone and many of the ships were lost. In addition, large foreign trading firms were established and ran their own ships, carried their own goods, and set up their own trading agencies on each island in competition with local ones. The local people did not have the connections with overseas buyers and sellers, or the familiarity with banking and other skills needed for a large mercantile business. After an interesting flourish, most of the indigenous businesses of last century folded up.[2] Not until the 1960s was there a major resurgence of business activity by islands people.

During the colonial era, a period of two to three generations, Pacific Islanders withdrew from active participation in the economy, apart from being passive labourers, passive buyers of bully beef, passive producers of fruit or copra. This must have been a peaceful period, a time of growing population and improving health, but it must also have been a period of great dullness, with very little apparent purpose in life. There was not much opportunity for people to achieve anything and few ways in which they could express themselves or develop their talents.

During this period a very tight set of communication lines developed between colonial powers and colonies, but the islands people could not participate significantly in any of them. Shipping lines developed between the U.S.A., Hawaii, and American Samoa; between France and her colonies of Tahiti and New Caledonia; between New Zealand, Niue, and the Cook Islands; between Australia and Papua; and between Germany and her then colonies of Western Samoa, Micronesia, and Northeast New Guinea.[3]

Reaction to dominance

The islanders were not necessarily happy about this state of affairs, but there was not much they could do about it. There was, during this period, a series of what we might call resistance movements, all of which were effectively suppressed because the islanders did not have sufficient skills, technology, or capital to organise, and the colonial governments (and more particularly the colonial trading companies) were in a much stronger position. In Fiji there were Apolosi's attempts over a number of years to get Fijians to boycott foreign trading firms and to set up their own trading companies. There was a major Tongan company of this type in the early years of this century. In the Cook Islands there were similar attempts by returned indigenous soldiers of the First World War. There was a co-operative movement in Nauru which was forcibly broken up by Australia, and there was the relatively successful Mau movement in Samoa, which for a period banned its members from trading with foreign firms.[4]

Usually the boycotts were more successful than the attempts to set up alternative commercial enterprises, because the latter had to sell to overseas trading firms which had their established links in the islands. So it was a period when the islanders had little effective participation, although they made various attempts to engage in more meaningful economic activities.

Co-operatives

After the Second World War came a period of mixed idealism, remorse, and self-interest when the colonial powers re-evaluated their past history and their future long-term interests. They decided to provide more opportunities for economic participation by the Pacific peoples, lest they be rejected and lose not only commercially and politically, but also strategically, as there was a fear of communism spreading.

These, as well as altruistic considerations, led to a general acceptance of the principle that the islands people should have a larger slice of the economy. The creation of the South Pacific Commission reflected this general feeling. It was to establish facilities that would tend to encourage the Pacific peoples to remain in a mutually acceptable association with the colonial powers. This included means to enable islanders to take a more meaningful part in economic activity.

Co-operatives were seen as the means by which this would be achieved and particularly during the 1950s they grew rapidly. In Kiribati and Tuvalu, co-operatives took over almost all commercial enterprise, as all foreign firms had moved out during the Second World War and were persuaded not to come back. To a lesser extent co-operatives spread throughout the Pacific though in the French territories they were marginal.[5]

Co-operatives have had a chequered career, some having done fairly well and some poorly, but the movement has survived and I think we will look back on it historically as a significant and moderately successful movement, given its goals and its scope. We must remember that when co-operatives were introduced the people had, for at least two generations, been effectively denied any meaningful participation in the economy, and had almost no experience in business affairs. They had very little education, and had been substantially, though unintentionally, deprived of their confidence in themselves. Not that they were all necessarily full of confidence before, but there are indications of a drop in self-confidence during the colonial period. Co-operatives provided them with specific skills, helped to restore some confidence, and enabled more meaningful participation in their own economic systems.

Co-operatives have contributed in other areas as well. For example, many successful Pacific Islands businessmen received their original training in commerce and book-keeping as co-operative managers or secretaries, and it is surprising how many of the early effective politicians in the Pacific also received their original training in this area. The first three countries in the Pacific to gain independence or self-government were led by men who spent years promoting the development of co-operative enterprises in their home countries: Prime Minister Fiame Mata'afa of Western Samoa, President Hammer de Roburt of Nauru, and Premier Albert Henry of the Cook Islands.

During the 1960s co-operatives reached something of a plateau and while they are likely to continue they are unlikely to become the major form of commerce. There has been some disillusionment with co-operatives because many people had unrealistic expectations for them. Thirty years ago, when the co-operative movement was spreading throughout the Pacific, I saw it as a realistic alternative to foreign investment. It took many years of repeated and continuing failures for me to realise two very important things:

1 That some co-operatives exploited the Pacific public as badly or worse than any other form of enterprise
2 That co-operatives are not 'naturally' adapted to Pacific cultures, as many people assumed.

I used to think their failure was due to lack of support from colonial governments, or to undermining by foreign firms, but in practice co-operatives have collapsed at least as much since independence as before. In several countries the co-operative movement has folded up completely since independence, and in most of those where it survives, it handles only a very small percentage of total trade. And while I am aware of some examples of undermining of co-operatives by business firms, careful research has convinced me that this is not the major problem. Many co-operatives have collapsed without any undermining and despite very substantial government subsidy and support. In fact, the only places where co-operatives have survived are where they receive very favourable treatment and extensive subsidy.

Naturally, in the early stages failure was often due to lack of skill or experience, but I am talking about the results *after* 30 and 40 years of training and experience. This experience, and considerable research evidence, leads me reluctantly to believe that some of the basic assumptions (including my own) about co-operatives as a system of economic organisation in the islands were false.

And we must remember that even when local co-operatives function effectively, they mainly sell Japanese transistors, New Zealand corned beef, Hong Kong clothes, and American coca-cola; and they buy local produce mainly to sell in Europe, Australasia, or the U.S.A. It is a world market that the co-operative members tend to insist on.

Government participation

With the disillusionment in co-operatives setting in during the late 1960s and 1970s, and with independence, there has been a great increase in state enterprises. Shipping was one area of government takeover. The governments of Tonga, and the Gilbert and Ellice Islands (later to become Kiribati and Tuvalu) took over all internal and some overseas shipping operations, and the government of Nauru has built up a fleet of large ships which operate throughout the Pacific Basin. Several other governments took lesser roles in internal shipping and the Pacific Forum Line (PFL), a consortium of Pacific governments, now runs an extensive network. Each ship is owned by a particular government, but operated by PFL. After a very difficult beginning, PFL may well become an efficient and effective organisation. National government shipping lines have had only moderate success, and some have been serious failures.

Most Pacific governments have set up both internal and international air services. Plagued by long distances, limited traffic, and escalating fuel prices, most have cost local taxpayers subsidies they can ill afford. Nevertheless, after some bitter experiences in the 1970s, it may be that more realistic goals in the 1980s will lead to their consolidation and rationalisation.

During most of the colonial era the marketing of produce was handled by private foreign firms, but during the 1960s many governments took over (or at least controlled more tightly) the marketing of export crops. This was partly a re-action to demands within the Pacific area itself, and partly a result of influence from colonial countries, especially Australia and New Zealand, where governments had come into power which favoured the marketing of primary produce being governmental or co-operative enterprises rather than private business. The present trend is for mixed private and governmental marketing.

In agriculture, the largest state enterprise by far is WESTEC — the Western Samoa Trust Estates Corporation, which usually employs about 3500 workers. Despite some successes, its overall record has been one of modest productivity, and heavy losses despite massive use of (sometimes waste of) foreign aid. State agricultural enterprises elsewhere in the Pacific seem not to have fared much better. But government participation in some selected aspects of the production process, as in the Fiji sugar industry, has a much better record.

In short, some government commercial enterprises have functioned well, and there is strong support for their continuation and expansion. But a depressing proportion have been inefficient and uneconomic. It is a sad reality that many government businesses have exploited the public (in terms of charging exorbitant prices, inefficient management, absorbing large and unnecessary subsidies which could be better used by or for the public, or providing low quality service) even worse than equivalent private enterprises.

So I have come reluctantly to the conclusion that, to the extent that co-operatives work well, they should be encouraged. Likewise, statutory or government enterprises which perform well now, or are likely to, should be fostered. But the experience so far suggests that they work much better in some roles than others, and that in these other roles the public and the nation is better off to take a more pragmatic approach, and facilitate a wider range of forms of economic organisation. An interesting experiment recently began in Fiji with a joint enterprise between a trade union and the government in the operation of certain airline services at Nadi airport. If it works well, good, expand it. But reluctantly, and I emphasise reluctantly because all of them would prefer to promote growth from within, all Pacific Islands governments have come to the conclusion that the national interest is better served by attracting overseas capital to fulfil certain selected functions. Privatisation, which is experiencing a period of popularity in

a)   Transport problems in the islands are acute. Photo (a) shows a Britten Norman Islander of Air Tungaru (the Kiribati national airline) making a regular call at an outlying atoll. Only coconuts thrive in the poor soil of these islets, that are seldom more than half a kilometre wide or a few kilometres long.

b)   This photo shows the problem of transport between islets. Where distances are short, permanent causeways have been made, and in other cases walkways have been erected, but in most cases people have to trudge through at low tide.

To get one's copra — almost the only export — to the ship often involves long journeys by canoe or bicycle. Some motor vehicles exist, but the price of copra does not often merit their use.

c)

To help overcome problems of international shipping connections, the Pacific islands nations set up the Pacific Forum Line. Here the *Fua Kavenga* arrives in Sydney with a cargo from the islands.

d)

the Western world, is also becoming a policy trend in the islands.

Indigenous businesses

The next move after governments got involved in the economy, especially since about 1965, was to increase the opportunities for Pacific Islanders to become businessmen. Some Pacific countries now place considerable emphasis on this policy. Most if not all have imported overseas consultants, set up special government agencies, development banks, and a network of services aimed to facilitate the emergence of a class of small-scale indigenous businessmen.[6]

The development of independent indigenous entrepreneurs may be of limited applicability. In the larger islands of Melanesia there is more room for it than in Polynesia, both because the Melanesian cultures are better adapted to it and because the isolated valleys and islands need small stores, work-shops, truck operators and so on. For this generation at least, but probably not for much longer, there is scope for the development of one-man businesses in the larger islands of Melanesia. There is less scope in Polynesia, however, partly because competitive business is less compatible with some aspects of Polynesian culture and personality, and partly because the islands are much more accessible. This accessibility leads to more foreign capital per head being attracted in.

The small local trader is at a great disadvantage against firms that operate branches throughout the Pacific and the world and which gain much of their income from monopoly handling rights on products ranging from motor-cars to whisky. Small local ship-owners find it very difficult to compete with large foreign-owned fleets. This is even more so with airlines. Slowly more and more functions in the economy are being taken over either by governments or by large-scale international capital. The proportion of total business handled by small businessmen is dwindling all the time.

The latest trend in economic change[7] (I prefer not to call it economic development because 'development' tends to have a false connotation of something inevitable and invariably desirable) is for combined indigenous-expatriate enterprises.

That is, a major foreign firm moves in and shares with local people. This has many advantages and it does facilitate participation, but in practice many of these organisations end up very substantially foreign owned, and with only token local participation.

The foreign firm, being much larger and more experienced, is more likely to establish a profitable operation, but the main task of a local subsidiary is to serve its foreign parent company. Its loyalty, not only its moral obligation but its legal obligation, is to make as much profit as it can for its shareholders, the vast majority of whom are foreign. This question of partnership between foreign and local business is likely to become a crucial political issue in the Pacific, and foreign firms seem to have been very successful recruiting local politicians (including heads of government and their families in some cases, and cabinet ministers in many cases) as their local partners!

One aspect of joint ventures that could have serious consequences is that the local participant is usually chosen from within a fairly small, elite class. This is usually a strongly politically affiliated and unrepresentative segment of the local population. Joint enterprise in these circumstances may increase the already substantial political power of the local business elite, and divorce it further from the common people. There is evidence of this in various parts of the Pacific. As those with political power gain more economic power, they can entrench themselves in a smaller and smaller, more and more exclusive, richer and indigenous but foreign-influenced elite. And that inevitably has political consequences, for when hereditary or other leaders divorce themselves from their people and align their interests more closely with foreign business, there is a danger that (as in other forms of divorce and remarriage) the children feel abandoned and tend to hate their step-mother. Such resentment can be hidden or muffled for a time and to a degree, but there are distinct limits. Partly the result will depend on how far the benefits are spread.

Tourism

Tourism is an industry that most Pacific governments are trying to promote. There is an interesting pattern here in relation to foreign investment and alternatives to it. In Fiji, Vanuatu, and the French colonies, the hotels and tourist trade are overwhelmingly owned by foreigners, to a smaller extent by non-indigenous locals and almost not at all by indigenous people. But in Tonga, Western Samoa, Kiribati, Nauru, Tuvalu, and Niue on the other hand, tourist hotels and related facilities are predominantly owned by local governments or indigenous business people. This is very interesting because quite commonly when one discusses such possibilities in countries where the tourist plant is not indigenously owned, one is assured that it cannot be done — even though it is being done rather successfully next door.

The Cook Islands is a particularly interesting case, because in Rarotonga, which has many more hotel beds than Fiji, relative to population size, there is a mix of foreign-owned and local-owned hotels and motels. Rarotonga has one of the highest tourist densities in the South Pacific. The largest hotel was owned jointly by the Cook Islands Government, Air New Zealand and the New Zealand Tourist Hotels Corporation, but it lost millions while the privately owned small hotels and motels, mostly owned and operated by Cook Islanders, got much higher occupancy rates and much better profitability. The largest hotel has now been taken over by a consortium involving the Cook Islands government and four tourist supply companies in New Zealand and the U.S.A.

One might say that some of the small countries listed above are somewhat special cases because they are isolated and need hotels mainly for official visitors rather than for tourists. This would apply to Niue, Tuvalu, Kiribati, and to some extent Nauru. But this is not the case with the Cook Islands, Tonga, and Samoa. Relative to their population sizes, their greater distance from central air routes, and the fact that they have less scenic and other diversity than Fiji or Vanuatu, they seem to have done much better than people a decade or two ago would have had us believe was possible.

Recent trends

The reality is a mix of co-operative, state and private capital, but the proportion of the economy in the hands of co-operatives has been declining steadily and is now in most cases miniscule; the proportion in state ownership is declining in favour of private enterprise, and the proportion of private capital that is foreign-owned is generally increasing. This is partly because potentials for savings in islands economies are limited, partly because islanders with funds to invest generally do so in the industrialised countries which they regard as safer, and partly because almost all countries actively solicit foreign investment.

When it comes to most forms of manufacturing, very few Pacific Islands have a sufficiently large market to justify it, and the distances and scale constrain export industry greatly. There have have been proposals for forming a Pacific Islands common market, but even that creates a market of only six million people spread over a vast area and each closer to much cheaper sources of most commodities. After at least ten years of encouragement for inter-islands trade it is still only about 2 per cent of total trade. Perhaps it could be lifted to 3 per cent, which would be a considerable improvement, but any goal beyond that in this century would be wishful thinking.

Under the South Pacific's non-reciprocal regional free trade agreement (SPARTECA) of 1980, Australia and New Zealand allow a wide range of agricultural and industrial products preferential access from Forum island states. This has benefitted mainly the countries with significant manufacturing capacity (especially Fiji), but despite its shortcomings it is regarded as a useful step in a direction which could lead to a wider free trade zone like the reciprocal New Zealand/Australia CER (Closer Economic Relations Programme) has provided.

Another area of growth has been in what are called 'tax havens', 'offshore finance centres' or 'international finance centres'. In brief, small countries with limited resources guarantee secrecy and no tax in return for licensing fees, a royalty on deposits and other spin-offs. Vanuatu, the largest and longest established centre, has over 100 banks registered, though many of them merely use Vila as a 'brass plate' for operations conducted elsewhere. Nauru, with no great need for employment or income, has only a limited tax haven. Tonga and the Cook Islands began in 1984, and the latter at least has grown rapidly. There may be money in it for a few countries (probably one per time zone) but certainly not for many.

Both the advantages and the ethics of the system are much debated. A recent article by Kevin Rafferty (in *Pacific Business Guide*, 1986) quotes Tonga's Minister of Finance as describing them as the 'fastest and easiest' way of providing jobs, income and a flow of money, whereas the Governor of Fiji's Reserve Bank says he remains to be convinced of their advantages.

Broadly, the small genuinely poor countries provide a loophole to let firms in rich countries avoid taxes and other payments. There is considerable concern that some are also used to 'launder' income from major international crime syndicates and drug dealers. And the potential political leverage of such powerful interests in tiny nations should not be overlooked.

The Pacific public is insisting on more goods, more services, more money. Where it has freedom of choice, it will elect governments that help it achieve those goals. I personally find the crass consumerism which has invaded the islands distasteful, inappropriate, and likely to disadvantage the islands in the long-term. But who wants to listen to that kind of nonsense from us academics and other privileged categories, who live in relative opulence and with comparatively lots of goods, sevices, money, and opportunities. Islands people have seen too many of us preach one thing for others but practice quite different things ourselves — if not when we are students, when our choice may be limited, as soon as we can thereafter.

Non-economic consequences need more attention

Insufficient attention has been given to the social and other costs of certain kinds of economic activity. Creating artificial demand for unnecessary goods and services irrespective of their use or value makes people worse off even though it shows up in the statistics as 'economic growth' and gives a false impression that welfare has been improved.[8]

The fact that the 'best of both cultures' does not necessarily evolve on its own is sadly demonstrated by the 'Mr Whippy' ice cream vans which prowl the slums of Port Moresby and other towns, coercing, by their jingling presence, poverty-stricken mothers to spend desperately needed money on valueless imported commodities which create their own demand, thus worsening the problem of undernourishment. I once heard the official who was responsible for granting licences for such businesses warmly and sincerely support this one as a contribution to 'economic development'.

The social costs of urbanisation and industrialisation also need more careful assessment. Urban people commit more crime, suffer more mental breakdown, produce more addicts, and cost much more in welfare services than villagers. In other words, the indigenous cultures provide a number of economic, social, and psychological services which are not adequately recognised. This is not necessarily an argument against urbanisation and industrialisation, both of which can contribute to better living. But they do not necessarily do so in practice. The economic development plans produced so far do not contain any realistic assessment of the additional money costs, let alone social and psychological costs, of these processes. For example, I suspect that when a fuller appreciation of the total costs of such industries as tourism is available, the industry will be required to contribute more to the public purse to compensate for the indirect costs with which it burdens the host community.[9]

Unemployment and migrant labour

Employment is a coming economic problem, as population is growing rapidly and in many islands exceeds employment opportunities (including those on the land). It is sometimes suggested that richer neighbours like Australia, New Zealand, Canada, and the U.S.A. should offer any unemployed surplus the opportunity to live there. This may be reasonable if the problem was temporary, or if the islands now had effective family planning (as do the countries to which they want to migrate). The countries mentioned are taking some, and I hope they take more, but it is unreasonable and naive for any country to breed unlimited numbers and expect others to take responsibility for the surplus. Not only do cultural differences make their absorption in large numbers more difficult, but most are unskilled.

Moreover, islands with adequate land or job opportunities are very reluctant to help their less fortunate neighbours. The Solomon Islands, with considerable surplus land, absorbed a few thousand landless Gilbertese in the colonial era, but refuses to help more. Papua New Guinea, with some vast empty spaces, has denied other islanders entry. Nauru uses Kiribati labour, but does not allow citizenship or even permanent residence. Tongans who call Australia 'racist' for accepting too few Tongan immigrants approve their own government's refusal of citizenship to the few Indians and others who were born in Tonga, or have lived and worked there for years, some of whom contribute very effectively to its economy. Western Samoa has evicted from its relatively ample lands some virtually landless Tongans, and the Cook Islands rightly insists on free entry and full privileges for Cook Islanders to New Zealand, but restricts other New Zealanders entering the Cook Islands. Niue, with considerable surplus land and a declining population has been particularly restrictive in allowing migrants in, though this policy was relaxed in 1986.

Even within some territories there is resistance to free migration of citizens seeking better economic opportunities. In the Trust Territory of the Pacific Islands, for example, people of some districts not only resented but actively resisted fellow citizens from other districts seeking jobs — even when these were available. Papua New Guinea and Solomon Islands suffer similar internal inflexibility.

Even in its economic effects, racism is a serious affliction. Undoubtedly the Pacific's white neighbours are guilty of it, but in practice most Islanders are equally racist at both a personal and a governmental level. When all parties realise that this is a universal problem with deep psychological and cultural as well as economic implications, there will be a better chance of remedial action.

Who aids who?

Paradoxically, restrictions on permanent migration lead to the poorer independent islands subsidising their rich neighbours!

The Tongan economy, for example, pays the heavy costs of raising and educating children who produce nothing but consume a lot. When they become potentially productive, however, the young men seek paid employment overseas. Women, as well as unfit and aged men, remain a relative drain on the reduced proportion of active men left in Tonga. New Zealand, Nauru, and the other countries employing Tongan labour gain by acquiring fit men, usually without their dependents, at minimal pay-rates and minimum overhead costs in short-term jobs. When they become redundant or old they are returned to Tonga. In other words, contract employment which New Zealanders call 'aid' to Tonga is more properly Tongan aid to New Zealand. For seasonal harvesting (which Fijians particularly undertook in New Zealand) Fiji in effect paid the unemployment benefits which New Zealand would have to pay during the off-season if New Zealand had a full work-force for these least desired tasks. (Incidentally, island villages have subsidised foreign-owned plantations in the islands in this way for over a century.) It was Fiji and Tonga governments which requested New Zealand to provide job opportunities for their under-employed citizens. It was not an exploitative plot by New Zealand to boost its economy with cheap island labour while the islands pay the overheads — but that is the way it will be increasingly regarded, and this analysis contains an element of truth.

Unskilled migrant labouring can be exciting if undertaken once or twice, but as a way of life it is culturally sterile and psychologically depressing. Permanent migration, on the other hand, can help the situation back home so long as it does not become a brain drain of the top talents.

The dangers of over-dependence

Income per capita, particularly locally generated income, has declined in many Pacific countries. For the twelve years 1960–72 (according to the World Bank Atlas 1974) GNP per capita declined or stagnated in Tonga, Western Samoa, and the Gilbert and Ellice Islands. Solomon Islands showed a marginal gain, but declined again towards the end of the period. There was general improvement in the mid 1970s, but the world economic depression, combined with rising populations and limited resources has led to a reduction again in real incomes in many countries in the 1980s. Many islands nations are becoming increasingly dependent on external aid, (though the Cook Islands and Kiribati have been reducing dependence). For example, in the 1950s Western Samoa paid for its imports with its exports. But by 1974 it imported over $14 million worth of goods and paid for only $4 million of it from its own production. Another $4 million came in remittances from Samoans working overseas, $1½ million from 'tourism' (in practice much of it from the living costs of aid officials and businessmen), and the largest amount ($5½ million) from aid and soft loans. The proportions were similar in 1980–83, the latest years for which data is available (e.g. in Western Samoa GDP declined by about 2.3 per cent per year during this period). This is becoming a common pattern for the smaller islands nations and territories.

The Pacific economies need aid, but much of it has benefited the donor countries more than the recipients. Beggars cannot be choosers, but it is probably to the advantage of the donors also to give more thought to long-term consequences. The aid relationship should generate opportunities rather than charity, confidence rather than humiliation, and self-reliance rather than dependence. This is the stated aim of both donors and recipients, but neither side does much to implement it: the political and bureaucratic power groups on both sides have much to gain from keeping the relationship as it is; and neither side is prepared to institute the sometimes painful reforms that would be necessary to get better value from the available resources. (A 1976 SPEC report, *More Effective Aid*, discusses these problems more fully.)

POWER

15 Dependence, independence, interdependence: Improving the options
Military dependence
Educational dependence
Economic dependence
Foreign investment
Wider spheres of dependence

11
Politics and government
Traditional and colonial

Political units in the Pacific are the smallest in the world, with 22 governments for 8 million people, or 42 if one adds the provincial governments of Papua New Guinea, each with its own Premier and ministers. The 17 countries and territories of Micronesia and Polynesia (excluding New Zealand and Hawaii) average only 50 000 people each, and those of Melanesia (excluding Papua New Guinea and Fiji) only 190 000.

Political structures are more diverse here than for any equivalent population in the world, and include a kingdom (Tonga), a dominion (Fiji), a state in which only chiefs can vote or be elected (Western Samoa), a republic (Nauru, the world's smallest independent nation), an associated state (the Cook Islands), a United Nations Trust Territory (the U.S. Trust Territory), an Unincorporated Territory (American Samoa), a Commonwealth (the Northern Marianas), a department (New Caledonia — of France), a province (West Irian — of Indonesia), and several other forms such as Easter Island which is constitutionally (though not otherwise) an 'integral part of Chile'. Papua New Guinea seems to be developing into a loose federation of twenty provincial governments. Besides these constitutional diversities are other differences which derive from much earlier forces.[1]

Traditional systems

Before European contact there were two main kinds of political system in the Pacific Islands: the aristocratic societies of Polynesia and Micronesia, and the more democratic societies of Melanesia. They are still very important in the 1980s. This classification into two systems is an over-simplification, because there was considerable diversity within these areas, and

even in aristocratic societies high birth was not the only determinant of leadership. But generally speaking the peoples of
New Guinea, the Solomon Islands, and Vanuatu lived in small
fragmented societies in which political power was achieved
more through skills in production, organisation, politics, and
war. To a substantial extent any man of proven ability was
acceptable as a leader. In Polynesia, on the other hand,
heredity was much more important, and although a few
outstanding individuals from lower ranks achieved high status
because of superlative performance in war or otherwise, being
a member of the aristocracy was a prime criterion for
leadership.[2]

The introduction of guns, swords, sailing ships, and
commerce by the early European traders gave certain Polynesian and Micronesian chiefs the opportunity to expand their
political power. They established kingdoms — on a much
larger scale and much more tightly organised than ever before,
but using the traditional aristocratic hierarchy of chiefs as the
basis of their organisation and government.[3]

This did not happen in Melanesia, largely because its traditional societies and beliefs did not, like the traditional aristocracies, provide such a convenient basis for the development
of kingdoms. Fiji was, in this and some other ways, like
Polynesia.

The Polynesian kingdoms had not been long established,
and were in some cases still being established, when European
colonial powers annexed or otherwise took effective control of
the various islands. The only kingdom which survived was the
Kingdom of Tonga.

Within these broad culture areas, some very fundamental
differences occur — even between people of a probably ident-
ical origin. For example, while the cultures of Samoa and
Tonga have a great deal in common, there are also radical
differences between them. These are of immense significance
even at a political level today. Some of the differences are probably due to environmental factors. Samoa is mountainous,
making unified control over large areas difficult; and the soil
very rocky, making agriculture arduous. So Samoans came to
depend heavily for their subsistence on breadfruit and bananas
which require almost no labour, but are conducive to consumption on an extended family basis. This form of subsistence is

congruent with the Samoan *aiga* system, with each aiga containing an average of about twelve persons under the strong and immediate control of a *matai*. It facilitates self-sufficiency at that level. This again is congruent with the integration of groups of aiga into a village community controlled at that level by the council of matai.

Tonga, on the other hand (and in particular the main island of Tongatapu which contains most of the population), was flat, fertile, and drier than Samoa. The basic food crop was the yam. Yams require intensive cultivation and care which is much more conducive to a higher degree of individualism in production than breadfruit, and this was and still is characteristic of Tonga. It is also congruent with more clearly identified individual rights to land which are also characteristic of Tonga today and seem always to have been so.

The relatively large, mountainous islands of Samoa were very difficult to conquer and unify — and nobody ever succeeded in doing so. And the fact that they were in sight of one another, and that winds and currents were such that one could not venture far without being carried westward with no chance of return, meant that navigational skills did not develop (the name Navigators Islands, given by an ignorant European visitor, was a misnomer).

Tonga's wide scatter of small islands with a diversity of distances and sea and wind conditions facilitated the emergence of the most sophisticated navigational system in the Pacific. This, with the relatively flat terrain, facilitated the conquest and significant degree of unitary control of Tonga, and the emergence of the only large-scale kingship in the Pacific before contact with industrialised societies. (It also led to the conquest of Samoa by Tonga.)

These and a number of other consequences of environmental difference are still of enormous cultural, social, and political significance in those countries today. Similar parallels could be drawn between various other Pacific societies.

Colonial systems

The colonial era is now coming to an end,[4] but as many Pacific Islanders still live under colonial rule it is of interest to look at some of its main features. Until the Second World War there were fifty years of relative stability, or stagnation, depending on one's point of view. Medical services were improved and populations increased, some low-level schooling, was instituted, roads and services were expanded, and centralised government was established.

The Second World War saw most of the northern and western Pacific Islands conquered by Japan and, without American aid, Australia and New Zealand could have been also. After the war the colonial powers began, through a mixture of idealism and self-interest, to take a new interest in the Pacific Islands. The South Pacific Commission was set up to facilitate social, economic, and medical development, and also to serve the interests of the colonial governments which directed and financed it. In the 1940s and 1950s at least it aimed to minimise United Nations activity in the Pacific, as it was feared that this would not be sympathetic to colonial governments. It also slowed down political development by prohibiting discussion of matters with political implications from all its agendas and programmes.[5]

The most striking differences in colonial policies were between the United Kingdom colonies, where chiefly systems were generally strengthened and made the basis of the colonial government, and the French colonies, where the chiefly systems were in most cases systematically destroyed. The French had a strongly nationalistic colonial policy which aimed, at least nominally, to imbue the islanders with French culture, whereas the English placed greater emphasis on the preservation of the indigenous culture.[6]

The United Kingdom in the 1960s and 1970s facilitated the independence of her colonies, and withdrew from the Pacific as a colonial power, but France still holds her colonies with determined tenacity. New Caledonia contains one of the world's largest deposits of nickel, as well as supplies of other minerals. French Polynesia is where France tests nuclear weapons, without which she would not be a world power. The new 200 mile Exclusive Economic Zone gives France, with her Pacific colonies, control of more water than almost any other nation on earth. And some of that water is rich in seabed minerals. France sees the 21st century as the century of the Pacific and wants access to the action.

Official French statements at the highest level oscillate between asserting that France's Pacific colonies are part of France and will remain so for ever, and on the other hand that the people can have independence whenever they want it, but that they do not want it. If the other colonial powers in the Pacific had followed this approach, there would not be a single independent country in the Pacific today. As the Prime Minister of Fiji, Ratu Sir Kamisese Mara, has frequently pointed out, there was no support for early independence for Fiji in the ruling Alliance Party, nor was it his own wish.[7] The United Kingdom exerted steady pressure over a period of years to facilitate that independence.

If the United Kingdom had followed the French policy and ensured that virtually no local people were given appropriate training or responsibility to take over, that Government radio and television maintained a constant barrage of misinformation about the virtues of remaining a colony and the horrors of independence, and made continuous threats that if people did vote for independence all aid would immediately be withdrawn, that all key staff and equipment would be withdrawn, and that their economy would be destroyed, Fiji would probably still be a colony. In French territories the above techniques are reinforced by the encouragement of immigration from France and its other colonies and ex-colonies, by the continuous harassment and intimidation of those who favour independence, as well as by heavy investment in the creation of dependence on French money, French language, French culture and so on. Whereas in the 1970s the ANZUS powers were pressing France to decolonise, this is now muted as they see France as an anti-Soviet influence. France greatly expanded its military forces in the islands in the 1980s.

In Vanuatu, when France was finally pressured into leaving (which would not have been possible were it not that the United Kingdom was keen to go) French officials were instructed to rip out telephones, air conditioners, and other equipment, take away all movable goods and make the situation as difficult as possible for the newly independent government, which France had tried to subvert in every possible way (for details of the process, from secret French official documents, see Van Trease, 1982).

DON'T BUY

please don't visit Hawaii

until we are able to save what's left!
Resort-travel-land interests are
ruining us - and our islands - to get
your money. Prices, taxes soar; wages
diminish. You can't buy <u>ALOHA</u>!

Honolulu, Hawaii

HAWAII RESIDENTS BUREAU

In New Caledonia, some significant powers were delegated in 1985 to four newly-created regional assemblies, in three of which Melanesians had the majority. But the new government in France in 1986 withdrew most of these powers, asserted more control from Paris and increased the number of French military personnel — already much the highest density of troops in any part of the South Pacific.

Australia had the largest colonial responsibility in the Pacific, for Papua New Guinea has more people than all other Pacific Islands put together. Australia's record was not inspiring, and by the end of it only between five and ten per cent of New Guinea people were literate. When it gained independence in 1975, Papua New Guinea was faced with an enormous task, for Australia did very little (except in the last few years) to promote the integration of its 700 separate language and culture groups into a single nation. The institution in which Australia developed the most cohesion and unity in Papua New Guinea was, unfortunately, the army.

The second largest colonial power until 1962 was the Netherlands, whose only colony in the islands was West New Guinea. Holland virtually ignored it for the first 100 years of control, but in the 1950s, after losing Indonesia, she instituted a huge development programme in West New Guinea. Despite ample staff and money, it was too late. Indonesian pressure, supported by American interests, made West New Guinea a part of Indonesia in 1963. In 1966, unrepresentative groups of Irian Jaya men were rounded up by Indonesian soldiers, intimidated, and given no choice but to 'vote unanimously' to join Indonesia. That was called 'The Act of Free Choice'! Despite Indonesian assertions to the contrary, Irian Jaya as it is now known, is for all practical purposes a colony; and by most criteria the worst administered colony in the Pacific.

I would not have believed the extent of the brutality, misunderstanding, and incompetence of Indonesian officials there if I had not seen it with my own eyes. The people would prefer to be independent or to join with Papua New Guinea but there is little possibility of their winning their continuing guerilla war for independence against Indonesia, at least not in this decade. Indonesia is, unfortunately, at least as self-centred in her relationship with her Pacific colony as France or the United States.[8] But one reason Indonesia is so unsuccessful as a colonial power is that she is so poor and so badly governed.

American colonial interests in the Pacific have been almost entirely military.[9] Hawaii can be equated with Irian Jaya in that Hawaii was incorporated into the U.S.A. as a result of a coup by Americans, and sixty years later Hawaii residents voted overwhelmingly in favour of becoming a state of the U.S.A. That is Indonesia's hope too — that after taking another people's territory by force, a generation or two of indoctrination and integration will lead them to like it.

Nevertheless there is a growing movement in Hawaii, particularly among persons of Hawaiian descent, to explore the possibilities of independence. Factors favouring Hawaii's continued membership of the U.S.A. are likely to decrease and those favouring a move towards independence to increase. The strongest support for independence is among the people of Hawaiian ancestry, which is the fastest growing sector of the population. The Hawaii economy has tremendous potential for autonomous existence (greater than any independent islands nation) from its agriculture, strategic value, tourism, and the fact that it has some of the most valuable real estate in the world. As part of the U.S.A., Hawaiians are becoming increasingly concerned about the possibility (or probability) of their destruction in a nuclear war, because America's largest offshore military bases are there.

Guam was acquired from Spain by U.S.A. military conquest in 1898. It remains a military fortress and the indigenous adult population has at times been outnumbered by Americans working directly or indirectly on U.S.A. military programmes.

American Samoa was acquired in 1899 to serve American naval interests and for over fifty years its people were governed by the commander of the naval base. In 1954, as a result of changes in military technology, it became obsolete and American Samoa was then handed to civilian, but still colonial, administration. By that time, it was so deeply dependent on the United States that there was a general wish to retain the dependence. The colonial power, moreover, despite some rhetoric to the contrary, has continued activities which deepen that dependency. When the then Prime Minister of Western Samoa, the Hon. Tupuola Efi, suggested several years ago that the two Samoas — so arbitrarily separated at the end of last century by the colonial powers — might at some future time be rejoined, the Governor of American Samoa asserted that it would never happen. Later, however, he accepted the possibility of future reunification. The key issue is going to be the extent to which American Samoa becomes again part of Samoa, as against the extent to which the independent state of Western Samoa becomes instead a part of America. Both processes are in train. Both will continue. The relative balance is the crucial issue.

The United States Trust Territory of the Pacific Islands (the Northern Marianas, Caroline Islands, and Marshall Islands) are the only remaining United Nations trusteeship in the world, not because they could not survive independently, but because of their strategic value to the United States. The U.S.A. Micronesian territories are now being launched into a new political status which the United States hopes will free it from continued United Nations supervision, and give the U.S.A. long-term effective control of that whole region. A constitutional lawyer opening a public meeting on the topic in Hawaii said that the first clause of the U.S.A. 'Compact of Free Association' with the Micronesian territories asserts that they will govern their own affairs, but every other clause denies it. And the most serious provisions for dependence are contained not in the compact itself, but in codicils attached to it, including, guarantees of exclusive U.S.A. military use of the islands for 50 years. One of the U.S.A. selling points in trying to make the new dependency more acceptable in the South Pacific is to claim that it is analogous to the relationship between the Cook Islands and New Zealand. This claim is untrue, except in relation to some insignificant details.

The Marianas have been incorporated into the United States (Guam as an 'Unincorporated Territory' and the Northern Marianas as a 'Commonwealth') as these are nearest to Asia and are of most value to America for military purposes. The United States will grant nominal self-government to the Marshall Islands, The Federated States of Melanesia (Kosrae, Ponape, Truk and Yap) and Palau (Belau) but will retain control of matters of significance to America. The planned extreme dependence on the U.S.A. is now a reality. The people of Guam and the Marianas voted overwhelmingly in favour of joining the U.S.A. — dependence does pay, and can increase security.

In addition, the United States controls such other islands as Wake, Johnson Island, Midway, the Aleutian Islands chain, and various others — all of which are directly involved in U.S.A. military operations.

New Zealand's colonial responsibilities in the Pacific were small, and her administrative record rather dull.[10] By comparison with the United Kingdom, France, and Holland, which used highly trained specialist staff, New Zealand's colonial officials were not well-equipped for the task. The administration was generally well-intentioned, but more effective in achieving improvements in welfare than in production. New Zealand's territories were probably fortunate to come under Maori ministers for most of the first half of this century — Sir James Carroll (Timi Kara), then Sir Maui Pomare, then Sir Apirana Ngata — who were concerned to improve social services and to minimise industrial and commercial developments which they feared might disrupt island cultures.

Although New Zealand did much more in primary education than most colonial powers, technical and higher education was grossly inadequate. The islanders are thus dependent to an unnecessary degree on foreign staff: much more than Fiji or Tonga for example. Many problems in the Cook Islands today are due to the fact that before self-government New Zealand had not prepared an adequate pool of trained, qualified, local manpower to undertake existing and emerging tasks. The Cook Islands is for all practical purposes independent, and Niue fully self-governing, but Tokelau is not as it has a total resident population of only 1600 people (more than half have migrated to New Zealand or Australia). But Cook, Niue, and Tokelau Islanders insist on retaining their New Zealand citizenship also as most of their people live in New Zealand anyway, and it widens their options.

Federation was seen by some people in the 1940s and 1950s as the best solution for the Pacific Islands. There were obvious advantages of scale to be gained from joining forces. Three main proposals have been put forward — one for a Melanesian federation to include New Guinea, the Solomon Islands, and

Vanuatu; one for a central Pacific federation based on Fiji, Tonga, and Samoa; and one for all the Pacific Islands. None of the proposals has come to fruition and none is likely to. The peoples are diverse, the cultures are different, the distances vast, and a federal government would add a large new burden of expense. Countries which have recently obtained independence from colonial powers are not likely to want a political federation which would curtail their independence, and reduce the number of attractive jobs as members of parliament, cabinet ministers, or heads of even tiny governments. Nevertheless, external pressure and internal convenience is likely to see the degree of real independence whittled down considerably over the coming years.[11]

12
Independence and after
The Pacific way?

Self-government and beyond

Even the most diverse forms of governmental organisation
today have much in common. They are based on bureaucracy,
upon hierarchies of control, laws, procedures, memoranda,
and telephones. But it is easy to overemphasise the similarities.
There are also substantial differences.

In the 1950s the idea of eventual self-government came to be
cautiously accepted, and in the 1960s complete independence
became almost universally adopted as the goal. Western Samoa
(1962), Nauru (1968), Tonga and Fiji (1970), Papua New Guinea
(1975), Solomon Islands and Tuvalu (1978), Kiribati (1979), and
Vanuatu (1980) are all independent. So are the Cook Islands
for all practical purposes, though this was not by declaration
but by de facto evolution from the time of self-government (in
1965).

The period since independence has been, in all cases, much
more politically stable than many people assumed it would be.
There may be future crises, but the outlook is promising. Each
island nation has difficult political problems to cope with. Fiji,
with its population delicately balanced between Indians and
Fijians, has a tremendous task ahead. It was at about that stage
of population balance between immigrant Englishmen and
resident Maoris in New Zealand that the race wars occurred.
A similar crisis in Fiji is unlikely, but not impossible, and the
welding of these two very different cultures, plus European,
Chinese, and other minorities into a unified nation, will be a
major task for another generation at least.

Tonga is one of the world's few remaining kingdoms. It is
not democratic, and most forms of power and privilege are

concentrated in the hands of a small, predominantly heredi-tary, elite, plus an expanding bureaucracy. Neither are noted for their efficiency. The climate of world opinion is no longer sympathetic to such a form of government, and this is increas-ingly so in Tonga also. But the aristocracy and its associated non-aristocratic elite, like any privileged minority in any human society, is unlikely to reshape the society voluntarily, either far enough or fast enough to meet the mounting desire for change.

In varying degrees Samoa, Tonga, and Fiji have all given constitutional and other privileges to hereditary chiefs. In the past, these chieftainships have had a number of advantages,[1] and the countries that achieved independence first were those with strong hereditary chieftainships. In future, however, the advantages of chiefly authority are likely to continue to decrease, and their disadvantages to multiply. This is particu-larly so because of the psychological effects which such rigid class levels have in inhibiting the development of the talents of the great majority of people. New Guinea, the Solomons, and Vanuatu never had such restrictive aristocratic systems. In the past this had disadvantages but in the future political and economic context they may be fortunate not to be burdened with a leadership system which is not well adapted to the aspirations or the economy of the new generation of Pacific Islanders.

New political forces are taking shape. Greatly increased urban employment has led to worker interests being expressed through political involvement by trade unions. Where non-traditional sectional interests are clearly distinct, political parties have emerged (significantly not in Tonga, and only recently in Western Samoa). Race is becoming a major focus for political alignment — islanders, Europeans, and Asians being the main categories — but in Micronesia and Melanesia there is also considerable political division between islanders on the basis of language or other cultural or regional origins, and in Fiji persons of mixed European-Fijian origin constitute a distinguishable political entity. Ideology too is becoming more important. As people become aware that alternative political systems are possible, imported ideologies are sought and examined. Some of them are likely to be of increasing political significance.

Pacific Islands political leaders are mainly elected, yet islands voters tend not to elect their own kind to high office, but rather to choose disproportionately urbanised, foreign-educated, and foreign-oriented candidates. This may indicate the direction of their aspirations.

It is not generally realised that in every Pacific country except Western Samoa, which did have a genuine indigenous independence movement, there was no really effective indigenous independence movement until it was stimulated from outside: especially from United Nations pressure and changes in the climate of world opinion.

Cultural continuities

The relative significance of traditional forms in the present-day structure and functioning of governments in the Pacific is closely related to the co-ordination at the national level, as well as the strength at the local level, of the culture concerned. The governments of Tonga and Western Samoa operate to a substantial degree on traditional precedents (the radical differences between the two countries are discussed in the previous chapter), despite their being formally cast in a Westminster mould. In the Marshall and Caroline Islands, traditional forms were very significant in the district legislatures, but very much less so in the 'federal' congress of Micronesia. This was because traditional patterns were relatively uniform at the district level but diverse at the 'federal' level.

Fijian precedents have significant force today, even though indigenous Fijians are a minority population in Fiji. In the Cook Islands, where traditional precedents are mainly of a ceremonial order, tradition is reflected in the House of Ariki (high chiefs) whose functions are confined largely to advising in matters of custom and protocol. In Melanesia, being characterised by great diversity, it is much more difficult to adopt local patterns directly as national models. But throughout Melanesia some adaptations are being made. The French territories, in government as in all else, are almost totally assimilated to the French model.

Societies in the eastern Pacific developed systems of government in which leadership was determined largely by accidents of birth reinforced by systematic thought control. 'Accident of birth' systems are now much less widespread in the world than they used to be. The decline has resulted partly from a weakening of beliefs about the rank or status of a person being determined by gods. Partly it is due to evidence showing (contrary to beliefs in such stratified societies) that ability in government and other skills is learnt rather than in-born, and that both high and low intelligence are found among both high ranking and low ranking persons. These changes in knowledge and belief, and the greater mobility of people, have led to a decrease in the importance of hereditary leadership.

Another reflection of the reduced value accorded to accident of birth is the relative status and effectiveness of governments where this is a primary criterion for obtaining power. The two most marked instances are Tonga and Western Samoa. Since last century they were looked up to throughout the islands as the leaders. This began to change in the 1960s. Once the most admired and respected, the systems of government of those two former models are now widely regarded by other islanders as constraints to achieving the goals to which they aspire.

The change of view is not without substance: Tonga and Western Samoa once had the highest proportions of highly educated manpower in the Pacific — now they have lower ratios than Papua New Guinea; once they were the most productive and had the highest standards of living — now they are among the lowest on both counts; once they were the most independent — now they are among the most dependent. Obviously there are many reasons for these changes, but the system of government is one. If, in a rapidly changing present, one puts too much emphasis on admiring one's past rather than creating unique adaptations for the future, one is soon left behind.

Why, it is often asked, has the Fiji government performed so effectively when Fiji recognises strong hereditary leadership? There are several reasons. One is that the political leadership is elected by universal suffrage, and that chiefs who wish to govern must prove their worth to the public. Ratu Sir Kamisese Mara, Prime Minister since independence, has indeed been re-elected on the basis of skilled performance. Another is that while there seems to have been some preference for those of rank in some government posts, this bias has not been acute. (Nevertheless, nepotism is a growing problem in Fiji.) Finally, the strong economic base for the Fiji government was built largely by non-Fijians, who also constitute the majority of the civil service.

Our beliefs are much influenced by our own interests. Those who do not themselves benefit from inherited rank do not want its hereditary privileges preserved. On the other hand, those who gain from traditional systems of privilege use traditional precedent to justify perpetuation or extension of their advantage.

Though more complex and elaborate, the traditional cultures of Tonga and Fiji may not survive as fully or as long as those of Papua New Guinea or Solomon Islands. This is because the hereditary chiefs of the former societies tend to insist that anything done in the name of tradition be to their advantage, whether in the distribution of goods, the opportunity to achieve, or the granting of the limelight and prestige roles. The unstated obverse is that this is to the commoners' disadvantage.

Today the commoners have alternative ways of interpreting their role, and alternative ways of doing things, and they increasingly use them. It is unlikely that many members of the privileged classes will be farsighted or public spirited enough to emphasise aspects of traditional society which do not reinforce the differences. By over-emphasising their own self-interest, they slowly cause the destruction of much of their culture. In Papua New Guinea and Solomon Islands, by contrast, more traditional activities involved population participation without subordination or deprivation. Everyone has more incentive to perpetuate them.

One reflection of the differences between societies where heredity is emphasised and those where leadership is achieved by the younger and more energetic shows up in the ages of cabinet ministers. The average age of the ministers in Solomon Islands, Papua New Guinea, and Vanuatu, for example, is probably ten to twenty years younger than that for Fiji, Tonga, or Samoa.

Personalised styles

Despite a great deal of talk about consensus as the 'natural' Pacific style of government, there is also considerable authoritarian control, both in the 'big man' systems of Melanesia and in aristocratic systems. While much depends on the social and cultural context, much also depends on the personalities of key individuals.

Why, for example, do so many of the most talented Tongans escape from Tonga (and so few return) whereas almost all Fijians of top talent remain at home? If it were the other way round it would be easy to suggest reasons why Fijians would want to leave: the competition from Indians, Europeans, and Chinese means that in this multiracial society Fijians can only hold a share of the top slots. In Tonga by contrast, every post is available for Tongans.

One of the important differences, I believe, is the style of leadership of the men at the top. The King of Tonga and President Hammer de Roburt of Nauru are men of outstanding ability. Almost no one doubted that each was the most outstanding man in his country. In both cases, however, this tended to lead the man concerned to behave not as though he were better than any other individual in the country, but as though he were better than all other individuals in the country put together. It led them not to draw out the potential talents of others to any significant degree and perhaps unintentionally to restrain their growth and contribution to those societies.

The reaction of Tongans and Nauruans was substantially different. Nauruans tended to withdraw from the competition and leave it to the President to run. Most of them had adequate incomes and could console themselves with excessive booze, food, overseas travel, and competitive giving. Very few Nauruans had the academic or professional qualifications that many Tongans have, and therefore they could not have moved into senior posts in other countries — and their own government had not given them much opportunity to occupy such posts — so the tendency was to sit at home and pay expatriates (in earlier years Europeans, but more recently Indians and others also) to run the country for them. Tongans do not have the Nauruans' income and they do have some openings abroad, but although the per capita income of all races in Fiji is about three times that of Tongans, that of rural Fijians is much the same.

In the Fiji case, the leadership style of Prime Minister Ratu Sir Kamisese Mara seems to be a significant factor in retaining

Father Walter Lini, one of the founders of the National Party (in 1971) which changed its name in 1977 to the Vanuaaku Party. Leader of the party and Prime Minister since the independence of Vanuatu in 1980, Father Lini here addresses a political rally.

Former Prime Minister Tupuola Efi (1976 to 1982) of Western Samoa with Albert Henry, first Premier (1965 to 1978) of the Cook Islands.

Toalipi Lauti, Tuvalu's first Prime Minister (1978 to 1981).

Peter Kenilorea, first Prime Minister of the Solomon Islands, 1978 to 1981 and 1984 to 1986.

the top talents at home. He expects senior Fijians both in the bureaucracy and in politics to innovate, to think problems through, and to communicate much more than his counterparts in Tonga or Nauru. A leading Tongan was amazed several years ago when he heard that one of the top political figures in Fiji (Ratu Sir Penaia Ganilau) had written to Dr. Nayacakalou, who was then lecturing at the University of Sydney, to request him to return to Fiji to take a senior post (which Dr. Nayacakalou did). The Tongan felt that both the King and the Prime Minister of Tonga would have considered such action below their dignity. If they had been prepared to do such things, my informant felt, and to delegate, listen, and show more of the humility that some other leaders show, significant numbers of leading Tongans of high ability who were overseas would have remained in the country.

To take another case, although a higher proportion of the Niue population migrated to New Zealand than Cook Islanders, it was my impression that Niue retained a higher proportion of its top civil servants than the Cook Islands. This, I think, related in part to the contrast between styles of leadership. They have similar constitutions, and the same relationship with New Zealand whereby Cook Islanders and Niueans can enter New Zealand at any time. But Premier Sir Robert Rex of Niue operates much more of a consensus pattern, has avoided the emergence of political parties, has not politicised the public service, and plays the role of a wise and experienced community elder. He unifies, heals, listens, and is humble.

Former Cook Islands Premier, Albert Henry, on the other hand, polarised, dramatised, asserted, and demanded the limelight. The Public Service in the Cook Islands became highly politicised. Nepotism and political favouritism were major

(Opposite, top left) President Hammer de Roburt of Nauru, 1968–76 and 1978 to present.

(Opposite, top right) Sir Thomas Davis, former Prime Minister of the Cook Islands, 1978 to 1981 and 1983 to present.

(Opposite, bottom left) Rt. Hon. Michael Somare, Papua New Guinea's first Prime Minister, 1975 to 1980 and 1982 to 1985.

(Opposite, bottom right) Premier Sir Robert R. Rex of Niue, the Pacific's longest serving head of government has never been effectively challenged.

problems. A number of Cook Islanders who live overseas alleged political victimisation or discrimination as a reason for their departure.

In 1978 Albert Henry's government was thrown out of office by a decision of the High Court, unique in Commonwealth history, for massive corruption in that year's election. Court and other evidence revealed that the corruption was not confined to elections. The Henry government had little under-standing of economics and the emphasis shifted to expanded (generally inefficient) services, while productivity declined markedly in agriculture, manufacturing, and construction. In terms of real value, Gross Domestic Product (GDP) declined from about NZ$8 million to $6 million between 1970 and 1978 and per capita income levels from $370 to $330. The percentage of GDP originating from productive activities declined from 45 per cent in 1970 to 27 per cent in 1978 (and that for agriculture from 22 to 17 per cent). The decline was offset by foreign aid, remittances from Cook Islanders abroad, and tourism.

The government of Sir Thomas Davis, which came to power in 1978, put considerable emphasis on restructuring the economy, with some success, despite world recession. Values of exports more than doubled within two years of the new government, and administrative efficiency seems to have improved — though not markedly. Nepotism and political favouritism in the granting of contracts, study awards, travel opportunities etc, seems to have been reduced immediately after the change of government, but to have escalated again (though not to former levels) within a few years. The popu-lation, which had steadily declined through migration in the Henry years, in 1984 and 1985 began to grow again, and the retention of talents seems to have improved.

Scope for creative adaptation

All governments contain much that is carried over from the past, plus some features that are constantly modified by current pressures. In creating governmental systems for the needs of tomorrow, there is room for much improvement. But Pacific people need not be overwhelmed into the wholesale adoption of foreign models. Most of the capitalist governments in the world today are based on structures designed for conditions in the seventeenth and eighteenth centuries. Communism was designed to solve the problems of last century. No government was designed for today's problems and conditions, still less for tomorrow's. The island nations can therefore afford to look at their own governmental systems afresh, and from the perspective of their own needs.

Bureaucratic organisation has an inevitable tendency to standardise and consequently to stultify. There is an urgent need for an effective, flexible linkage between the government and the young and creative sectors of the population. This may be more readily achieved among the small populations of the Pacific than in the vast populations of Asia or Europe.

The hungry bureaucracies

Alas, not much of the scope for creative adaptation has been grasped as yet. It is constrained by a lack of confidence, a hangover from colonial patterns, and by the new dependency on foreign governments and foreign experts who come overwhelmingly from the countries which were colonial powers in the Pacific (as one islands cynic observed, the Colonial Offices of the metropolitan powers are more powerful than ever, but are now named Ministries of Foreign Affairs).

The demand for greatly expanded services, the availability of aid, the limited pool of top talent yet available, the cultural value placed on leisure, and a widespread opposition to commercial enterprise, have led to the rapid growth of relatively inefficient bureaucracies. In many Pacific countries today the worst exploitation of the public (in terms of the distribution of the available cash, resources, and privileges) is by their own governments. It is the more difficult to correct because it is seldom realised, let alone admitted.

Other problems include nepotism and political favouritism (which are often linked in small societies). In countries with very small populations it is inevitable that there will be many 'interlocking directorates', in business, politics, the bureaucracy, and all other forms of organisation. The small total populations are made effectively much smaller by the concentration of higher education, power, and privilege in the hands of small, often inter-marrying, mutual-supporting, and self-perpetuating elites based on traditional privilege and/or professional background. (Incidentally, at a conference of persons in charge of staff training for all Pacific governments held in 1981, it was the unanimous view of all present that political favouritism and/or nepotism was perhaps the greatest single problem in selection of personnel for study awards in almost all Pacific countries.)

The great majority of the people in positions of power, and of the young elite at the Pacific universities, are sons and daughters of that small minority in the previous generation who were either ministers of religion, civil servants, persons of hereditary privilege, or engaged in commerce. This too is not generally realised, though it is to be expected and occurs to some extent in any human society. But the speed with which it has grown, and the size of the gap between privileged and underprivileged which has developed in most countries, is contrary to both the image and the stated intention of most governments.

In many countries there are also allegations of government transport (land, sea, and air), staff and other resources being deflected for the personal benefit of those in power. There are also concerns about the spreading tendency for persons in power to benefit from unethical (though sometimes legal) acceptance of commissions, shares, services, and even direct payments to themselves or their families. Papua New Guinea, Fiji, Tonga, and Western Samoa may suffer from these problems more than the other countries, but their apparently expanding presence everywhere has been a factor in the apparent reduction in public confidence, increased cynicism, corruption and crime. The model set by the leaders is vitally important (as studies of corruption elsewhere show) in the extent to which this problem becomes entrenched in any society. To the extent that it is considered inevitable that 'all power corrupts' this is a good reason for constraints on the powerful. The Kiribati constitution does not allow any person to hold the presidency for more than three terms; and Belau and the Federated States of Micronesia have a limit of two consecutive terms.

Growing external commitments and attractions

Pacific Prime Ministers, Premiers, Presidents, and Cabinet Ministers spend more and more time away from their countries attending each others' conferences and celebrations. When at home they are tied down increasingly by entertaining visiting political leaders, ambassadors, international agency personnel, and lots of others. The proportion of time left over to keep effective contact with their own people is ever reducing.

As the scale of foreign involvement becomes more complex, it gives more scope to manipulate others or to be manipulated. The world's major powers have been represented in the islands since independence. 1976 saw China and the U.S.S.R. come formally into the islands picture, and to establish diplomatic ties and aid relationships. Their presence was invited by several Pacific governments, at least in part to improve bargaining relations with the established aid sources, the former colonial powers. This inevitable step involves the Pacific governments and people, for good or ill, more closely in world political movements, where very large powers call much of the tune. How far Pacific governments can co-ordinate their leverage in responding to big powers remains a major question for the coming decade, though the 1980s has seen a significant reduction in independence and greatly increased penetration and manipulation by U.S.A. in particular.

Achievements so far

The independent Pacific Islands nations are the only region of the Third World where governments are regularly chosen by election and where the democratic process is respected and followed. Professor Yash Ghai observed in 1981 that he was not aware of a single change of government in Africa, ever, as a result of democratic elections.

The independence constitutions of the Pacific nations are all observed, again the only region of the Third World where this is generally so. Papua New Guinea has one of the most comprehensive constitutions in the world — probably too complex — whereas Vanuatu has one of the simplest. Most have been modified (though none drastically) by the processes provided for adapting to changing needs.

There are no political prisoners, no cases of governments torturing or killing their opponents, no outlawed parties, and no use of military forces against their own people in any independent Pacific nation. And monetary dependence is in most cases moderate. These are considerable achievements.

The independent governments have generally operated at a high level of integrity by world standards, though recent years has seen some tarnishing of that integrity by some leaders. External pressures in particular are likely to lead to further erosion in the coming years. The pressures are not only from foreign governments and trans-national corporations, each pursuing its respective interests, but also from international thugs and confidence men, who have already taken in a disturbing number of Pacific governments and leaders. We may come to look back on the 1970s as the high point in Pacific Islands independence.

It is usual, when reviewing progress since independence, to compare factors with the pre-independence situation. This 'backwards' comparison is important and necessary, but sometimes over-emphasised to the neglect of 'sideways' comparison. If we compare the progress in education, for example, or health, or infrastructure in 1987 with that in 1967 we can see tremendous progress over that achieved in the colonial situation. But if we compare the situation in independent countries in 1987 with that in the Pacifics' remaining dependent territories in 1987, on many criteria we find the opposite: that the improvement of these facilities in the dependent territories is greater than in the independent states. Moreover, much of the progress in the independent states is financed by the former colonial powers. Such facts are naturally unpalatable, but we need to be aware of them, even though services are far from the only factors in assessing the merits of various degrees of independence.

13
Intra-Pacific relations
Co-operation and competition

The growing regional network

The attainment of self-government and independence by island nations in the 1960s and 1970s loosened ties with former colonial powers, but the geographical units so created are the smallest in the world. Apart from Papua New Guinea and Fiji, an average Pacific Island nation contains only about 90 000 people. Thus they are too small to carry out effectively a whole range of functions which would be normal in larger nations. Functions which require a large population base were formerly undertaken by the metropolitan powers. Now the advantages of joint action by Pacific governments, training institutions, churches, businesses, unions, and other organisations are being explored and used increasingly.

By world standards regional co-operation among the Pacific countries and territories has achieved a great deal in a short time. Over 250 regional organisations now operate in the Pacific; a generation ago there were almost none.

Some people think of regionalism only in terms of inter-governmental activity. Fortunately that is only a part of it. Inter-governmental linkages are indeed important, but they are also brittle: a dispute in one field may directly influence or threaten other supposedly unrelated organisations. The region's strength lies in the multiplicity of the fibres making up the web, and the fact that each serves a different interest group, and involves a different set of people. This 'collective dynamic' in Pacific regionalism is difficult to quantify, but its existence is evident and its significance substantial. In addition to the vital role of governments, regional religious bodies, business and worker associations, learned and professional societies, and cultural, sporting and other organisations constitute

the network of co-operation and interaction on which a significant degree of Pacific unity has already been built.

Critics are often heard to say that regional co-operation
'doesn't work', but there is abundant evidence that it does. The
more important issues are for *what purposes*, among *which partners*, at *what times*, are *which tasks* better undertaken on a
regional basis (whether the region be the whole Pacific, or part
of the Pacific), than on a smaller scale (for example, nation or
district) or larger (multinational or world).

Another common view is that 'they won't last'. The
surprising feature has been the unexpectedly high rate of
survival to date. There is no particular virtue in an organisation
being regional (or national or world-wide or any other kind).
And one would expect a number to have gone out of existence
because of inadequate resources, unrealistic goals, political
tensions, staff disputes, or otherwise. Again, the record to date
shows fewer of these inadequacies than might be expected.

Regional co-operation in the Pacific is facilitated by water
boundaries (the only land boundary — that between Papua
New Guinea and West New Guinea — is a source of constant
tension), by the absence of major ideological differences, and
by the fact that extensive close contact is recent (and thus there
are few hangovers of historical conflict). Also the fact that
governments are generally stable and freely elected (again with
the exception of West New Guinea) results in mutual respect,
there is some feeling of common ethnic heritage *vis-à-vis*
surrounding populations, there is relatively frequent and
harmonious contact between leaders, and relations are charac-
terized by flexibility, informality, and pragmatism.

On the other hand regional co-operation is constrained by
national interest (leaders get their positions through national
votes, not regional ones), by bilateral pressures from industrialised nations on the Pacific rim, by the absence of major
common external threats, and by the fact that sanctions to
enforce compliance with regional agreements are hard to
apply.

The Pacific is not aiming for integration, in the sense of
moving towards a single islands state or federation, but
towards more functional and pragmatic co-operation.

The five umbrellas

Many regional organisations fit under one or other of five umbrella organisations — the South Pacific Forum (the annual meeting of Pacific Prime Ministers, Presidents, Premiers), the South Pacific Commission, the University of the South Pacific, the Pacific Conference of Churches, and the United Nations. The fit is far from exact — it is probably better that it is not — and organisations under an umbrella are not necessarily subordinate. For example, the Festival of Pacific Arts comes within the orbit of the South Pacific Commission, which provides secretarial services for it, but it is controlled by its own independent council; the Church of Melanesia belongs to the Pacific Conference of Churches, but is not subordinate to it; the South Pacific Air Transport Council is facilitated by SPEC but is not controlled by it; the South Pacific Creative Arts Society is associated with the University of the South Pacific (as is common for cultural and learned societies anywhere) but has no legal connection with it. And the umbrellas are themselves related: all members of the Forum are also members of the South Pacific Commission, most are represented on the University Council, and several belong to the United Nations.

Many organisations do not fit readily into any of the above loose categories. These include such women's organisations as the Pan Pacific and South East Asia Womens Association, the Pacific Womens Association and the Young Women's Christian Association's Pacific Regional Office; or professional associations like the Conference of Asia and Pacific Accountants, South Pacific Dental Secretariat and various others, though the South Pacific Commission could perhaps serve a useful role assisting professional associations.

What region for what purpose?

While the great distances add expense and difficulty to regional co-operation (for example the South Pacific Commission's area is about 10 000 km west to east by 5000 km north to south), small areas and populations make co-operative efforts more effective in many fields. Rapid communications facilitate such efforts.

Loyalties and feelings of identification evolve from the level of the family and local community to a concentration at the level of the new nation, from the continuing but possibly diminishing importance of cultural and geographical sub-regions (Melanesia, Micronesia, and Polynesia) to an increasing awareness of identification at the level of the Pacific Islands as a whole. The growth of regional awareness is clearly demonstrated by the tremendous expansion of regional organisations, often unconscious of the existence of each other. They are based on inter-governmental, religious, commercial, educational, technical, cultural, sporting, and other common interests. In addition national institutions are increasingly offering use of their facilities to close neighbours.

Most services are best provided at a national or lower level, for example district, village, or household. Which services can be of higher quality, or lower cost, and/or greater efficiency or satisfaction, if provided jointly by more than one nation? For some purposes, the best combination might involve only a few (like the Cook Islands/Niue/New Zealand/Joint Shipping Service); for other purposes it is the independent Pacific plus selected neighbours, as with The South Pacific Forum. For some it is all the Pacific countries and territories with a wide range of others, for example the South Pacific Commission; for a few others it is part of a world body, as with the United Nations Development Advisory Team for the South Pacific.

Among the easiest and most effective regional organisations are those for the sharing of experiences and accommodation of mutual needs, such as the South Pacific Ports Conference, and those providing specific services which require specialised skills and a base larger than a single nation, like the Committee for Co-ordination of Joint Prospecting for Mineral Resources in South Pacific Off-Shore Areas — known as CCOP-SOPAC. Among the most difficult ones to set up are those involving highly competitive commercial activities, like Air Pacific and the Pacific Forum Line of cargo ships. They often have difficulties in reconciling divergent commercial and political goals.

The pattern of formation

The whole of the last century saw the establishment of only about ten organisations on a regional basis, most of them by churches, a few by colonial governments, and one by a learned society — the Polynesian Society. The first half of the present century, until the end of the Second World War, witnessed another dozen or so emerge — about double the rate of the previous century. Again most were religious and a few colonial: all were established and managed by Europeans.

The first sign of change came with the formation of the South Pacific Commission in 1947, and about ten others within the next decade. The first half of the decade of 1960s saw another dozen or so, and its second half, another 32. In the first half of the 1970s another 40 were formed, and in the second half many more. The total is now over 250, excluding voluntary agencies. (A Directory of Pacific Regional Institutions prepared by the Institute of Pacific Studies of the University of the South Pacific, was published by ESCAP in 1982; another is in preparation.)

The centre of gravity is moving westwards

Last century the centre of gravity in the islands was located in Polynesia, where effective centralised governments were established in the 1800s. It then moved to Fiji after that became the centre of the British empire in the islands, with a consequent centralisation of trade, higher education, and the creation of an administrative/political elite. This gave Fiji a great advantage in regional politics after independence because its leaders, having been educated earlier and further, had little competition in becoming leaders of the Pacific. In the early stages this leadership seems to have been used altruistically for the benefit of all islands, and was widely appreciated. But by the late 1970s it was becoming clear to the other countries that Fiji's role in regional co-operation was being used in such a way that, while the main costs of most forms of regional co-operation were being paid by external donors, and intended to be for the equitable benefit of all islands countries, Fiji was the main beneficiary.[1]

A process of offering attractive terms for the initial establishment of regional facilities in Suva and then slowly manipulating the factors in its own favour, has given Fiji considerable short-term advantage, but probably greater long-term disadvantage. Jamaica, once the centre of the British empire in the

Caribbean, likewise became the centre for Caribbean region-alism. But having used its advantage to its own benefit in relation to its neighbours, within twenty years Jamaica was no longer the centre of regional co-operation.

In the same way, if Fiji continues to allow the accidents of colonial history to disadvantage its neighbours, it is likely to be left isolated by the end of this century. The Central Medical School, built by external donors to serve the whole English-speaking Pacific, was highly successful. But after some decades it became the Fiji School of Medicine and its service to the region became a token, only large enough to ensure that it qualified for regional aid. The Derrick Technical Institute, set up by the United Kingdom to serve all United Kingdom terri-tories in the Pacific, became absorbed into the Fiji Institute of Technology within 20 years; Air Pacific, set up by colonial powers, aimed to transfer its assets to a consortium of Pacific nations, but became Fiji's national airline within a decade; the South Pacific Telecommunications College, financed by the EEC for all Pacific countries, was taken over by Fiji as a nation-ally-operated college even before the concrete had set. There is some apprehension about the fate of other regional facilities located in Fiji.

There is no need here to go into the details of the process. Fiji generally claims that it is because others will not meet their share of the costs. But the most common reply of the others is that they are happy to pay an equitable share, but that Fiji insists on disproportionate benefits for its economy and its people. The Fiji government's practices guarantee big advan-tages for Fiji citizens over those of other member countries. Immigration practices discriminate heavily against islanders from outside Fiji, and those who do enter face a range of official and unofficial discrimination against them and their families in relation to employment, housing and other loans, scholarships, finance, civil rights, and otherwise.

To take a few examples, the 66 jobs for Pacific Islanders in the *regional* programme of the United Nations Development Programme (in 1982) were all held by Fiji citizens; when a member government asked if it could have just one or two of its nationals employed as hostesses in the airline of which it was supposed to be an equal partner this was refused by Fiji;

and in eighteen years at the University of the South Pacific almost every islander appointed from outside Fiji has been unnecessarily delayed or harassed and in some cases frustrated to the point of withdrawal.

Once the concrete is poured, any regional institution is to some extent a hostage of the host nation, and the more regional facilities that are concentrated in one country, the greater that country's leverage. This realisation is leading to growing pressure for a spread in locations of headquarters of regional institutions. Telecommunications, improved air links, and the rapid spread of computing and other services make this feasible.

If co-operative regional activity is too centralised the central nation becomes the main beneficiary, usually playing down its benefits and over-rating its costs, until the peripheral smaller countries turn elsewhere — at which stage the central nation is likely to be the main loser. A major reason for the collapse of the Caribbean Federation was the disproportionate benefits derived by Jamaica. Likewise Kenya's taking of the lion's share was a major issue in the collapse of the East African Community. Unless the benefits of Pacific regional co-operation are more realistically shared, not only will the Pacific nations be worse off, but the leverage of the superpowers will be so much greater.

The spreading of regional institutions is likely to be predominantly westward. Many people are just waking up to the reality that in the Pacific islands (excluding Hawaii) 76 per cent of the people are Melanesians, only 8 per cent Polynesian, 4 per cent Micronesian, 10 per cent Asian, and 2 per cent European. And within Melanesia the growing strength lies in the Pidgin-speaking nations (Papua New Guinea, Solomon Islands, and Vanuatu). If we exclude West New Guinea (as it is unlikely to be able to win its ongoing guerilla war for independence from Indonesia in the foreseeable future), 91 per cent of all Melanesians live in those three Pidgin-speaking countries. They became independent later, and were left less infrastructure by the departing colonial powers, but they have much more resources (for example they have vastly more minerals, and few people realise that Solomon Islands is more than 50 per cent larger than Fiji).

Ethnicity and commonality: basis for co-operation or division?

The three major cultural divisions of the Pacific — Melanesia, Micronesia, and Polynesia — do not form the basis for many regional organisations, though significant parts of each area do. It must be remembered that the concept of these areas is based on similarity of cultures, not necessarily on their past interaction, which was limited. Nevertheless, members of particular cultural areas do 'pull together' at times within larger regional bodies, and in ad hoc decision-making. There is also, in most cases, more interaction between neighbours sharing the same culture area, than between neighbours of different cultures. The three culture areas are still significant for Pacific politics.

Unlike some other parts of the world each nation of the Pacific is very different from the others in language, culture, and feelings of identity. Yet despite there being more language fragmentation here than in any other part of the world, when people want to co-operate with their neighbours, their common 'Pacificness' can be emphasised. This is increasingly done.

All Pacific Island nations draw both on neighbours and on metropolitan countries. Yet most have expressed a desire to draw more on other Pacific Islanders. The lack of fuller utilisation of the potential is attributed to several constraints: the shortage of qualified islanders, though in many fields more are available than is commonly assumed; metropolitan countries paying to get their own nationals in but generally resisting paying for even lower-cost, more appropriately qualified islanders to do the same job; metropolitan countries having diplomatic offices, aid missions etc, that actively 'push' their nationals; a fear still in many places that fellow islanders are not as good as foreigners; the hiring of staff from other Pacific countries is at times resented by the country they are hired from; and fear of further domination by Fiji.

More effective regional use of existing Pacific talents is an urgent need in order to supply skills and to develop talents and confidence. This may be facilitated by the establishment in 1982 of the Pacific Regional Advisory Service (which was absorbed by SPEC in 1985) for this purpose, but so far its achievements have been quite modest.

National allegiance in regional activity

Regional organisations are staffed largely by citizens of the member nations (plus small numbers of specialists from outside the region). Several factors make national allegiance a more significant factor than it might otherwise be. The first is that most staff in most regional organisations are citizens of the country in which that organisation is based. Even though this is less apparent at the higher levels than the lower, it applies to almost every organisation — and perhaps to all. Staff from other countries of the region working for regional organisations are generally on temporary secondment — most commonly for three years. Most of them come from particular national governments (or for the religious organisations from particular national churches). It is to those that they will return and those are the places where their contribution is most likely to be evaluated, not so much in terms of what they did for the region as what they did for their own country from their regional base. Naturally everyone has more contacts with people in his or her own country, knows the context better, knows where particular services of his or her institution might be most helpfully applied to their country, and has most commitment there.

The above factors apply to some extent in any international organisation, but are more pronounced in the Pacific Islands due to the general resistance to providing secure long-term employment to people from outside the host country; the general resistance to granting citizenship to outsiders, and the very significant cultural and other differences between Pacific Islands nations. If regional institutions are to work effectively, therefore, action is needed to offset these inevitable, but re-ducible, nationalist tendencies. Many Caribbean countries, for example, allow people from one country to take citizenship in another if they are working there, without losing their original citizenship. Dual citizenship is also allowed by Australia and New Zealand, and many other countries in similar cases. The restrictions on movement between islands states are an additional incentive to the most talented Pacific people to migrate outside the region rather than join or remain in a regional service.

Spheres of intensive co-operation

Areas of influence of the former (in some cases present) colonial powers remain significant in most aid arrangements involving Pacific Islands nations and territories. There is a lot of interaction between United States territories: the Territory of Guam, the Commonwealth of Northern Marianas, the Republic of Palau, the Federated States of Micronesia, the Marshall Islands, the Territory of American Samoa, and the State of Hawaii. U.S.A. is encouraging American influence to spread into the South Pacific from these intermediary points. France's Pacific territories remain tightly linked to France and to each other, and in 1985 France established a new high-powered committee on French Pacific affairs to reinforce its interests. There is considerable co-operation between former United Kingdom colonies.

The United Nations pattern of setting up institutions in Asia covering the 'Asia-Pacific' region has led to an increasing link with Asia in some activities. Over twenty organisations now serve Asia and the Pacific Islands jointly. Owing to radical differences in size and needs, and the vast distances between them, however, Pacific Islands governments prefer separate facilities for the Pacific. But Papua New Guinea now attends ASEAN (the Association of South East Asian Nations) and SPEC now has co-operative relations with ASEAN. Nevertheless much the greatest co-operation is still between Commonwealth Pacific countries.

The importance of the network

A significant feature of co-operation in the Pacific Islands is not the individial institution or source, but the network. Co-operation between political leaders is greatly facilitated by a network of economic, social, cultural, professional, and other linkages. Each reinforces the other as awareness of the region grows with increased personal and institutional links. In addition, as services are commonly added to existing institutions, a deeper understanding and further utilisation of the network calls for an awareness of the whole pattern. Regional linkages will never be the dominant linkages for Pacific Islands states as they are so small, and the nations on the Pacific rim so large. Regional inter-governmental activity accounts for only about three per cent of total governmental expenditure, but it provides some useful services and a higher degree of political cohesion and bargaining power than could be achieved without it.

14
Extra-Pacific relations
Extremes of scale

The world's largest superpowers are on the Pacific rim. But the world's smallest micropowers are the Pacific Islands nations. The imbalance is extreme, but that does not mean that the situation is hopeless. In fact relative to size the Pacific Islands nations have better options than most. But it does require us to be realistic about what is and what is not achievable.

Let's get the relationship into perspective. In *population* there are about 2500 million people in countries on the Pacific rim, as against only 8 million Pacific Islanders. Pacific Islanders are outnumbered more than 300 to 1. *Wealth* shows a similar disproportion. In *education* the U.S.A., Japan, and Australia have about *10* times the tertiary educated manpower per 1000 of population that Pacific Islands have, and the islands are not catching up. *Military power* shows an even worse imbalance. Only three Pacific Islands countries have military forces and those are very small.

Superpower involvement

For most of this century the main superpower in relation to the Pacific was the United Kingdom, but it is now finished so far as the islands are concerned. For the 1980s the superpower in the Pacific is the United States, though not necessarily for much longer. I would expect America's power in relation to the Pacific Islands to increase for a few years and then go into a permanent decline.

As noted earlier, U.S.A. interest in the islands has always been mainly military. Hawaii, whose independence was broken by a coup organised by American business and military interests was then developed into the biggest U.S.A. military base off the mainland. Guam, too, was converted into an enormous military base (it was from there that much of the bombing of Vietnam was done) and American Samoa served as a naval base for more than half a century. Then at the end of the Second World War the U.S.A. took the Mariana, Caroline, and Marshall Islands by military action from Japan and is likely to maintain the controlling influence there for a long time. By the Monroe Doctrine the U.S.A. arrogates to itself a controlling interest down the whole Pacific coast of both North and South America.

ANZUS, the military alliance that links Australia, New Zealand and the U.S.A., came into being after World War II, particularly to defend the former two partners from Japan, which had nearly overwhelmed them. The U.S.A. felt increasingly less threatened by Japan in the Pacific and correspondingly more by China (the northern Marianas Islands were for years a secret CIA training base for a planned invasion of China) and as relations with China thawed, by U.S.S.R. The assumed 'peril' changed from yellow to red. When ANZUS was created, and for many years thereafter, Australia accepted certain strategic 'responsibilities' for islands west of Fiji and New Zealand for islands to the east, providing a sort of southern defensive quarantine like the Monroe Doctrine.

As islands nations became independent, the same broad strategic pattern continued, but with U.S.A. becoming more directly involved. In the late 1970s, in return for relinquishing spurious claims which the U.S.A. had long made to some islands in the Cook Islands, Kiribati, and Tuvalu those countries were persuaded to grant treaties giving the U.S.A. considerable control in strategic matters. With the Reagan administration in U.S.A. moving to the right, and Labour governments in Australia and New Zealand to the left, the ANZUS relationship weakened. When in 1985 New Zealand decided against admitting nuclear warships to its ports, heavy U.S.A. pressure was applied, and ANZUS is now in abeyance. The network of linkages the U.S.A. military had been developing with the heads of several islands governments since the 1970s began to be drawn upon.

Of the English-speaking colonial powers in the Pacific, the U.S.A. has been the most imperialist in terms of authoritarian government, force-feeding of its values and culture, and 'protection' from alternative influences and opportunities. The U.S.A. is the only colonial power to have run most of its Pacific colonies, most of the time, by direct military rule. The Solomon Plan, commissioned by President Kennedy on 18 April 1962, set out the process by which the long-term dependence of Micronesia would be assured by a permanent relationship within the U.S.A. framework. When the secret plan was leaked, the U.S.A. government denied that it had been adopted, but its strategies were implemented systematically and achieved the intended goal.

The Solomon Plan spelled out the method by which Micronesians would be conditioned to vote to remain with the U.S.A. when the United Nations insisted on a plebiscite to determine the political future of the territory. It aimed to devise the 'minimum capital investment and operating program to insure a favourable vote in the plebiscite', and to resolve the 'conflicting interests of Micronesians, the United Nations, and the United States along lines satisfactory to the U.S.A. Congress.' It recognised that the U.S.A. policy in Micronesia was contrary to both 'the anti-colonial movement that has just about completed sweeping the world', and to the U.S.A. government's stated policy against acquiring more territory, but also noted that as more than 95 per cent of the budget came from America (the local economy having been effectively destroyed by the U.S.A. administration) 'the importance of those funds in influencing a favourable plebiscite result is obvious.'

The plan's provisions included appointing Americans with the specific task of developing Micronesian opinion 'in favour of permanent affiliation' with the U.S.A. and spreading U.S.A. propaganda through radio, adult education, and other media; sending all the more intelligent Micronesian students to study in America, and sending Micronesian leaders there for study tours; 'introduction in the school system of U.S.A.-oriented curriculum changes and patriotic rituals'; bringing in the Peace Corps because of its importance to 'plebiscite attitudes'; and offering government employees and all wage earners 'specific inducements to seek affiliation with the U.S.A.'.

The mission recommended 'a reasonable appearance of self-government' while in fact retaining 'adequate control' by the

U.S.A. (For further details see the book by Donald McHenry, who later became U.S.A. Ambassador to the United Nations). France has been working on similar principles in its Pacific colonies. U.S.A. journalist Joseph Murphy estimated in 1982 that America had 'about the same economic and military control (of Micronesia) that the U.S.S.R. had of Poland' (*Marshall Islands Journal*, 22/1/1982).

U.S.A. official policy in the Pacific Islands was spelled out in December 1981 by Noel C. Koch, then the head of the International Security Affairs division of the U.S.A. Ministry of Defense. He noted that the presence of 9400 U.S.A. military personnel in Guam and the U.S. Trust Territory 'underscores our intention of preserving U.S.A. interests . . . and continues to show interest in achieving a position of consequence in the Pacific Islands states.' American Samoa, he said, provided America with 'a potential point for power projection in the South Pacific . . .'. He emphasised the strategic importance of all U.S.A. territories in the Pacific, which were 'inextricably linked to overall U.S. foreign policy and economic interests'. As the goal of maximising U.S.A. interests depended on 'close and friendly relations' with Pacific people and governments, the Department of Defense, he explained, has a 'strong and continuing interest in the success of initiatives and programmes undertaken by other agencies' of the U.S.A. government in the islands.

These initiatives were set out at the same time by Assistant Secretary of State John Holdridge, who said that to advance its interests in the islands, the U.S.A. was increasing its diplomatic representation, offering more influential islanders trips to America 'which has had a very positive impact', supporting regional co-operation, 'co-ordinating closely with Australia and New Zealand', expanding its aid, resolving territorial claims, using the Peace Corps, getting more involved in communications in the region, and sending more naval vessels through the islands. He observed that the U.S.A. expected its Pacific territories 'to play a valuable role as links between the United States and the island countries', and that it had 'already benefited from contributions which the territories have made to our foreign policy activities in the region.' By way of example, Governor Peter Coleman of American Samoa and his staff, through their 'knowledge of the region and of their fellow islanders, had facilitated working out arrangements (with independent island countries) that were of benefit both to the United States and to American Samoa.' Governor Paul Calvo of Guam was likewise credited with helping the United States in its relations with its neighbours.

Having effective control over the kinds of governments and economies in the Pacific Islands is very significant to U.S.A. interest throughout the Pacific rim. It is cheaper, easier, and more acceptable to the U.S.A. to wield influence over the Pacific Islands indirectly, though it is building tremendous direct control of Pacific media and of some islands governments. It is the modern equivalent of what the British colonial system called 'indirect rule'. That role in the Pacific is 'sub-contracted' in part to satellite states which have in the last decade or so moved into the American orbit from the U.K. — Australia in particular plays that mediator role and New Zealand to a lesser extent. Some foreign powers, particularly the U.S.A., tend to use Fiji as a pivotal state through which to apply leverage on other Pacific countries. That gives Fiji a short-term advantage, but is likely to lead to its isolation in the longer term.

Australia's interest in the Pacific is exemplified by the fact that it has more diplomatic posts there than any other country. There is extensive trade, investment, tourism, aid and military involvement. The same is true of New Zealand but to a much lesser extent (New Zealand has less than one-fifth of the popu-lation and closer to one-tenth of the wealth of Australia). And large numbers of islanders go to both countries for higher education, employment and even permanent residence. But the role of both countries, though major, is often over-estimated: many companies which are nominally Australian or New Zealand are in fact mainly owned in the Americas, Asia or Europe; much of the military activity from those countries is subsidiary to that of U.S.A.; and the bulk of trade is in fact with Asia and Europe, not with Australia and New Zealand.

The biggest changes for the Pacific Islands in the 1980s and 1990s will come from the north: first and strongest from Japan, which began its involvement in the islands with large numbers of settlers in Hawaii, then as the colonial power over Micro-nesia from 1914 to 1944, with some thousands of businessmen and workers in New Caledonia and a few in Fiji and Tonga

(all of whom were deported in World War II). Her administration of Micronesia was efficient but ruthless. The economy
boomed, but so many Japanese settlers were brought in that
they soon outnumbered the Micronesians. Japan's record as a
colonial power in the islands was not good. Her attempt to
conquer the Pacific militarily in World War II came disturbingly
close to fruition. Her future record as a neo-colonial power is
an unknown quantity, but a matter of some concern to many.
Japan has embassies or consulates in the larger islands states,
while Papua New Guinea, Fiji, and Nauru have offices in
Tokyo. Trade is overwhelmingly in Japans' favour, the main
imports being PNG copper, New Caledonia nickel, Solomon
Islands timber, and fish caught under license in most islands
economic zones; in the other direction Japanese vehicles and
electronic equipment have virtually taken over the islands
market.

Japanese aid is substantial, and Japanese experts, volunteers,
businessmen, tourists and researchers are now in evidence
throughout the region.

But the day of single superpowers is now over. Regionalism
is becoming a major basis for mobilising power. Japan initiated
the concept of a Pacific Basin community, and Japan is likely
to be the major beneficiary from it. But it is probably an inevitable next stage in Pacific politics. It aims to pull together the
capitalist economies of the Pacific rim: Japan and the U.S.A.,
South Korea, Australia and New Zealand. The ASEAN nations
(Singapore, Malaysia, Indonesia, Philippines, Thailand, and
Brunei) and the Pacific Islands nations are reluctant participants but in many ways involved nevertheless. China and the
Pacific states of Latin America may or may not be involved.

In an informal sense the Pacific Basin community is already
a reality, and formalising it will only give recognition to a
grouping that in many ways already functions. The exact form
it will take still has to be worked out — presumably it will start
with a softening up process through the media, educational
and cultural exchanges, and some liberalising of trade, plus
political leverage and a military backup which won't get much
publicity but which will be very influential. Pacific Islands
intellectuals and students will oppose this in principle, but
once it is converted into trips, conferences, scholarships,

exchange schemes, money, jobs in international organisations arising from it, etc many of these people will be the most enthusiastic and most over-represented participants from this part of the world.

China's first indirect contacts came with the first human settlers to Polynesia, Micronesia, and eastern Melanesia, who carried some elements of language and culture that can be traced to south China. And over the past 120 years immigration has resulted in small Chinese and/or part-Chinese minorities in almost every islands nation. Western Samoa was first to establish diplomatic relations with China, then Fiji (both in 1975), Papua New Guinea in 1976, Kiribati in 1980, and Vanuatu in 1982. There are substantial Chinese embassies in Apia, Suva, and Port Moresby, but only Papua New Guinea has an embassy in Beijing.

Trade between these five countries and China, though still small, had grown to US$50 million in 1984, with the balance in the islands favour (mainly due to PNG copper and Fiji sugar). Raw materials from Melanesia and marine products from throughout the region are likely to be of growing interest to China. The strategic dimension of China's interest first became apparent when Chinese missiles were tested in the South Pacific in 1980. Irritated reactions from Pacific governments led to an apology from Beijing for not having informed them adequately. There have been no more tests in this region.

China's foreign policy emphasises expanding its influence with Third World countries, especially in the Pacific Basin, and relations with small islands states (which have equal voting power with China in regional and international forums) can be developed more economically than with big countries. China has welcomed many islands leaders on official visits and has sent its Vice-President twice and Party Secretary Hu Yao Bang once to the islands. It has encouraged cultural ties and established a small but generally effective aid programme.

To turn to the U.S.S.R., its Pacific coast is becoming more significant and it is an enormous military power. Obviously it would like to be the major source of influence in the Pacific Islands but the U.S.A. is already firmly in control. If there is a Third World War, the U.S.A. and U.S.S.R. could destroy or neutralise each other as world powers, in which case Japan might become the Pacific superpower even more quickly. If there is no such war in our time, the U.S.A. and Japan will probably be able to minimise the influence of the U.S.S.R. in the Pacific. But some of the middle-sized powers, especially some ASEAN nations and other powers of east Asia and Mexico, could become increasingly influential. One relative advantage of the U.S.A. is that its major interests and strategies are widely known. Those of the U.S.S.R. are not.

U.S.S.R. has no embassies (though some countries have minimal diplomatic relations via the Soviet embassy in Canberra). Papua New Guinea and Fiji have declined requests for resident embassies, but the Vanuatu government was in 1986 considering allowing a resident Soviet embassy. And also unlike China, there has been no high-level visits of government leaders in either direction. Soviet fishing boats operate under license in New Zealand, Kiribati, and Vanuatu, and other countries are considering similar arrangements. But trade, cultural exchange or other contact is minimal. And despite its extensive border on the Pacific Ocean, involvement with the islands has been minimal since the visits of Russian explorers early last century. But having a long Pacific coast, and noting expanding American military and political activity in the region, U.S.S.R. fears a NATO type alliance blocking it from participating in Pacific affairs and has responded with a big expansion to its Pacific fleet.

But whenever there is strong competition for leadership, the competitors will pay a high price for someone from the other side to break ranks. The price the U.S.S.R. or its satellites will be prepared to pay will no doubt increase, and the bidding by the U.S.A. and its satellites will have to increase to hold the Pacific Islands in the Western bloc. The temptation to break ranks will increase, and maintaining Pacific Islands unity will almost certainly become more difficult as big power rivalry increases. Personally I think integrity in international relations pays. Fiji has built a reputation for reliability in its foreign relations. That reputation, justifiably earned, is a valuable asset from which the country has benefitted. The few Pacific countries whose leaders have sought short-term gain from deviousness in external relations seem not to have benefited in the long run.

It is sometimes claimed that the Pacific Islands nations are non-aligned politically. But the truth is the opposite: all except Vanuatu are so firmly aligned with the Western bloc that they really do not belong in a non-aligned movement (not that the non-aligned movement is necessarily non-aligned!). Being non-aligned is hardly possible in a highly polarised world. But it is unlikely that all islands nations will remain so consistently within the Western bloc. Only Vanuatu had a policy of not having diplomatic relations with either superpower, until 1986 when it invited both, still trying to steer a middle course.

Pacific Islands nations would obviously prefer to be truly non-aligned, but that option is not available to them. If they had to choose between Americans and Russians, there is no doubt in my mind that the Americans are the lesser (though not much lesser) of the two evils. When one has no choice but to be part of someone else's empire, it is probably better to choose the one that is richest, softest, and has a language and culture that you understand and can deal with. And the U.S.A. has a more flexible society which accommodates more options. But abroad it supports many military dictatorships (and helps them into power in many cases) and American history in the short time it has been a world power shows that it will be as ruthless as Russia if that suits its interests. To paraphrase Lord Acton, the greater the power, the more corrupt its use is likely to be.

On the Russian side one only needs to think of the ruthless crushing of many governments, most recently such places as Hungary, Czechoslovakia, Afghanistan, and Poland; and on the American side the equally ruthless overthrow of popular governments and/or U.S.A. military occupations in support of dictatorships in Argentina, Nicaragua (beginning in 1853 and including the installation from 1927 to 1933 of the brutal Somoza dynasty which ruled until 1981); the military occupation of Haiti, the Dominican Republic and Cuba for more than a decade, and more recently of Grenada; the invasion of Vietnam, the overthrow of elected governments in Guatemala, Brazil, and Chile, and the support for repressive governments in South Africa, Asia, and Latin America.

It is not that the Russians and Americans are more ruthless than others in the pursuit of their own self-interest. It is just that, at this phase of history, they have the power. Pacific Islanders may find in the next decade or so that China and Japan are even more concerned with their own self-interest and may be even less scrupulous in the pursuit of it.

France's superpower aspirations

In the mid 1950s France was the most progressive colonial power in the Pacific: New Caledonia and French Polynesia had elected cabinets and a considerable degree of self-government. Then from the late 1950s these policies were reversed and direct control from Paris reintroduced. Being a nuclear power was crucial to France's perception of its role in the world, and this necessitated regular testing. With the independence of Algeria (where France used to test nuclear bombs), and with strong opposition at home, it was decided to use French Polynesia for this purpose. Other strategic goals as well as political and economic ambitions in the Pacific Basin as a whole, have led France to entrench itself more firmly in its colonies (giving them the highest consumption standards in the Pacific in the process) and to adopt more aggressive policies in relation to its Pacific neighbours.

In 1985 President Mitterand established a high level Council for the Pacific, chaired by the President and involving several ministers in Paris, ambassadors in Pacific rim (including those in U.S.A. and Japan) and islands nations, and heads of France's Pacific colonies. In 1986 Gaston Flosse, elected leader of the local government in French Polynesia and also elected representative to the French Parliament, was appointed to the French cabinet as Secretary of State for Pacific Affairs as the first time anyone from the Pacific has held a significant role in the French government. And an Université Francaise du Pacifique was formally instituted in September 1986, with the openly declared aims of countering 'Anglo-Saxon' influences and spreading French culture and political influence. The governing body of this University of the Pacific, however, is chosen by France and is exclusively French citizens. The local government of French Polynesia, the colony where it is to have its headquarters, was not informed until a detailed programme of decisions taken in Paris was released.

Relations with South Pacific Forum nations have deteriorated, mainly because of nuclear testing and the continued colonial presence, but also because of the style of France's relations with islands nations which is characterised by assertion, condescension and minimal consultation. It remains to be seen whether France's new policy of expanded aid and aggressive participation in regional affairs will achieve her goal of being an accepted member of the Pacific community in the 21st century.

The frontier power brokers

Governments are far from the only external influences. A significant hazard facing all Pacific nations today is the unethical businessman with powerful political links. Mainly from America so far, some are also appearing from Asia (especially Singapore, Thailand, India, and the Philippines) as well as Australia and elsewhere.

Classic cases include the Phoenix Foundation of the U.S.A. which was instrumental in the Santo rebellion in Vanuatu and for a short time set up a rebel government there; Stabihon Associates whose activities nearly toppled the government of Western Samoa in the late 1970s; the Bank of the South Pacific which in the short time before its founder was goaled in the U.S.A. achieved enormous influence in Tonga; the fall of the government in Tuvalu in 1982 was attributed to the activities of an American real estate dealer; and Albert Henry's Cook Islands Party won the 1978 elections only through the involvement of a U.S.A. stamp dealer — the party was later deposed from office by a unique High Court judgement and the stamp dealer prosecuted. (In very small countries where stamp sales are a major source of government revenue, stamp dealers who acquire monopolies can wield alarming political influence.) These are just a few of many cases of deep involvement of individual foreign businessmen in Pacific Islands nations. Because of the very small size of the governments, the power of such people is at times extreme. More disturbing still is the recent interest in some islands from major international crime figures — and the closeness of their relations with some political leaders.

Less spectacular, but more pervasive, is the influence of more conventional business, both the big multinationals and smaller enterprises, some of which become very influential in Pacific Islands politics. When Frappier said in the 1960s that a 'number of U.S. advertising agencies are directly involved in Latin American politics through their handling of political campaigns and government advertising' it seemed to have no relevance to the Pacific. But advertising agencies have now emerged here too, derive their main income from multinational corporations, and increasingly find that those interests are even better served if they also support and influence political parties which are sympathetic to such interests. In the larger Pacific countries particularly, but also in some smaller ones, the agents of business are increasingly politically involved.

Foreign trade unions have some effect in the larger islands, but as the Pacific is primarily rural this influence is not yet extensive. But it is perhaps significant that the Asian–American Free Labour Institute claimed credit, in its application for further funds in 1986, for having reduced Pacific trade unions' support for a Pacific nuclear-free zone 'due to the close collaboration and friendship nurtured between AAFLI and South Pacific trade union leaders'. When the Kiribati Government signed a fishing agreement with U.S.S.R., the Kiribati politician who moved a vote of no confidence in the President (unsuccessfully) had recently been financed by AAFLI.

External religious influences, as mentioned earlier, tend to be mainly fundamentalist Christian and politically ultra-conservative, though Islam is being actively promoted in Irian Jaya, Fiji, New Caledonia and even Tonga — whose constitution forbids non-Christian religions.

Imperialism of any kind can succeed only via the involvement of local collaborators, mediators, or middle-men. These are not hard to find anywhere in the world if the price is high enough. They are always found among the elite. Moreover we must always be aware not only of pressures from without, but also of suction from within. In other words, all power systems have a tendency to push out into areas which are weaker than themselves, and weak areas have a tendency to suck in aspects of stronger areas. The key question is, how can the 'dependent' areas strengthen their bargaining position and their confidence so that they do not suck in unintentionally more dominance from external systems than they want, and how can they more effectively build resistance to diminish the extent of unwanted external pressure? This calls for a much more sensitive awareness of how both the suction and the push operate, and of the alternatives.

Salvaging the remnants

Before looking at the influence or leverage of external powers in the Pacific Islands, let's look first at those that already have almost total control of Pacific Islands. The U.S.A. has incorporated Hawaii, Guam, Northern Marianas, American Samoa, Wake, Midway, Palmyra, the Aleutians and various others as part of the U.S.A. The Marshall Islands, Palau, and Federated States of Micronesia are to be nominally self-governing but with the U.S.A. holding all the major leverage. *All the north Pacific Islands, then, have already been taken over by the U.S.A.*

To the west the Indonesians have taken West New Guinea, (or more accurately they were given it by the U.S.A. in a trade-off for not opposing the invasion of Vietnam). West New Guinea is the second largest group of people in the Pacific Islands (about 1.2 million) and Indonesia runs it as a military colony.

In the east Chile will retain its hold on Easter Island. Again this is a military administration.

In the south New Zealand has long since been taken over by Europeans. And Melanesians are the minority in Fiji and New Caledonia (though possibly not for long in either place).

The most likely channels through which the U.S.S.R. might become involved appear at the moment to be New Caledonia where French imperialism is so pervasive that any external support may be welcomed by those seeking a more just society for the Melanesian population, or Vanuatu. Such a possibility in Vanuatu has been considerably reduced since independence was attained with the help of Papua New Guinea's forces. It is a sad reality that almost no other Pacific country was prepared to help a genuinely-elected government from being subverted by foreign interests.

It is almost inevitable that Soviet involvement will increase from its present minimum. The only potential gain for the Pacific is as an alternative lever for islanders to lean on if the Pacific Basin group (especially Japan, the U.S.A., and Australia) don't provide for them adequately. In 1985 after years of U.S.A. purse-seiners taking fish in Kiribati waters without payment (whereas Japan, Korea, Taiwan do pay) and with their government's support, Kiribati leased fishing rights to U.S.S.R. (as New Zealand has done for many years). Several other nations are considering fishing leases to U.S.S.R. despite strong pressure from the ANZUS partners not to do so.

What options are available to the Pacific Islands nations in getting the best possible deal from the enormous and competing powers all around them? They can do little to stop them, and are obviously better advised to work towards as deep an understanding as they can get of the likely future realities.

One urgent need is for a Pacific Islands 'think tank' — an institution geared to collecting data, sorting out options, heightening public awareness, and drawing on the best minds available. Japan's Nomura Research Institute is one of several that have been doing their homework on the future of the Pacific, and very effectively it seems. The Brookings Institute in America is one of many that has been helping the U.S.A. find the best solutions in the Pacific. New Zealand has its Commission on the Future, and so on. The University of the South Pacific should undertake some more focussed thinking on the future, perhaps in co-operation with SPEC and the South Pacific Commission. So far the Pacific has had to respond belatedly to the big powers' proposals. It would be in a much stronger position if it clarified its own options — and to do so needs a continous, open, responsive programme. The danger is that those with big power interests in the Pacific would want to fund such a programme, influence its direction, and even subvert its activities to serve its own interests — a considerable danger with the Pacific Islands Development Program in Honolulu.

The Pacific Islands states are likely to gain more from fuller co-ordination — which does not necessarily mean unified action. Compared with most parts of the world, Pacific regional co-operation so far has been relatively successful, but it would be unrealistic to expect (or even to aim for) too high a degree of co-operation when interests are so diverse, and when the short-term payoff to the country that plays the role of Judas is so high.

A closed Pacific Islands region would be a club of the weak and that would be of little value. One doesn't get strength from joining only with the weak. Most strength can come from joining the strong — though that usually means paying a higher price in dependency on a range of fronts.

In monetary terms at least the largest short-term gains will come from the region splitting up, and each island nation attaching itself to one major power, with multiple strings to at least some other powers. This is already the case: the U.S.A. controls the North Pacific almost totally (and is likely to aim to attain maximum leverage over Kiribati, Western Samoa and the Cook Islands); Australia is the overwhelming external influence for Papua New Guinea and increasingly for the rest of independent Melanesia; New Zealand is for the Cook Islands, Niue, and Tokelau; France is in New Caledonia, Tahiti, Wallis and Futuna. Japan and China are going to find a place in the Pacific — a very powerful place — but the stronger their role becomes, the more the small islands states are likely to see common interests with their present big partners.

While in the short-term the Pacific islands nations could do best by playing off one big power against the other, the Western bloc powers are likely to limit that by developing a co-ordinated strategy towards the Pacific Islands. And playing outside the Western bloc is a bigger gamble involving high stakes. But some such play seems inevitable.

Selective interference

Pacific Islands leaders speak frequently about the need to avoid or negate external interference. The concept has popular support. But even superficial awareness of the actions of leaders shows that they not only condone external interference but constantly actively encourage and solicit it. Probably few areas in the world solicit as much external interference as Fiji, Tonga, or Papua New Guinea. It is simply a question of terminology — interference which helps those in power is not discussed, or is redefined as positive assistance. That which helps the opposition, or any categories which do not support those currently in power, is condemned as interference. It is amazing how effectively much of the relatively vast external interference is channelled to serve the mutual interests of those involved on both sides of the relationship.

External involvement of all kinds in the Pacific increased dramatically towards and during 1985, particularly in strategic issues. It is not likely to decrease in the foreseeable future, and leads to increases in every activity from subsidies to congruent religious organisations, trade unions, women's groups, media, etc, as well as direct action in trade, education, government, and even spying. 'Strategic denial' becomes a cover for a wide-ranging pattern of penetration and manipulation.

15
Dependence, independence, interdependence
Improving the options

Being constitutionally independent does not make a country politically independent, let alone economically, culturally, or otherwise. As the constitutionally independent Pacific Islands become more and more dependent in other respects — and they are going to become even more so — there is a great deal of talk about increasing self-reliance. With the increasingly effective communication of ideas and transport of goods throughout the world, self-reliance becomes less and less feasible — at least in the conventional sense.

The more popular aim now is for balanced interdependence: acknowledging the increasing multiplicity of external impacts, but aiming to balance them with equivalent internally generated resources, goods, and ideas. But balanced interdependence between small island states and populous, powerful nations is unlikely, even in trade; much less so in relation to military, political, media, cultural, and other influences. Nevertheless, most Pacific Islanders have wider options than groups of similar size almost anywhere else in the world. Nobody is independent today, and the crucial issue is what extent of dependence is considered acceptable, or inevitable, in what area of life, at what costs, weighed against what benefits.

And when we speak of independence, whose independence do we refer to? For example in French Polynesia, which is constitutionally dependent on France, although many powers are held by French officials responsible to Paris, the local elected Assembly and Cabinet have considerable powers in local affairs. On these criteria the average Tahitian is probably more independent than the average Tongan commoner. In each case a very small elite power group rationalises its monopoly on power: in Tonga by accident of birth, and in the French colonies by accident of history.

We are being naive when we imply, as we often do, that any form of dependence is bad. As communication becomes more effective, dependence of many types will deepen — irrespective of whether political systems are capitalist, socialist, or otherwise. The task Pacific Islands nations are facing is how to get the best deal out of the relationship with bigger powers — a sort of living cost/benefit struggle in which the bargaining advantages of the small powers are likely to get less rather than more. The indirect remote control from Washington, Canberra, Tokyo, Moscow, and other major power centres is getting more extensive and more effective — to the Pacific's disadvantage.

Military dependence

It seems to be an unfortunate reality of human life, perhaps of all living organisms, that the ultimate determinant of position in a hierarchy of dependence is real or assumed physical power. Obviously it is far from the only factor in a complex world, but aggression quickly polarises people, and the reality of the world today is a polarisation between the U.S.A. and the U.S.S.R. Everybody else is stacked in some set of direct or indirect array under one or other of those two umbrellas. This is unfortunate, because many of the smaller countries would be much better off if they could be freed from both umbrellas — not a very likely possibility.

Perhaps a better alternative is to distance and insulate island nations from some of the greater excesses of the two superpowers. Father Walter Lini, Prime Minister of Vanuatu, said Pacific peoples were very much afraid of both the U.S.S.R. and U.S.A., because too much influence from either of them would mean 'to risk losing our independence, politically and otherwise' (*Pacific Islands Monthly*, December 1981). The Prime Minister was well aware that both superpowers support repressive regimes anywhere, provided they reciprocate that superpower's support. Dictatorships are easier for superpowers to manipulate than democracies. Techniques of protective insulation include reducing involvement with the superpowers, diversifying links with larger countries than one's own, co-operating with Pacific neighbours on appropriate issues, and trying to avoid the kinds of extreme internal

polarisation which would give either superpower a rationalisation to intervene directly.

Both superpowers gain from accentuating the danger of the other in their dealings with smaller nations under their umbrella. Each expends tremendous effort to convince its subordinates that the other superpower is motivated by self-interest, intent on imposing its will, and that its philosophy is a snare and a delusion. Both are probably right!

When I was in the Caribbean in 1981, and explained the relative peace and progress of Pacific nations, I was warned in several countries that I was talking like they talked in the 1960s, before the U.S.A. and the U.S.S.R. began to exert major pressures in the region. The increased big-power involvement in the Pacific in the 1980s has led to much more polarisation and tension.

Direct military dependence was from each metropolitan power to its colonies, with the exception that Australia and New Zealand participated in military matters in the United Kingdom colonies and expanded that involvement after independence. The first significant U.S.A. involvement was in 1976 when it supplied Fiji, at a nominal price, with ships to establish a small navy. This has increased significantly since, with full-time U.S.A. military personnel in training and liaison roles, and supply of equipment. A formal military aid programme was begun in 1985. Military activity in the region was co-ordinated by the ANZUS partners (with the French territories less closely involved) but since New Zealand's denial of nuclear ship visits and deteriorating relations between France and the South Pacific Forum states, this situation is less cohesive, giving the islands states somewhat wider options within the ANZUS/French framework.

Educational dependence

Dependence in education and training is deep and likely to get much deeper. As the level of education increases, so does

Specialised education is provided by a number of regional institutions serving many Pacific countries. Above, the interdenominational Pacific Theological College teaches in both French and English. Below, students from many countries study at the University of the South Pacific.

the level of dependence on foreign money, foreign staff, foreign equipment, foreign teaching materials and ideas. The lower levels of education are in many respects dependent on higher levels: for example, primary school teachers are trained in teachers colleges; secondary school teachers are trained in universities largely, but not totally, within the Pacific region; and university staff are trained — almost 100 per cent of them — in larger universities outside the Pacific Islands.

We university people, both staff and students, usually decry dependence on others and assert that they should be more self-reliant, while insisting on more dependence for ourselves. We demand more foreign financed buildings, equipment, scholarships, trips, conferences, perquisites and so on. Even local staff salaries at Pacific Islands universities are subsidised from overseas, and always have been. I never see anyone resist it. Most of us speak in favour of greater self-reliance and reduced dependence, but unless students and staff alike demonstrate the principle a little more in practice, we can hardly be expected to be taken very seriously by governments or the public.

Most graduates of the Pacific Islands universities have had all their fees, food, accommodation, etc paid, and have not been required to undertake any work or make any reciprocal contribution in cash or kind or effort during the whole of their training. And in a high percentage of cases they are on holidays for more than half the time that they study (because most university students only study 34 weeks per year). This is hardly the way to prepare people for either a self-reliant independence, or for any effectively balanced interdependence, when the people they will be dealing with, both those from Australasia and the Americas on the one hand and increasingly from Japan, China, and other East Asian countries on the other, have generally had to go through a tougher formative experience.

Although some students at the Pacific universities are full-time workers taking part-time studies, they constitute only a minority of the total number of graduates. And many students work during some of their vacations, but a high proportion do not. This would not be possible were it not for the heavy dependence on foreign assistance, which students and staff usually in practice demand ever more. Some students are bonded to refund a small proportion of the money spent on them after they begin full-time employment, but that seems to me to begin four years too late.

A high percentage of the new Pacific Islander elites are graduating with the experience that for their four years or so of crucial training they were on holiday for half as much time they were at study, and were not required to contribute significantly towards their study costs. They have learned the rhetoric of preaching self-reliance but practicing dependence. If a high proportion of such people become concentrated in the power roles in Pacific Islands societies, no real increase in self-reliance seems likely.

Almost all of those students whom I have heard cry against dependence themselves refuse opportunities to do their post-graduate studies either in the Pacific or in other parts of the Third World. They insist on being associated with the most colonial and imperial institutions of education, and build elaborate rationalisations to justify their inconsistency.

A decision which may be very important in relation to educational dependency was that announced in 1981 by the Prime Minister, Malcolm Fraser, to the effect that Australia was preparing to become the higher education centre for Southeast Asia and the Pacific Islands. Partly this will be through Australian scholarships, with selection largely on examination results, which clearly favours the children of the established bureaucratic, political, and commercial elite. And secondly by privately financed education which only the commercial, political, and bureaucratic elites will be able to afford.

Some of these potentially very influential students will return to the islands and gain disproportionate access to powerful positions. And most of them will have more knowledge of, friendly contacts in, and nostalgic memories of Australia than they will of the Pacific Islands. Most who do not return will presumably stay in Australia which thus attracts a significant percentage of the very best islands talents to become Australians. For the the northern Pacific Islands, the U.S.A. has for two decades played the same role, as New Zealand has for the Cook Islands, Niue, Tokelau, and to a lesser extent, Western Samoa.

One of the interesting phenomena to observe is the way in which islands countries (particularly in Polynesia and Fiji) complain that the brain drain to industrialised countries takes away some of their most intelligent, most innovative, most motivated people. Yet all those countries maintain vastly discriminatory immigration practices to ensure that few if any intelligent, innovative, motivated people can come in. So it is hard to be too sympathetic when one hears the complaints of inertia, inadequate enterprise, or lack of motivation.

Economic dependence

The two main kinds of economic dependence concern foreign aid (largely by overseas governments) and foreign investment (largely by private businesses). Every Pacific leader preaches self-reliance but practises maximal dependence. And if he didn't his electors would soon vote him out. They too insist on the rhetoric of self-reliance and the reality of dependence.

In 1981, Canada's Prime Minister, Pierre Trudeau, opened the new University of the South Pacific Science Building which had been financed by Canadian aid. After Canada had agreed to the university's request for a building, their aid policy shifted in favour of more rural projects and the poorest nations, so they tried to withdraw from this project or at least reduce the size of the building. The university objected as strongly as it could (in other words, fought as hard as possible for maximum dependence) and the building came into being. Pierre Trudeau did not open that building at his wish — but on our insistence.

And at the official opening the public begging for more aid from Mr Trudeau seemed humiliating to many of those present. Canada was not selling more aid, it was the potential recipients who kept begging for it. And this is the case to a larger extent than we care to admit in aid relationships. We are aware, and rightly, of the power and influence derived by the pressure from without in aid relationships, but we give inadequate recognition to the suction from within.

When the King of Tonga invited the Russians to discuss aid, in a ploy to push Australia and New Zealand and others to make Tonga more dependent, Tongans did not object to his forcing of the pace of dependence — even though the countries being forced did not want to give more aid and refused to give more until Tonga used the strategic threat. Most Pacific Islanders even saw it as a victory for Tonga, once the most truly independent nation in the Pacific, that it had so intentionally increased its dependence. It is now one of the most dependent nations in the Pacific.

Everyone appreciates that there is no such thing as aid without strings, but anyone in the islands also soon learns that the amount of string that different donors use, and the tightness with which they tie the recipients, and the kickbacks that they squeeze out of them, differ greatly. The crucial question is the extent to which the money and services are aid to the recipients as against aid to the donor. Within the donor country, there develops an industry that lives off servicing, siphoning, or hijacking the aid that was labelled for others. The United States and Japan seem to have developed these self-interest techniques further than most. To quote one example (one could quote many), the United States A.I.D. made a grant, with a fan-fare of publicity, of about one million dollars a year for five years in the name of the Ur versity of the South Pacific for the stated purpose:

> To promote agricultural productivity and further socio-economic development for the rural people of the South Pacific region. . . .

Bearing that stated purpose in mind, let me now quote from an official report of the Hawaii Department of Planning and Economic Development on Hawaii's relations with other Pacific Islands, which begins with a strongly supportive statement from Governor Ariyoshi:

> Two related pieces of legislation and a new U.S.
> commitment to development assistance in the Pacific
> Islands have come together in 1978 to offer Hawaii an
> opportunity to establish itself as a world centre for tropical
> agriculture and aquaculture, and to play a pivotal role in
> developing the food resources of the Pacific Islands.

The report notes that under the 'Food for Peace Act' funds labelled as helping food production in the Third World were payable only to U.S.A. universities. The University of Hawaii was approved as the executing agency for the $5½ million labelled for the University of the South Pacific. The report says that this 'aid' to the Pacific would have four main effects:

1 There will be an infusion of federal funds to upgrade the University of Hawaii College of Tropical Agriculture. . . .

2 The University of Hawaii College of Tropical Agriculture will be a focus and a funnel for U.S. contributions to . . . the Pacific Islands. . . .

3 Similar programs involving the University of Hawaii School of Public Health and the U.H. Sea Grant programs can be devised. . . .

4 These international programs would lead to desired University of Hawaii expansion, providing more employment for local faculty and staff. . . .

One might say that these two perspectives — the one presented to Pacific people of the aid being of help to them, and the other presented to Hawaii people to show how the aid helps them, are mutually compatible. It would be nice if they were, but A.I.D. policy was to pay the first 40 per cent of 'Food For Peace' Funds labelled as aid to the Pacific's rural poor to the State of Hawaii in the name of fictitious 'overhead costs'. (This was ultimately reduced in the case above after strong protests, but it remains unethical.) And most of the rest of the money was paid not to the implied recipient but to the University of Hawaii and to Cornell University. Only twenty per cent of the money went to the 'recipient' institution, and part of that to house visiting American staff. It is too early for an objective cost-benefit analysis of the overall exercise, though the experience so far is distressing. In my experience the main beneficiaries of programs of this kind are the foreign academics and institutions involved in what is so nicely termed the 'delivery' of the aid.

Appropriate scholarships and training for Pacific Islands students are generally appreciated and valuable. But the reports of foreign consultants and academics litter the shelves of government offices throughout the islands. Some of them have been of considerable value, probably somewhat more have not been worth the time and money spent on them. For most of them, the Pacific would have been neither better nor worse off — it is just more unread paper. A balance sheet for the post independence phase of Pacific history would probably show that one of the significant factors that will be seen to have retarded development is the so-called development expert. There is indeed a potential for external expertise to be useful to the Pacific, but as in other unbalanced power relationships (including academic research) those with the power so often execute the projects in the way that achieves their own goals.

The Hawaii State document quoted above said that it was the state government's policy to have all U.S.A. aid to the Pacific Islands managed by the State of Hawaii. That is likely to be wonderful for Hawaii but disastrous for the islands. Hawaii would use it to maximise the supply of goods and services from Hawaii, which for most skills and most commodities is one of the most expensive sources on earth.

If the recipients of aid complain about it, why do they accept it? This is a complex question, but to touch on several key elements in it: first, given the vast gap between the relative poverty of most islands nations and the wealth of industrialised powers on the rim, a popular demand for aid develops. The dependency mentality has deepened greatly in the islands in the last decade, and if the Governments in power do not get the aid, the Oppositions will attack them and offer to get more. Another factor is that the donor has most of the power over setting the terms. There is a very strong ethical responsibility on the part of donors not to misuse their bargaining advantage, but they often do — sometimes even when they do not intend to — because the pressures, contacts, values, and ideas derive from within the donor's national context. Moreover, the psychological feeling of indebtedness does not allow recipients to 'look the gift-horse in the mouth'.

Even though the U.S.A. gives little aid, it concentrates what it gives in the high visibility public appeal areas and makes a public fuss about it: it focusses on media and communications, education of the elite, and the Peace Corps. Like the other seven or eight volunteer organisations working in the Pacific, the Peace Corps provides some useful skills and creates a generally favourable image.

Future challenges to U.S.A. power are likely to come first
and foremost from Japan, which has long had expansionist
ambitions in the islands and is now acquiring the wherewithal
to bring them to fruition. China is still sufficiently weak that
it opposes expansionism, but as China's economic and political
strength grows, that is likely to change. The U.S.S.R. would
obviously like to challenge the American position, but the only
realistic weapon they have for achieving it is the military.
Nobody in the islands can speak their language, nobody is
interested in their culture, they are of little significance for
trade, and their political system is not attractive. The only
factor the U.S.S.R. has in its favour in the islands is as an alter-
nate source of support for any group or nation that is dis-
enchanted with the existing order. But Russian attempts to get
a foothold in the islands so far have had minimal success. One
effective way to minimise Soviet influence would be for the
existing powers to ensure that France is not allowed to de-
stabilise or subvert the elected government of Vanuatu, and to
ensure that New Caledonia and French Polynesia are assisted
to a realistic independence; another would be for U.S.A. to
reduce its aggressive penetration of islands affairs.

Foreign investment

I landed in China in 1981 and was amazed to see enormous
advertisements for Japanese products, and to hear that some
huge new factory complexes were joint ventures with foreign
capital. Great blocks of flats were being constructed by Hong
Kong businesses. I found it hard to digest. On another visit in
1985 the process had gone much further.

What was the significance of this for the Pacific islands? Was
it, as some see it, the ultimate disaster, precluding the much
better alternative of independent development? Or was it, as
others see it, the result of bitter experience of the ineffective-
ness and frustration of attempts at development from within?
Or something of each?

When the largest country in the world decides that it is in
its interest to make significant concessions to exploiting some
of the advantages (and having to put up with the concomitant
disadvantages) of foreign capital, then the more extreme

proposals for self-reliance that one sometimes hears in the Pacific (by people who preach rather than practice such principles) probably do not have much chance of realisation. Almost every Pacific government has an active policy of attracting foreign capital. Even though such policies are selective, most are seeking more than they can get. There is an inevitable price on it, and this price will get higher as time goes on, but for the present it is seen by most governments as the best way to introduce the more complex commercial and industrial skills and to reduce unemployment.

Wider spheres of dependence

There are other very important areas of dependence: on foreign media, foreign ideologies, foreign patterns of thinking and doing and consuming. Foreign foods, more conveniently packaged, more easily stored, and vigorously advertised, are taking over even from the more nutritious and less expensive local equivalents. The degree of dependence, unfortunately, is likely to increase rather than to lessen, at least partly because many of those who speak against foreign ideologies and systems and consumption patterns are those most addicted to them.

I hope these comments do not appear too pessimistic. They are intended to be realistic. In a world of increasing complexity and interaction, the prospects for the Pacific Islands nations are better than for most of the world's people. But being so small, the islands are particularly vulnerable. Much will depend on how the people of influence in all walks of life in the Pacific utilise the options available to them. Rhetoric won't help: it is realistic assessment, effective negotiation, integrity in leadership, and making sure that words are matched by actions, that will minimise dependence and make the Pacific as free as it is ever likely to be.

Notes

1 People

1. For summaries of information on Asian origins of Pacific peoples see Golson, 1972; Kirk and Szathmary, 1985. For data on plant origins see Barrau, 1963. Though an earlier form of man had lived in the Indonesian region for much longer, modern man (*Homo sapiens*) seems not to have been there for more than 100 000 years or so before spreading to New 1961; Spate, 1979, 1984 and forthcoming; Howe, 1984.
2. Suggs, 1960.
3. For broad classifications of Pacific languages see Grace, 1968; Biggs, 1967; Tryon, 1985; and Pawley and Green, 1985.
4. For archaeological and linguistic evidence for the origins of particular Pacific societies see Green, 1966; Bellwood, 1979; Jennings, 1979; Pawley and Green, 1985. Kirch, 1986, summarises the evidence to date and wisely cautions against taking any of these views as definitive or proven, as much more archaeological research remains to be done.
5. Wynne, 1966.
6. *Highlights* (Saipan) 15 June 1975.
7. Many instances of accidental as well as planned voyages are cited in Sharp, 1963, and Dening, 1963. An interesting study of what would happen to canoes drifting at random, given the existing current, wind and other conditions, is given by Levison and Ward, 1972.
8. The expansion of Europe into the Pacific has been extensively documented. Some of the major references include: Grattan, 1963; Morrell, 1966; Oliver, 1961; Spate, 1979, 1984 and forthcoming; Howe, 1984.
9. Te Rangi Hiroa (Sir Peter Buck), 1966, presents a major study of the adaptation of Maori culture to the New Zealand environment.
10. For human ecology and adaptation in the Pacific Islands see Fosberg, 1965.
11. For Chinese see Coppenrath, 1967; Moench, 1963; Yee 1976;
12. Gillion, 1962; Mayer, 1972; Ali, 1980; Crocombe, 1981; Lal, 1983.
13. Dewey, 1964.
14. The Japanese took these islands from Germany during the First World War and lost them during the Second World War to the United States, which still effectively controls them under 'Compacts of Free Association.' The Japanese were repatriated when the U.S.A. took over. The story of the Japanese mandate is told in Clyde, 1967.

15. Daws, 1968; Lind, 1967.
16. Tapol, 1984.
17. Most tourism studies, including those by international agencies, are biased in favour of the foreign tourist operators. Studies of the effects of tourism on the host community include Mahoney, 1970; Cottington, 1970; Rajotte and Crocombe, 1981.
18. Some people find it hard to credit such a number of ancestors, but allowing 25 years per generation, and remembering that everyone at each stage had 2 parents, then we had 4 grandparents 2 generations ago, 8 great-grandparents at 3 generations, 16 at 4 generations, 32 at 5 generations, 64 at 6, 128 at 7, 256 at 8 generations and 512 at 9 generations.
19. This from an average of only between 3 and 4 children born to each person per generation.
20. This situation was being approached in the early 1960s at the time of Lind's study, but has since become a reality.
21. Serjeantson, S.W. et al, 1982.
22. There are many studies of particular migratory patterns and some general data is contained in McArthur, 1961. More detailed studies include those by Ward, 1971; Chapman, 1985; Connell, 1986; and Hayes, 1984.
23. For information on urbanisation in the Pacific see Harré, 1973; the case of Suva see Monsell-Davis, 1986.
24. Crocombe, 1985.

2   Culture

1. A general survey of each of the culture areas is contained in Oliver, 1961 (chapters 4–6). For ancient Polynesian society the most comprehensive study is that by Goldman, 1970; for Micronesia, Mason, 1968. For Melanesia, Brookfield's 1971 geographical study contains a survey of principles of social grouping in chapter 9.
2. A useful article highlighting the contrast is that by Sahlins, 1963.
3. A detailed description of one such system is contained in Nayacakalou, 1955 and 1957.
4. Mason, 1959.
5. Hughes, 1971.
6. Carano and Sanchez, 1965, page 104.
7. Fiji Education Commission, page 26. Alvin Toffler's *Future Shock* points out more fully the value of cultural diversity even in highly industrialised nations.
8. In two brief but significant articles, John Kasaipwalova and Kumulau Tawali express different views on this topic in *New Guinea Writing*. Referring to culture in a wider sense than just the creative arts, the latter author advocated a return to past tradition, whereas the former emphasised the need to create a new tradition, unique to New Guinea, and expressing the values and aspirations of New Guineans of today.
9. Firth, 1958, page 198.
10. An example was the establishment of the periodical *Nakamel* in Vanuatu.

Named after the traditional indigenous meeting house, it was owned and operated by, and represented the interests of, foreign businessmen.
11. Crocombe, 1984, 'Education, Enjoyment and Integrity in Tourism,' *Contours*, vol. 8.

3   Personality

1. The most comprehensive summary of the data for Polynesia and Micronesia is that by Levy. Localised studies include those by Beaglehole in New Zealand, Hawaii, and the Cook Islands; Levy in the Society Islands; Ritchie in New Zealand; and Spiro in the Caroline Islands. For details of these studies, see Bibliography.
2. Gallimore and Howard, 1969.
3. Howard, 1966.
4. This pattern of extensive filial respect in Fijian society is commented on by Nayacakalou, 1955 and 1957; Ravuvu, 1984; Sahlins, 1962, and others.
5. For a society where many traditional values were retained in the process of modernisation see Hagen (1962) on Japan. Japan is a classic case of retention of key personality traits. For information on young Fijians in urban Suva see Monsell-Davis, 1986.

4   Language

1. Tryon, 1985. But the possibility of other influences, even from as far away as North Africa, cannot be ignored — see Fell, 1980.
2. Pawley and Green, 1985: 175–7.
3. Samoan is the language of Western Samoa and American Samoa, and the languages of Tokelau and Tuvalu are very closely related and mutually intelligible. It is also spoken by about 150 000 Samoans who now live permanently in New Zealand, Hawaii, and California.
4. Indonesian is the official language of Irian Jaya (West New Guinea); French of New Caledonia, Loyalty Islands, Wallis and Futuna, the Society Islands and other groups of French Polynesia, and partly of Vanuatu; Spanish in Easter Island. English is the 'second language' elsewhere in the Pacific.
5. This process has perhaps gone furthest in French Polynesia — the Society, Tuamotu, Marquesas, Gambier, and Austral Islands (see Prevost, pages 256–60). The same trend has gone a considerable distance in the Cook Islands and Fiji. Dr. Stefan Wurm (personal communication), a specialist in New Guinea languages, has expressed the view that 150 of Papua and New Guinea's 700 languages are likely to be still actively spoken in one hundred years' time.
6. Moreover, the mental stimulus of learning another culture has value in itself, and is generally done in time that would not be otherwise actively used.
7. Many islanders fail to realise the necessity for this. English people who teach English in England still require a great deal of formal training to do so effectively with the complexities of today's world, and the same appiles with any other language.

8. Four different viewpoints are expressed in *New Guinea* under the title, 'The future of Pidgin', in vol. 2, no. 2 June-July, 1969. See also, references below to Mihalic and Salisbury.
9. *Pacific Islands Monthly*, vol. 42, no. 4, April 1971, page 29.

5   Tradition

1. For a statement by a leading political figure see Tamasese, 1970. For the views of Pacific Islands writers and intellectuals see such periodicals as *Kakamora Reporter* and *O'o* in Solomon Islands; *Dialogue, Ondobondo,* and *Papua New Guinea Writing* in Papua New Guinea; *Moana* in Samoa; *Purua* in the Cook Islands; *Faikava* in Tonga; *Sinnet* in Fiji; and regional publications like *Kovave, Mana, Mana Review, Pacific Perspective,* student publications of the Pacific universities, and other expressions of local opinion.
2. As Dr Gerald Arbuckle has pointed out, the right is associated with a corresponding obligation to consider the needs of all others, particularly the disadvantaged, both within the islands concerned and without. The principle of interdependence is of increasing relevance.
3. Readers are also referred to Dr Schmidt's interesting paper on the future of the Samoan *fale*.
4. As has been shown in the writings of such people as Fanon, Memmi and Mannoni.
5. Firth, 1961, page 161.
6. We now see such statements as 'We, the people of Melanesia, are a group . . . ' (*Kakamora Reporter* May 1971, page 5), which would have had little if any meaning a few years ago.
7. In the late 1970s Western Samoa suffered from an epidemic of suicide by young people, but this now seems to have subsided — though it seems to indicate serious stresses among the youth.
8. Beier, page 4.
9. Some American Samoans see themselves as having the best of both worlds, being almost totally financed by the U.S.A. while retaining some aspects of their own culture. Others see themselves 'hooked' on total aid, and fast losing the prospect of ever getting off it. Like any form of addiction, it can be euphoric in the early stages.
10. Some Tongans have moved into important roles as business and professional men as well as skilled artisans in various countries, but language differences as well as limited educational facilities have resulted in a larger proportion of migrant workers being in the low-skill categories.
11. The present King of Tonga, when Prime Minister, advocated a vigorous family planning programme, but public support was then negligible. New official efforts are having some success.

6   Belief

1. Of the very considerable volume of this material which has been recorded, the works by the Chadwicks, Radin, and Williamson listed in the Bibliography give a good introduction and include useful bibliographies.

Taylor's bibliography is also useful for this purpose. Langdon, 1975, explores the evidence for some syncretism with 16th century Spanish Catholicism in Tahiti and several other islands.

2. *Catalyst*, vol. 1, no. 2, page 84. See also Deverell, 1986.
3. Crocombe, 1982. Garrett, 1982, provides an interesting account of the history of Christianity in the Pacific from its inception to the present time.
4. For example, studies by Alan Howard (see Bibliography) show that the much greater success of Rotumans than of Fijians in professions, business and industry is associated with differences in the social organisation, values, and philosophies of the two groups.
5. For an excellent analysis of a variety of Fijian ceremonies and the distribution of costs and benefits, see the last chapter of Ravuvu, 1987.

7   Social organisation

1. See Bryden and Faber, pages 81–2.

8   Creative arts

1. A recent trend, apparently increasing, is for the islanders themselves to be consumers of local craft manufactures which had been almost exclusively for export. Harry Dansey recently reported that the main buyers of *piupiu* and other traditional Maori garments are now themselves Maori. Some high quality Pacific Islands artifacts find a major market among indigenous Hawaiians.
2. For example, Masiofo Fetaui Mata'afa recently noted that the use of certain sacred ceremonies for entertainment 'undermines that aspect of our culture which has retained our identity and dignity'.
3. In an unpublished address at the University of the South Pacific.
4. Mata'afa, pages 6–7.
5. *Kakamora Reporter*, Sept. 1971, no. 19, page 3.

9   Land

1. An overview of Pacific land tenure systems is given in Crocombe 1986 particularly chapters 1 and 16.
2. This is illustrated for Fiji by Nayacakalou, 1965.
3. The result is illustrated by an instance quoted by Judge Jock McAuley, of the Cook Islands Lands Court. A four-acre block in Rarotonga was registered earlier this century in the names of twenty members of a particular family. It now has registered legal owners with as little as one five thousand and fortieth part of a share in the land, and land is divided into sixteen shares.
4. Van Trease, 1986.
5. Saussol, 1982.
6. Gilson, 1970.
7. Crocombe, 1986, chapter 16.

10   Economy

1. See for example, Pospisil for a detailed study of a Melanesian traditional monetary system.
2. This phase of the history of the Pacific has not yet been adequately documented.
3. Oliver, 1961, (chapter 9) provides some information on this topic, but I am not aware of any comprehensive study of it.
4. For movements in Fiji, Tonga, Samoa, and Kiribati see Couper, 1986; for the Cook Islands, Gilson, 1977; for Nauru, Viviani, 1970 (pages 61–2); for Samoa, Davidson, 1967 (chapter 5); and for the Pacific as a whole see Hempenstall and Rutherford, 1984.
5. A full study of co-operatives in the Pacific has not been made, but a detailed study of the most extensive co-operative movement in the Pacific (that of Papua New Guinea) is contained in Singh, 1973; and for Vanuatu, Ponter, 1986.
6. This has been a major point of contention in relation to the Papua New Guinea economy. Even in 1972 Australians operated barbers shops, taxis, an estimated 94 per cent of all retail trading, and a host of other small enterprises, many of which New Guineans could operate given appropriate provisions. An extensive debate on this topic appears in the journal *New Guinea*, vol. 3, nos. 1 and 4, and vol. 4, nos. 1, 2, and 3. See also Crocombe, 1972. Since the Reagan administration took over in U.S.A., the 1980s has seen considerable encouragement and financial support from U.S.A. for small island businesses as it is congruent with American strategic and economic goals in the Pacific.
7. For a comprehensive review of Pacific economies see Fairbairn, 1985.
8. For examples of rural villagers selling *kava* to buy beer, coke, and cordial; selling fresh taro to buy less nutritious white bread; selling coffee beans at ten cents a pound and buying back instant coffee at several dollars a pound; exporting peanuts and buying back canned American peanuts at fourteen times the price; being persuaded to buy sunglasses by false fears of eye damage artificially generated by advertisers, and vitamin pills and processed foods by irresponsible implications about their benefits, see Crocombe, 1971. All these show up in economic statistics as 'growth'. Likewise, increasing malnutrition in Samoa is said to be linked with excessive consumption of imported white flour and canned fish and such local 'development' as ice-cream and softdrink factories built with the aid of government tax concessions.
9. The substantial psychiatric and social costs of intensive tourism on the local community are discussed in relation to Hawaii by Cottington and Mahoney. Some common fallacies about assumed monetary advantages from tourism are discussed in the articles by Levitt and Gulati, and by Bryden and Faber. Bolabola's study of serious decline in child nutrition in the region of Fiji's luxury hotel complex makes disturbing reading.

11   Politics and government

1. Basic information on the constitutional and governmental structures is contained in Crocombe and Ali, 1982, 1983, and 1984.

2. For further details of the respective systems see Goldman, 1970, and Sahlins, 1963.
3. For details of actual and emerging kingdoms last century see Daws for Hawaii, Langdon for Tahiti, Gilson for Samoa and the Cook islands, Latukefu for Tonga, Derrick for Fiji, and Maude for Kiribati, and Howe generally.
4. For a summary of the decolonisation process in the Pacific see Davidson, 1971, or Crocombe and Ali, 1982, 1983 and 1984.
5. A comprehensive study of the South Pacific Commission has been written by T.R. Smith, a former Secretary-General. See also Neemia, 1986.
6. The contrast is apparent in the comparison of Langdon's study with that of Derrick. It is interesting that France still supports traditional royalty in Wallis and Futuna and that the United Kingdom reduced the power of chiefs in the northern Gilbert Islands. There are clear (not necessarily 'good') reasons for these anomalies.
7. See Keith-Reid, 1985.
8. One of the few studies of politics in Papua New Guinea and West Irian in a single book is Hastings, 1969. For Irian Jaya see Tapol, 1984.
9. For American Samoa see Gray, 1960; for Guam see Carano and Sanchez, 1965; for the United States Trust Territory see Meller, 1969, or Crocombe and Ali, 1983.
10. Details of New Zealand's administrative record in the islands are given in Crocombe, 1962; Davidson, 1967; Gilson, 1977; Ross, 1969; and Stone, 1971.
11. Interesting references on government and politics in the Bibliography include: Davidson for Western Samoa; Haas, Stone and Crocombe for the Cook Islands; Latukefu for Tonga; Meller for US Micronesia; Van Trease for Kiribati; Kalauni for Niue; Larmour for Solomon Islands; Nayacakalou and Fisk for Fiji; Dornoy for New Caledonia; Tagupa for French Polynesia; and for the Pacific as a whole, Crocombe and Ali.

12   Independence and after

1. Their effectiveness has been prolonged somewhat by the practice which a distinguished Polynesian has termed 'rank marries ability'.

13   Intra-Pacific relations

1. See Neemia, 1986.

14   Extra-Pacific relations

1. See Tapol 1984, Ali & Crocombe 1982, chapter 1.

Further reading

About one new book a day is published on the Pacific Islands, and much more is contained in academic and professional journals. C.R.H. Taylor's *Pacific Bibliography* contains details of about 16 000 publications relating to people in the Pacific, and that is much less than half the total published to date, excluding vast amounts in magazines and newspapers.

The following recommended readings are a brief personal selection. They are divided into three sections: those dealing with the first 50 000 years — the period before contact with industrial technology; then the last 400 or so years — the period since Spanish contact; and finally the present or recent past. Fuller details of each are given in the Bibliography. As much very interesting material is continually being published in journals, a brief selection of the best of them is also given.

The first 50 000 years

Barrau, *Plants and the Migrations of Pacific peoples*
Bellwood, *Man's Conquest of the Pacific*
Chadwick, 'The Oral Literature of Polynesia'
Goldman, *Ancient Polynesian Society*
Golson, *Polynesian Navigation*
Golson, 'The Remarkable History of Indo-Pacific Man'
Green, 'Linguistic Subgrouping . . . Implications for Prehistoric Settlement.'
Highland, *Polynesian Culture History*
Hiroa, *Vikings of the Pacific*
Hiroa, *The Coming of the Maori*
Howells, *The Pacific Islanders*
Jennings, *The Prehistory of Polynesia*
Kirk and Szathmary, *Out of Asia: Peopling . . . the Pacific*
Levy, *Personality Studies in Polynesia and Micronesia*

Maude, *The Evolution of the Gilbertese Boti*
Parke, 'A Short History of Rotuma'
The Journal of the Polynesian Society also contains considerable material on this period.

The last 400 years

Oskar Spate's trilogy is much the most comprehensive.
Oliver's *The Pacific Islands* and Grattan's *The South Pacific To 1900* and *The South Pacific Since 1900* give valuable summaries of this whole era, though they were written a generation ago and much new information has come to light since.
Kerry Howe's *Where the Waves Fall* is the most recent study of the early impact of foreign influences in the islands.

For Melanesia

Ali et al, *Politics in Melanesia*
Angiki et al, *The Road Out: Rural Development in Solomon Islands*
Brookfield, *Colonialism, Development and Independence: the Case of Melanesia*
Fisk, *The Political Economy of Independent Fiji*
Kiki, *Ten Thousand Years in a Lifetime*
Lasaqa, *The Fijian People*
Lini et al, *Vanuatu*
Nayacakalou, *Fijian Leadership*
Ravuvu, *The Fijian Way of Life*
Routledge, *Matanitu*
Scarr, *Fragments of Empire*
Tijibaou et al, *Kanake: the Melanesian Way*
Various authors, *The History of Melanesia*
Ward, *The Politics of Melanesia*

For Micronesia

Bataua et al, *Kiribati: A Changing Atoll Culture*
Carano and Sanchez, *A Complete History of Guam*
McHenry, *Micronesia: Trust Betrayed*
Meller, *The Congress of Micronesia*
Tabai et al, *Politics in Kiribati*
Teiwaki et al, *Politics in Micronesia*
Various, *Kiribati; Aspects of History*
Viviani, *Nauru*

For Polynesia

Ali and Crocombe, *Politics in Polynesia*
Davis et al, *Cook Islands Politics: The Inside Story*

Daws, *Shoal of Time: A History of the Hawaiian Islands*
Davidson, *Samoa mo Samoa*
Fatiaki et al, *Rotuma: Split Island*
Gilson, *Samoa, 1830 to 1900*
Gilson, *The Cook Islands, 1820 to 1915*
Hau'ofa, *Our Crowded Islands*
Langdon, *Tahiti: Island of Love*
Latukefu, *Church and State in Tonga*
Lind, *Hawaii's People*
Rutherford, *Friendly Islands*
Tupouniua et al, *The Pacific Way: Social Issues in National Development*
Various authors, *Tuvalu: A History*
Vilitama et al, *Niue: A History of the Island*

For the Pacific as a whole

Ali et al, *Pacific Indians: Profiles from Twenty Countries*
Akau'ola et al, *Pacific Tourism: As Islanders See It*
Crocombe, *Land Tenure in the Pacific*
Crocombe, *The Pacific Way: An Emerging Identity*
Fairbairn, *Island Economies: Studies from the South Pacific*
Garrett, *To Live Among the Stars: Christian Origins in Oceania*
Powles et al, *Pacific Courts and Justice*
Subramani, *South Pacific Literature*
Tausie, *Art in the New Pacific*

Some leading journals concerned with Pacific affairs

Of more than a hundred periodicals published about the Pacific Islands, the most useful for the general reader probably include:

The Journal of Pacific History. Published since 1965. This is a journal of high quality.

Pacific Perspective, published twice yearly since 1972, focuses on current economic, social, and political issues in the Pacific area. It is published by the South Pacific Social Sciences Association, Box 5083, Raiwaqa, Suva, Fiji. The Association also publishes a monograph series.

The Journal of the Polynesian Society, a quarterly since 1892, is the longest established journal dealing with the societies and cultures of the Pacific. The address of the Polynesian Society is Anthropology Department, University of Auckland, Private Bag, Auckland, New Zealand.

The South Pacific Bulletin, an attractively illustrated quarterly containing brief articles concerned with technical, social and economic development, was produced by the South Pacific Commission, Box 306, Haymarket, N.S.W., 2000, Australia, for about thirty years but recently ceased publication.

New Guinea and Australia, the Pacific and South East Asia (generally known simply as New Guinea) was a quarterly journal of comment from 1966 to 1976, and dealt with current economic, political, and social affairs pertaining mainly to New Guinea, but also to other parts of the pacific.

Journal de la Société des Océanistes is a high quality quarterly published in France and dealing with Tahiti, New Caledonia, Vanuatu, Loyalty Islands, Wallis and Futuna, as well as with the rest of the Pacific. Much of the text is in French, but some is in English. The address is Musée de l'Homme, Paris 16E, France.

Pacific Islands Communication, the journal of the Pacific Islands News Association (PINA) is published twice yearly. It began in 1972, based at the East West Center, but in 1985 was transferred at PINA's request to a base at the Institute of Pacific Studies, University of the South Pacific, Box 1168, Suva, Fiji.

Pacific Viewpoint is a geographically-oriented biennial journal which deals with the Pacific Islands and with Pacific borderlands in Southeast Asia and South America. It is obtainable from the Geography Department, Victoria University, Box 196, Wellington, New Zealand.

Kovave is a high quality literary journal concerned with the Pacific Islands. The editor and almost all contributors are Pacific Islanders. The address is care of Institute of Papua New Guinea Studies, Boroko, Papua New Guinea. The Institute also publishes a high quality series of monographs.

The Institute of Pacific Studies of the University of the South Pacific, Box 1168, Suva, Fiji, began in 1977 publishing a series of books and monographs, mainly by Pacific Islands writers. Monographs include:

Island Economies
Pacific Courts and Justice
Education for Rural Development
Land Tenure in Vanuatu (and parallel volumes for several countries)
Kiribati: Aspects of History (parallel volumes on Niue, Tuvalu, Solomon Islands)
To Live Among the Stars: Christian Origins in Oceania
Polynesian Missions to Melanesia
Slavers in Paradise
Art in the New Pacific (also in French as *Art du Pacifique*)
Land, People and Government: Public Lands Policy in the South Pacific
Fishermen of Tonga
Beyond Pandemonium: From New Hebrides to Vanuatu
Vanuatu
Politics of Kiribati (and parallel volumes for Solomon Islands, Cook Islands)
Politics in Melanesia (and parallel volumes for Melanesia & Micronesia)
The South Pacific
Foreign Forces in Pacific Islands Politics
Pacific Literature
Pacific Indians
Zoloveke: A Man from Choiseul

The Cook Islands, 1820–1950
The Fijian Way of Life

and over 100 other volumes.

Mana, the journal of the South Pacific Creative Arts Society (Box 5083, Raiwaqa, Suva, Fiji), is the largest and best known outlet for Pacific poets, novelists, dramatists, and other creative artists. It has generally published two journals per year since 1972, plus about 30 books of poetry, drama, short stories etc by Pacific Islands writers.

In addition to the above journals and organisations which are concerned with the Pacific as a whole, or particular segments of it, there are also many which deal with particular nations.

Bibliography

Akau'ola, Lata, et al, 1980. *Pacific Tourism: As Islanders See It*, University of the South Pacific, Suva.

Ali, Ahmed, 1980. *Plantation to Politics*, University of the South Pacific, Suva.

Ali, A., et al., 1981. *Pacific Indians: Profiles from Twenty Countries*, University of the South Pacific, Suva.

Ali, Ahmed and Crocombe, Ron (eds), 1982. *Politics in Melanesia*; 1983; *Foreign Forces in Pacific Politics; Politics in Polynesia*; 1984; *Politics in Micronesia*, University of the South Pacific, Suva.

Baraniko, Mikaere, et al, 1979. *Kiribati: Aspects of History*, University of the South Pacific, Suva.

Barrau, Jacques, 1963. *Plants and the Migrations of Pacific Peoples*, Bishop Museum Press, Honolulu.

Bataua, Batiri et al, 1985. *Kiribati: A Changing Atoll Culture*, University of the South Pacific, Suva.

Beaglehole, Ernest, 1939. *Some Modern Hawaiians*, University of Hawaii Research Publication no. 19, Honolulu.

Beaglehole, Ernest, 1957. *Social Change in the South Pacific: Rarotonga and Aitutaki*, George Allen and Unwin, London.

Beaglehole, Ernest and Pearl, 1946. *Some Modern Maoris*, Oxford University Press, London.

Beier, Ulli, 1971. 'The Potential Role of the University of the South Pacific in Encouraging the Arts', Suva (mimeo).

Bellwood, Peter, 1979. *Man's Conquest of the Pacific*, Oxford University Press, New York.

Benton, Richard, 1982. *The Flight of the Amokura*, New Zealand Council for Educational Research, Wellington.

Biggs, Bruce, 1967. 'The Past Twenty Years in Polynesian Linguistics', in Highland, G.A. (editor), *Polynesian Culture History*.

Bolabola, Cema, 1981. 'Does Tourism cause Malnutrition; They seem to be Connected,' *Pacific Perspective*, vol. 10, no. 1, pages 72–7.

Brookfield, H.C. 1971. *Melanesia: A Geographical Interpretation of an Island World*, Methuen, London.

Brookfield, H.C. 1973. *Colonialism, Development and Independence: The Case of the Melanesian Islands in the South Pacific*, Cambridge University Press, London.

Bryden, John and Faber, Mike, 1971. 'Multiplying the Tourist Multiplier', *Social and Economic Studies*, vol. 20, no. 1, pages 61–82.

Carano, Paul and Sanchez, Pedro, 1965. *A Complete history of Guam*, Tuttle, Rutland.

Carpenter, Edmund, 1972. *Oh! What a Blow that Phantom Gave Me*, Doubleday, New York.

Catalyst, 1971. Editor, Kevin Murphy, Port Moresby.

Chadwick, H.M. and N.K., 1940. 'The Oral Literature of Polynesia' in *The Growth of Literature*, vol. 3, Cambridge University Press, London.

Chapman, Murray (editor), 1985. *Mobility and Identity in the Island Pacific*, University of the South Pacific, Suva, and Victoria University, Wellington.

Clyde, Paul H., 1967. *Japan's Pacific Mandate*, Kennikat Press, New York.

Connell, John, 1986. *Migration, Employment and Development in the South Pacific*, South Pacific Commission, Noumea.

Coppenrath, Gerald, 1967. *Les Chinois de Tahiti*, Société des Océanistes Publication no. 21, Musée de l'Homme, Paris.

Cottington, Frances, 1970. 'Socio-psychiatric Effects of Luxury Hotel Development on a Rural Population' unpublished report, Honolulu.

Couper, A.D., 1968. 'Protest Movements and Proto-cooperatives in the Pacific Islands', *Journal of the Polynesian Society*, vol. 77, pages 263–74.

Crocombe, R.G., 1962. 'Development and Regression in New Zealand's Island Territories', *Pacific Viewpoint*, vol. 3, pages 17–32.

Crocombe, R.G., (editor), 1986. *Land Tenure in the Pacific*, Oxford, Melbourne, and University of the South Pacific.

Crocombe, R.G., 1971. 'Economic Development and Social Change in Fiji: a review article', *Journal of the Polynesian Society*, vol. 80, pages 505–20.

Crocombe, R.G., 1972. 'Australian and New Guinean Interests in the New Guinea Economy', in Stevens, F.S. (editor), *Racism: the Australian Experience*, vol. 3, Australian and New Zealand Book Co., Sydney.

Crocombe, R.G., 1975. 'France in the Pacific', *New Guinea*, vol. 9, no. 4.

Crocombe, R.G., 1985. 'The Pan Pacific Person', *Pacific Perspective*, vol. 12, no. 2.

Crocombe, Ron (editor), 1978. *Cook Islands Politics: the Inside Story*, Polynesian Press, Auckland.

Crocombe, Ron and Marjorie (eds), 1982. *Polynesian Missions in Melanesia*, University of the South Pacific, Suva.

Dansey, Harry, 1971. 'Age-old skill . . .', *Auckland Star*, 27 August.

Davidson, J.W., 1967. *Samoa mo Samoa: The Emergence of the Independent State of Western Samoa*, Oxford University Press, Melbourne.

Davidson, J.W., 1971. 'The Decolonization of Oceania', *Journal of Pacific History*, vol. 6, pages 133–50.

Daws, Gavan, 1968. *Shoal of Time: a History of the Hawaiian Islands*, Macmillan, New York.

Dening, G., 1963. 'The Geographical Knowledge of the Polynesians and the Nature of Inter-island Contact', in Golson (below).

Derrick, R.A., 1963. *A History of Fiji*, Government Printer, Suva.

Deverell, Bruce (editor), 1986. *Pacific Rituals: Living or Dying*, University of the South Pacific, Suva.

Dewey, Alice, 1964. 'The Noumea Javanese', *South Pacific Bulletin*, vol. 14, no. 4.

Dornoy, Myriam, 1984. *Politics in New Caledonia*, Sydney University Press.

Fairbairn, Te'o I.J., 1985. *Island Economies*, University of the South Pacific, Suva.

Fanon, Frantz, 1967. *The Wretched of the Earth*, Penguin Books, London.

Fell, Barry, 1980. *Saga America*, Times Books, New York.

Fiji Education Commission, 1969. *Education for Modern Fiji*, Government Printer, Suva.

Firth, Raymond, 1958. *Human Types*, Mentor Books, New York.

Firth, Raymond, 1961. *History and Traditions of Tikopia*, Polynesian Society, Wellington.

Fisk, E.K., 1970. *The Political Economy of Independent Fiji*, Australian National University Press, Canberra.

Fosberg, F.R., 1965. *Man's Place in the Island Ecosystem*, Bishop Museum Press, Honolulu.

Fry, Gregory E., 1981. 'Regionalism and International Politics of the South Pacific', *Pacific Affairs*, vol. 84, pp 455–84.

Gallimore, Ronald and Howard, Allan (eds), 1969. *Studies in a Hawaiian. Community: na Makamaka o Nanakuli*, Bishop Museum Press, Honolulu.

Garrett, John, 1982. *To Live Among the Stars: Christian Origins in Oceania*, University of the South Pacific and World Council of Churches, Suva and Geneva.

Gillion, Kenneth, 1962. *Fiji's Indian Migrants*, Oxford University Press, Melbourne.

Gilson, R.P., 1970. *Samoa 1830 to 1900: the Politics of a Multicultural Community*, Oxford University Press, Melbourne.

Gilson, R.P. 1977. *The Cook Islands 1820–1930*, Victoria University Press, Wellington.

Goldman, Irving, 1970. *Ancient Polynesian Society*, University of Chicago Press.

Golson, Jack (editor), 1963. *Polynesian Navigation*, Polynesian Society, Wellington.

Golson, Jack, 1972. 'The Remarkable History of Indo-Pacific Man', *Journal of Pacific History*, vol. 7, pages 5–25.

Grace, G.W., 1968. 'Classification of the Languages of the Pacific', in Vayda, A.P. (editor), *Peoples and Cultures of the Pacific*, the Natural History Press, New York.

Grattan, F.J.H., 1948. *An Introduction to Samoan Custom*, Samoa Printing and Publishing Co., Apia.

Grattan, C. Hartley, 1963. *The South Pacific to 1900*, University of Michigan Press, Ann Arbor.

Gray, J.A.C., 1960. *Amerika Samoa*, U.S. Naval Institute, Annapolis.

Green, Roger, 1966. 'Linguistic Subgrouping within Polynesia: the Implications for Prehistoric Settlement', *Journal of the Polynesian Society*, vol. 75, pages 6–38.

Harding, Thomas G., 1967. *Voyagers of the Vitiaz Straits*, University of Washington Press, Seattle.

Harré, John, (editor), 1973. *Living in Town*, South Pacific Social Sciences Association, Suva.

Hastings, Peter, 1969. *New Guinea: Problems and Prospects*, Longman Cheshire Melbourne.

Hau'ofa, Epeli, 1975. *Mekeo*, Australian National University Press, Canberra.

Hawthorn, Harry B., 1971. 'The Survival of Small Societies' *Anthropologica*, n.s., vol. 13, no. 1, pages 63–84.

Hayes, Geoffrey, 1984. *International Migration in the Pacific Islands*, ESCAP Conference on International Migration, Manila, November.

Hempenstall, Peter and Rutherford Noel, 1984. *Protest and Dissent in the Colonial Pacific*, University of the South Pacific, Suva.

Highland, G.A., (editor), 1967. *Polynesian Culture History*, Bishop Museum Press, Honolulu.

Hiroa, Te Rangi (Sir Peter Buck), 1966. *The Coming of the Maori*, Maori Purposes Fund Board, Wellington.

Hiroa, Te Rangi, 1964. *Vikings of the Pacific*, Chicago University Press, Chicago.

Hooper, Anthony (editor), 1986. *Culture and Class in the South Pacific*, Institute of Pacific Studies, University of the South Pacific, Suva.

Howard, Alan, 1966. 'Plasticity, Achievement and Adaptation in Developing Economies', *Human Organisation*, vol. 25, no. 4, pages 265–72. For a summary, see his book *Learning to be Rotuman*, Columbia University Teacher's College Press.

Howe, Kerry, 1984. *Where the Waves Fall: A New South Sea Islands History from First Settlement to Colonial Rule*, University of Hawaii Press, Honolulu.

Howells, William, 1973. *The Pacific Islanders*, Reeds, Wellington.

Hughes, Ian, 1971. *Recent Neolithic Trade in New Guinea*, unpublished PhD. thesis, Australian National University, Canberra.

Jennings, Jesse (editor), 1979. *The Prehistory of Polynesia*, Australian National University, Canberra.

de Josselin de Jong, P.E., 1953. 'The Kon-Tiki Theory of Pacific Migrations', *Bijdragen tot de taal — , land and volkerkunde*, vol. 109, pages 1–22.

Kakamora Reporter, 1969–1973. Editors, Henry Raraka and Ella Bugotu, Honiara.

Kasaipwalova, John, 1971. 'What is Cultural Reconstruction', *New Guinea Writing*, no. 3, pages 14–17.

Keith-Reid, Robert, 1985. 'Ratu Sir Kamisese Mara: Memories of the First 15 years,' *Islands Business*, December.

Kele-Kele, Kalkot, M., 1978. *New Hebrides: the Road to Independence*, South Pacific Social Sciences Association, Suva.

Kiki, Albert Maori, 1968. *Ten Thousand Years in a Lifetime*, Longman Cheshire, Melbourne

Kirch, Patrick, 1986. 'Rethinking East Polynesian Prehistory', *Journal of the Polynesian Society*, vol. 95, no. 1, pp 9–40.

Kirk, Robert and Szathmary, Emoke (eds), 1985. *Out of Asia: Peopling the Americas and the Pacific*, Journal of Pacific History Monograph, Australian National University, Canberra.

Kissling, Christopher (editor), 1984. *Transport and Communication for Pacific Microstates*, University of the South Pacific, Suva.

Lal, Brij, 1983. *Girmitiyas: The Origins of Fiji Indians*, Journal of Pacific History Monograph, Australian National University, Canberra.

Langdon, Robert, 1968. *Tahiti: Island of Love*, Pacific Publications, Sydney.

Langdon, Robert, 1975. *The Lost Caraval*, Pacific Publications, Sydney.

Langdon, Robert and Tryon, Darrell, 1983. *The Language of Easter Island . . .,*

Brigham Young University, Laie.

Larmour, Peter and Qalo, Ropati, 1985. *Decentralization in the South Pacific*, University of the South Pacific, Suva.

Larmour, Peter (editor), 1983. *Solomon Islands Politics*, University of the South Pacific, Suva.

Lasaqa, Isireli, 1984. *The Fijian People*, Australian National University Press, Canberra.

Latukefu, Sione, 1967. 'Tonga after Queen Salote', *Journal of Pacific History*, vol. 2, pages 159–62.

Latukefu, Sione, 1972. 'The Place of Tradition in Modernisation', *Journal of the Papua New Guinea Society*.

Latukefu, Sione, 1974. *Church and State in Tonga*, Australian National University Press, Canberra.

Levison, M., Ward, R.G., and Webb, J.W., 1972. *The Settlement of Polynesia: a Computer Simulation*, University of Minnesota Press, Minneapolis.

Levitt, Karl, and Gulati, Iqbal, 1970. 'Income Effect of Tourist Spending', *Social and Economic Studies*, vol. 19, no. 3, pages 326–43.

Levy, Robert, 1968. 'On Getting Angry in the Society Islands', in *Mental Health Methods in Asia and the Pacific*, Caudill, William and Lin, Tsung-Yi (editors), East West Center press, Honolulu.

Levy, Robert, 1969. *Personality Studies in Polynesia and Micronesia: Stability and Change*, Social Science Research Institute paper no. 8, University of Hawaii, Honolulu.

Levy, Robert, 1969. 'Child Management Structure in Tahitian Families', *Journal of the Polynesian Society*, vol. 78, pages 35–43.

Lind, Andrew, 1967. *Hawaii's People*, University of Hawaii Press, Honolulu.

Lini, Walter, et al, 1980. *Vanuatu*, University of the South Pacific, Suva.

Lockwood, Brian, 1971. *Samoan Village Economy*, Oxford University Press, Melbourne.

McArthur, Norma, 1961. *Island Populations of the Pacific*, Australian National University Press, Canberra.

McHenry, Donald, 1975. *Micronesia, Trust Betrayed*, Carnegie Endowment for International Peace, Washington

Mahoney, Carl, 1970. 'Tourism and Urbanisation: the Lesson of the Outer Hawaiian Islands', Second South Pacific Seminar, Suva, in Harré (above).

Mannoni, Dominique, O., 1956. *Prospero and Caliban: the Psychology of Colonization*, Praeger, New York.

Mason, Leonard, 1959. 'Suprafamilial Authority and Economic Process in Micronesian Atolls', *Humanités*, vol. 5, no. 1, pages 87–118.

Mason, Leonard, 1968. 'The Ethnology of Micronesia', in Vayda, Peter, (editor), *Peoples and Cultures of the Pacific*, The Natural History Press, New York.

Mata'afa, Masiofo Fetaui, 1971. 'Regional Trade and Tourism in the South Pacific', Fiji Tourism Convention, Suva.

Maude, H.E., 1963. *The Evolution of the Gilbertese Boti*, Polynesian Society, Wellington.

Maude, H.E., 1970. 'Baiteke and Binoka of Abenama' in Davidson J.W. and Scarr, Deryck, *Pacific Islands Portraits*, Australian National Unviersity Press, Canberra.

Maude, H.E., 1981. *Slavers in Paradise*, University of the South Pacific, Suva.

Mayer, Adrian, 1963. *Indians in Fiji*, Oxford University Press, London.

Mayer, Adrian, 1972. *Peasants in the Pacific: a Study of Fiji Indian Rural Society*, (revised edition) Routledge and Kegan Paul, London.

Meller, Norman, 1969. *The Congress of Micronesia*, University of Hawaii Press, Honolulu.

Memmi, Albert, 1965. *The Coloniser and the Colonised*, Orion Books, New York.

Mihalic, Francis, 1957. *Grammar and Dictionary of Neo-Melanesian*, Westmead Printing, Sydney.

Moench, Richard, 1963. 'A Preliminary Report on Chinese Social and Economic Organisation in the Society Islands, in Spoehr, Alexander (editor), *Pacific Port Towns and Cities*, Bishop Museum Press, Honolulu.

Monsell-Davis, Michael (editor), 1986. *Fijians in Town*, University of the South Pacific, Suva.

Moore, Mike, 1982. *A Pacific Parliament*, University of the South Pacific, Suva.

Morrell, W.P., 1966. *Britain in the Pacific Islands*, Clarendon Press, Oxford.

Nayacakalou, R.R., 1955 and 1957. 'The Fijian System of Kinship and Marriage', *Journal of the Polynesian Society*, vol. 64, pages 44–55 and vol. 66, pages 44–59.

Nayacakalou, R.R., 1965. 'The Bifurcation and Amalgamation of Fijian Lineages over a Period of Fitty Years', *Proceedings of the Fiji Society for 1960 and 1961*, Suva.

Nayacakalou, R.R., 1981. *Fijian Leadership*, University of the South Pacific, Suva.

Neemia, Uentabo, F., 1986. *Co-operation and Conflict: Costs, Benefits and National Interests in Pacific Regional Cooperation*, University of the South Pacific, Suva.

Nettleford, Rex, 1979. *Caribbean Cultural Identity: The Case of Jamaica*, vol. 47, UCLA Latin American Center Publications, Los Angeles.

Nwoko, Demas, 1970. 'Search for a New African Theatre', *Presence Africaine: Cultural Review of the Negro World*, no. 75, pages 49–75.

Oliver, Douglas, 1961. *The Pacific Islands*, Natural History Library, New York.

Parke, Aubrey, 1971. 'A Short History of Rotuma', *Transactions and Proceedings of the Fiji Society*.

Pawley, Andrew and Green, Roger C., 1985. 'The Proto-Oceanic Language Community,' in Kirk and Szathmary (above).

Ponter, Brian, 1986. *Co-operatives in Vanuatu*, University of the South Pacific, Suva.

Pospisil, Leopold, 1963. *Kaupauku Papuan Economy*, Yale University Publications in Anthropology no. 67, New Haven.

Prevost, P.J.C., 1970, 'L'expansion de la zone d'influence de la langue Tahitienne', *Journal de la Societé des Océanistes*, vol. 26, no. 28, pages 256–60.

Radin, P., 1957. *Primitive Man as Philosopher*, Dover Books, New York.

Radin, P., 1957. *Primitive Religion*, Dover Books, New York.

Rajotte, Freda, and Ron Crocombe (eds), 1981. *Pacific Tourism: As Islanders See It*, University of the South Pacific, Suva.

Ravuvu, Asesela, 1984. *The Fijian Way of Life*, University of the South Pacific, Suva.

Ravuvu, Asesela, 1987. *The Fijian Ethos*, University of the South Pacific, Suva.

Ritchie, James, 1956. *Basic Personality in Rakau*, Victoria University Publications in Psychology no. 8, Wellington.

Ritchie, James, 1963. *The Making of a Maori*, Reed, Wellington.

Rose, Hilary, 1971. *Pangloss and Jeremiah in Science*, quoted by J.R. Price in *Australian National University News*, vol. 6, no. 2, page 15.

Ross, Angus (editor), 1969. *New Zealand's Record in the Pacific Islands in the Twentieth Century*, Longman Paul, Auckland.

Routledge, David, 1985. *Matanitu: The Struggle for Power in Early Fiji*, University of the South Pacific, Suva.

Russell, Tom, 1970. 'The 1970 Constitution for the Solomon Islands', *The Politics of Melanesia*, University of Papua New Guinea, Port Moresby.

Rutherford, Noel, 1971. *Shirley Baker and the King of Tonga*, Oxford University Press, Melbourne.

Rutherford, Noel, 1977. *Friendly Islands: a History of Tonga*, Oxford Universy Press, Melbourne.

Saemala, Francis, 1979. *Our Independent Solomon Islands*, University of the South Pacific, Suva.

Sahlins, Marshall, 1962. *Moala*, University of Michigan Press, Ann Arbor.

Sahlins, Marshall, 1963. 'Poor man, rich man, big man, chief: Political Types in Melanesia and Polynesia', in Hogbin, Ian and Hiatt, L.R., *Readings in Australian and Pacific Anthropology*, Melbourne University Press, Melbourne.

Salisbury, Richard, 1967. 'Pidgin's Respectable Past', *New Guinea*, vol. 2, no. 2.

Saussol, Alain, 1979. *L'Heritage: Essai sur le problème foncier Melanesien en Nouvelle Caledonie*, Société des Océanistes, Publication no. 40, Musée de L'Homme, Paris.

Scarr, Deryck, 1968. *Fragments of Empire: A History of the Western Pacific High Commission 1877–1914*, Australian National University Press, Canberra.

Schmidt, Karl, 1971. 'The Future of the Samoan Fale: Societal and Mental Health'. (Unpublished manuscript.)

Serjeantsen, S.W. et al, 1982. 'HLA Antigens in Four Pacific Populations,' *Annals of Human Biology*, vol. 9, page 69.

Sharp, Andrew, 1963. *Ancient Voyagers in Polynesia*, Paul's, Auckland.

Singh, Sumer, 1972. *Cooperatives in Papua New Guinea*, New Guinea Research Bulletin, Canberra.

Souter, Gavan, 1963. *New Guinea: the Last Unknown*, Angus and Robertson, Sydney.

Spate, O.H.K., 1979, *The Spanish Lake*; 1984, *Monopolists and Freebooters*; forthcoming 3rd and final vol; Australian National University Press, Canberra.

Spiro, Melford, 1959. 'Cultural Heritage, Personal Tensions and Mental Illness in a South Sea Culture', in Opler, M.K. (editor), *Culture and Mental Health*, Macmillan, New York.

Stone, David, 1971. *Self-rule in the Cook Islands: the Government and Politics of a New Micro-state*, unpublished PhD. thesis, Australian National University, Canberra.

Subramani, 1985. *South Pacific Literature*, University of the South Pacific, Suva.

Suggs, Robert C., 1960. *The Island Civilisations of Polynesia*, Mentor Books, New York.

Tabai, Ieremia, et al, 1980. *The Politics of Kiribati*, University of the South Pacific, Suva.

Tagupa, William, 1976. *Politics in French Polynesia: 1945–1975*, New Zealand Institute of International Affairs, Wellington.

Tamasese, Tupua, 1970. *Western Samoa Faces the Modern World*, New Zealand Institute of International Affairs, Wellington.

Tapol, 1984. *West Papua, The Obliteration of a People*, Tapol, London.

Taylor, C.R.H., 1965. *A Pacific Bibliography*, Clarendon Press, Oxford.

Te Rangi Hiroa (Sir Peter Buck), 1966. *The Coming of the Maori*, Wellington.

Thompson, V. and Adloff, R., 1970. *The French Pacific Islands*, University of California, Berkeley.

Toffler, Alvin, 1971. *Future Shock*, Bantam Books, London.

Tryon, Darrell, 1985. 'Peopling the Pacific: A Linguistic Appraisal,' in Kirk and Szathmary (above).

Tudor, Judy, 1972. *Pacific Islands Yearbook*, eleventh edition, Pacific Publications, Sydney.

Ulufa'alu, Bart, 1983. 'The Development of Political Parties' in Larmour, 1983 (above).

Van Trease, Howard, 1982. Series of articles in *Pacific Islands Monthly*, July, August, September.

Van Trease, Howard, 1986. *Land Policy in Vanuatu*, University of the South Pacific, Suva.

Various authors, 1969. *History of Melanesia*, University of Papua New Guinea, Port Moresby.

Viviani, Nancy, 1970. *Nauru: Phosphate and Political Progress*, Australian National University Press, Canberra.

Ward, Marion (editor), 1970. *The Politics of Melanesia*, University of Papua New Guinea, Port Moresby.

Ward, R. Gerard, 1971. 'Internal Migration and Urbanisation in Papua New Guinea', in *Population Growth and Socio-economic Change*, New Guinea Research Bulletin no. 42, Canberra.

Wenkam, Robert, 1971. *Proposal for a System of Oceanic Historical and Recreational Parks in Micronesia*, Saipan, U.S.T.T., (mimeo).

Williamson, R.W., 1933. *Religious and Cosmic beliefs of Central Polynesia*, Cambridge University Press, Cambridge.

Wynne, Barry, 1966. *The Man who Refused to Die: Teehu Makimare's 2000 Mile Drift . . .*, Souvenir Press, London.

Yee, Sin Joan, 1976. *The Chinese in the Pacific*, South Pacific Social Sciences Association, Suva.

Yen, Douglas, 1963. 'Sweet potato variation and its relation to human migration in the Pacific', in Barrau (above).

Basic facts

About Pacific Islands nations and territories

Land: Total area 976 047 km² of which:
    Melanesia comprises 949 034 km²   97.2%
    (of which Papua New Guinea and Irian Jaya
    comprise 872 243 km² or 89.5%)
    Polynesia (excluding New Zealand) comprises
    23 914 km²   2.5%
    (or excluding New Zealand and Hawaii 8052 km²
    or 0.8%)
    Micronesia comprises 3099 km²   0.3%

                                                   100.0%

Water: In contrast to land, Melanesia controls only
about 32% of the Pacific's marine resources
claimed by islands states and territories (2 km²
per person). This compares with Micronesia's
32% (32 km² per person) and Polynesia's 36%
(20 km² per person).

Population: Total 8 176 961 (1986 estimates) of
which countries and territories in:
    Melanesia contain 6 154 596   75.3%
    (Papua New Guinea and Irian Jaya alone contain
    4 865 696 or 59.5%)
    Polynesia (excluding New Zealand)
    contain 1 664 565   20.3%
    (or excluding New Zealand and Hawaii contain
    only 517 865 or 6.3%)
    Micronesia contain 357 800   4.4%

                                                   100.0%

Population density 8.4 per km^2

Ethnic components (excluding New Zealand and Hawaii):

Melanesian people comprise 76%, Polynesian 8%, Micronesian 4%, Asian (assuming 250 000 Indonesians in Irian Jaya) 10%, and Europeans 2%.

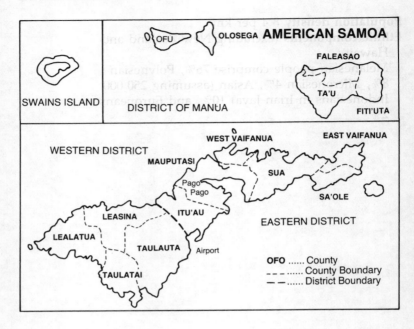

AMERICAN SAMOA

Population 35 300 (1985); Growth rate 1.8%; Density 179 per km². Mainly Samoan, with minor groups of Tongans, Koreans, Americans, and Japanese.

Land area 197 km²; per person 0.005 km²

Sea area 390 000 km²; per person 11 km²

Gross national product US$140 million (1983 est.); per person US$4130 (World Bank)

Aid US$57 million (1986 est.); per person US$1615

Main sources of income Tinned fish and other fish products, remittances from Samoans in the U.S.A.; aid from the U.S.A.

System of government Until last century ruled by chiefly families, often in transient unions.

1900, Unincorporated Territory of the U.S.A. in partition of Samoa between U.S.A. and Germany (the latter now being independent Western Samoa)

1900–1951, Administered by U.S.A. Navy.

1951–present, Administered through the U.S.A. Department of the Interior.

Territorial governing bodies (under U.S.A. Federal Government) Senate of Matai (family heads) elected under Samoan custom (18 members), but a constitutional review begun in 1985 may lead to its being elected by popular ballot. House of Representatives by popular election (21 members).

Local Government 3 Districts, 16 Counties and 59 Village Councils.

Political parties Formally none, but the main factions are closely identified with either the U.S.A. Democratic or Republican parties.

Head of State President of the U.S.A.

Head of Government The elected Governor, who exercises his authority under the direction of the US Secretary of the Interior. First elected Governor 1977 to 1984 — Hon. Peter Tali Coleman; 1984 to present — Hon A.P. Lutali.

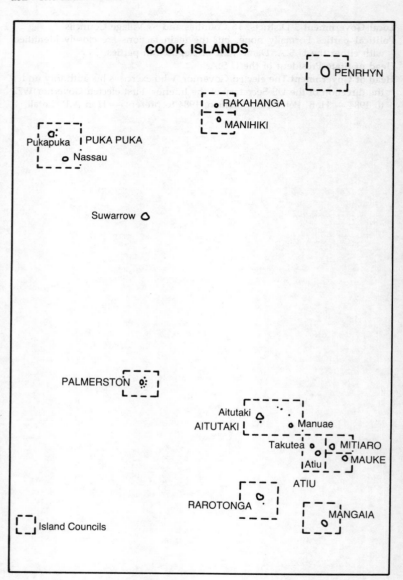

COOK ISLANDS

O PENRHYN

RAKAHANGA
MANIHIKI

Puka Puka
Pukapuka
Nassau

Suwarrow O

PALMERSTON

Aitutaki
AITUTAKI
Manuae

Takutea MITIARO
MAUKE
Atiu

ATIU

RAROTONGA

MANGAIA

Island Councils

COOK ISLANDS

Population 18 400 (1986 est.); growth rate negative 1980–84 owing to migration to New Zealand and Australia. Slight positive growth 1985–6; density 77 per km². Mainly Polynesian with some Europeans on Rarotonga

Land area 240 km²; per person 0.13 km²

Sea area 1 830 000 km²; per person 99.5 km²

Gross domestic product NZ$32.4 million (1983 est.); per person NZ$1837 (unofficial)

Aid NZ$18 million (1985 est.); per person NZ$978

Main sources of income Tourism, fruit products, pearl shell, remittances from Cook Islanders abroad, postage stamps, aid mainly from New Zealand.

System of government Each district or island generally autonomous under tribal chieftainship.

1888 British Protectorate, Federal Parliament established

1901 Annexed by New Zealand, Federal Council dissolved 1912

1946 Legislative Council formed, and replaced in 1957 by Legislative Assembly, which in 1964 unanimously chose self-government (from 1965) in association with New Zealand, which was responsible for foreign affairs and defence at the beginning. Foreign affairs was progressively taken over by the Cook Islands Government, and a full Ministry of Foreign Affairs established in 1983. Defence was not an issue until 1985 (there are no military personnel or bases in the Cook Islands) when, reacting to New Zealand's banning of nuclear ships, the Cook Islands created a portfolio of Minister of Defence.

Citizenship All Cook Islanders in practice hold dual citizenship, Cook Islands and New Zealand.

National governing bodies Legislative Assembly — 24 elected members (including 1 representing Cook Islanders overseas); House of Ariki with 21 Ariki (hereditary chiefs) with nominal powers only.

Local Government Separate (mainly elected but some ex officio members) Island Council for each island. Rarotonga, also has Vaka (District) Councils and Village Committees.

Political parties Democratic Party, Cook Islands Party (each of which is split into two factions).

Head of State 1981–84 Sir Gaven Donne

1984–present Hon. Tangaroa Tangaroa

Head of Government

1965–78 Albert Henry (Premier)

1978–83 Sir Thomas Davis (Premier to 1981 then Prime Minister by change of constitution)

April to Nov. 1983 Geoffrey Henry (Prime Minister);

Nov. 1983 to present Sir Thomas Davis (Prime Minister) as head of a Coalition of most of the Democratic Party and some of the Cook Islands Party.

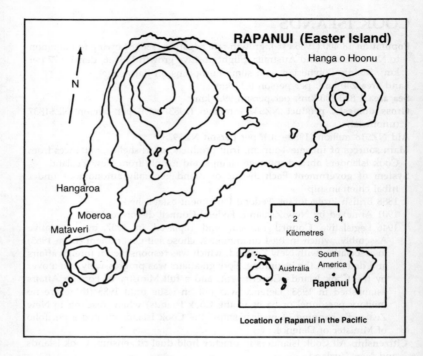

EASTER ISLAND (RAPANUI)

Population 2300 (1986 est.); Growth rate 2%; Density 14 per km².

Main ethnic components Polynesians about 75%; Chilean Mainlanders and others about 25%.

Land area 166 km², per person 0.07 km²

Main sources of income Government employment, tourism (approx US$1 000 000 per year), wood.

GNP Not available.

System of government

To 1861, Separate local chiefdoms

1861–1877, Local warlords supported by expatriates

1878–1888, French Protectorate (unofficial) and local restored monarchy

1888–1966, Colony of Chile

1965 Revolt in favour of independence put down by Chile

1966–present, integral part of the Chilean State

Political parties Since the overthrow of the elected government of Dr Salvador Allende on 11 September 1973, political parties in Chile have been effectively banned.

Appointed officials

Head of Government and Head of State President General Augusto Pinochet Ugarte of Chile

Governor Senor Sergio Rapu Haoa

Municipal Major Senor Samuel Cardinali Rakomio

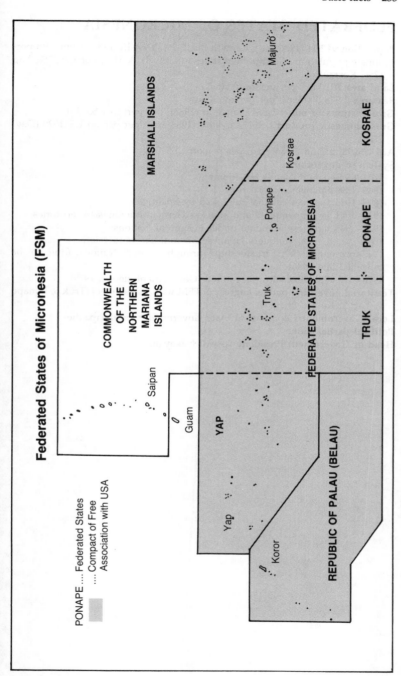

Federated States of Micronesia (FSM)

PONAPE.....Federated States
.....Compact of Free
Association with USA

FEDERATED STATES OF MICRONESIA

Population 94 534 (1986 est.); Growth rate 3.3%; Density 135 per km². Proportionate population of component states in 1980: Truk 51%, Ponape 31%, Yap 12%, Kosrae 6%.

Land area 701 km²; per person 0.009 km²

Sea area 2 978 000 km²; per person 37 km²

Gross national product US$111 million (1983); per person US$1301

Gross domestic product US$172 million (1986 est.); per person US$1820 (Dev. Plan)

Aid US$92 million (1986 est.); per person US$1018

System of government

To 1885 Separate islands chiefdoms

1885–1899 Spanish colonial rule

1899–1914 German colonial rule (sold by Spain)

1914–1921 Japan conquers and annexes German Micronesian territories

1921–1945 Japanese Mandate under League of Nations

1945   U.S.A. conquers Japanese Micronesian possessions

1947–present U.S.A. trusteeship through United Nations (due to be cancelled late 1986)

1978–   FSM Constitution ratified (Government elected 1979)

Territorial governing body Congress of FSM with 14 members (Truk 6, Ponape 4, Yap 2, Kosrae 2)

Local Government 4 component State Governments, municipalities.

Political parties None

Head of Government President Tosiwo Nakayama

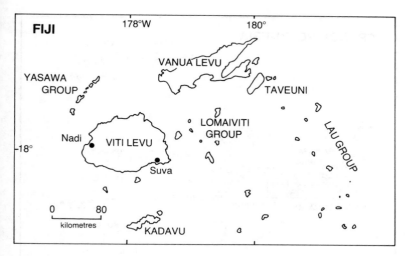

FIJI

Population 714 000 (1986 est.); Growth rate 2%; Density 39 per km². (Indians
49%, Fijians 45%, small communities of Europeans, Chinese and others).
Land area 18 272 km²; per person 0.026 km²
Sea area 1 290 000 km²; per person 2 km²
Gross national product F$1106 million (1983); per person F$1646 (Fiji Govt.)
Gross domestic product F$682 million (1983); per person F$1016
Aid F$29 million (1985 est.); per person F$41
Main sources of income Sugar, tourism, copra, industry, aid.
System of government To 1871, separate tribal chiefdoms
    1871–73 Independent Monarchy
    1874–1970 United Kingdom Colony
    Since 1970 Independent Dominion, member of Commonwealth
National governing bodies House of Representatives (52 members with
    separate seats for Fijian, Indian, and General Elector categories); Senate (21
    members nominated by Prime Minister, Leader of Opposition and Council
    of Chiefs) giving an average of 10 members per 100 000 of population.
Local Government Municipal and Provincial Councils and District Advisory
    Councils. The Fijian Administration and the Council of Chiefs have a special
    role in relation to the Fijian people.
Political parties (with number of seats in House of Representatives in 1986)
    Alliance, in power since before independence (29).
    National Federation Party/Western United Front Coalition (23).
    Fijian Nationalist Party (nil). Labour Party, formed 1985 (nil).
Head of Government Prime Minister, Ratu Sir Kamisese Mara, since inde-
    pendence in 1970 and Chief Minister in the preceding period of self-
    government.
Head of State Governor General
    1970–73 Sir Robert Foster
    1973–82 Ratu Sir George Cakobau
    1982–   Ratu Sir Penaia Ganilau.

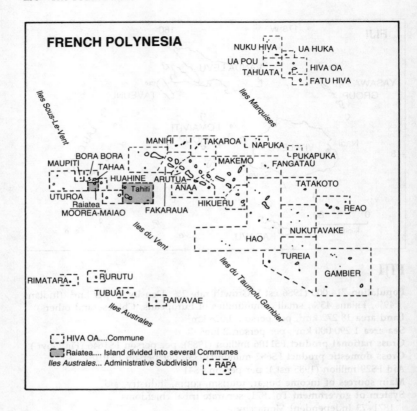

FRENCH POLYNESIA

Population 181 400 (1986 est.); Growth rate 3%; Density 55 per km². (Polynesians about 70%, others mainly European and Chinese).

Land area 3265 km²; per person 0.018 per km²

Sea area 5 030 000 km²; per person 27 km²

Gross national product US$1260 million (1983 est.); per person US$8190 (World Bank)

Aid US$500 million (1986 est.); per capita US$2250

Main sources of income French military activity and aid, tourism, copra, vanilla, pearl shell.

System of government To 1800s independent chiefdoms.

Mid-1800s Tahiti became the centre of power under the Pomare monarchs. Britain refused to grant a Protectorate.

1842 French protectorate over Pomare domains. Gradually extended.

1957 Reconstituted as French Polynesia, a Territory of France, with government control vested in the French High Commissioner.

1977 New Statute gives more local autonomy

1985 Autonomie Interne (partial self-government) from 29 June

Territorial governing bodies Territorial Assembly (41 elected members) whose members elected 6 persons to the Government Council. Represented in Paris by an elected Senator and two elected Deputies.

Local Government Communes for each island or district.

Political parties (and numbers of seats won in March 1986 elections). Tahoera'a Huira'atira (21), Amuitahira'a no Porinesia (7), Here Ai'a Ta'atiraa Porinesia (4), Ia Mana te Nuna's (3), Tavini Huiraatira no Porinesia (2), three others (1 each).

Head of Government French High Commissioner, who is Chairman of Government Council, Mr Pierre Angeli

Head of State President of France.

President of Territorial Assembly M. Gaston Flosse.

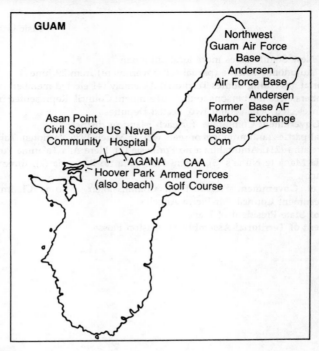

GUAM

Population 120 500 (1986 est.); Growth rate 2%; Density 220 per km² (About 24 000 of the total are U.S.A. military and their dependents)

Land area 549 km²; per person 0.005 km²

Sea area 218 000 km²; per person 1.8 km²

Gross national product US$690 million (1983 est.); per person US$6070 (World Bank)

Aid US$38.2 million (1983); per person US$317

Main sources of income Most of the population is directly or indirectly dependent on U.S.A. military expenditure which in 1983 amounted to US$712 million; Tourism is also significant.

System of government Previously Chamorros organised in matrilineal clans
1565 Spain took possession
1899 Annexed by U.S.A. after Spanish-American war
1950 An unincorporated Territory of the U.S.A.
At this time Guam residents and descendants were given U.S.A. citizenship. A local commission in 1986 was drafting an act for submission to the U.S.A. Congress to restructure the Territory's status to that of a U.S.A. Commonwealth.

Territorial governing body Legislative Assembly of 21 Senators (One non-voting delegate is also elected to U.S.A. House of Representatives)

Local Government 19 municipalities.

Political parties Democratic and Republican.

Head of State President of the U.S.A.

Head of Government 1986 to present — Governor Joseph Ada; 1983 to present — Governor Ricardo J. Bordallo; 1979 to 1982 Governor Paul Calvo.

Delegate to U.S.A. House of Representatives Congressman Ben G. Blaz.

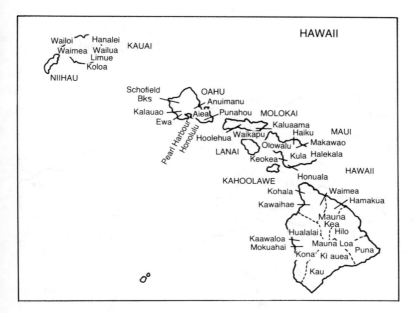

HAWAII

Population 1 118 600 (1983) (includes 125 300 military personnel and their dependents, and 107 500 tourists); Growth rate 1970–80 25.3%; Ethnic composition (1982) Caucasian 25%, Japanese 22%, Chinese 5%, Filipino 12%, Hawaiian 1%, Part Hawaiian 18%, Korean 2%, Black 1%, Puerto Rican 1%, Samoan 1%, Others 12%.

Land area 16 641 km²; per person 0.015 km²; density 67 per km²

Sea area 2 157 985 km²; per person 1.9 km²

Gross state product US$13 billion (1981); per person US$11 622

Main sources of income Tourism, military expenditure, sugar.

System of government To 1810 separate tribal chiefdoms
   1810–93 Hawaiian monarchy
   1893–98 U.S.A. coup to establish Republic of Hawaii
   1898–1900 U.S.A interim government
   1900 Annexed by U.S.A.
   1959 50th State of U.S.A.

State governing bodies (Under U.S.A. Federal Government) House of Representatives (51 members with 2 year term) and Senate (25 members with 4 year term, staggered). Universal suffrage for resident U.S.A. citizens 18 and over. No communal or restricted representation. One elected representative in U.S.A. Senate and two in U.S.A. Congress.

Local Government 9 Counties, 28 Neighbourhood Boards.

Political parties Democrat, Republican and several small parties. The Democrats control both Houses.

Head of National Government President of U.S.A.

Head of State Government 1974–1986 Governor George Ariyoshi.

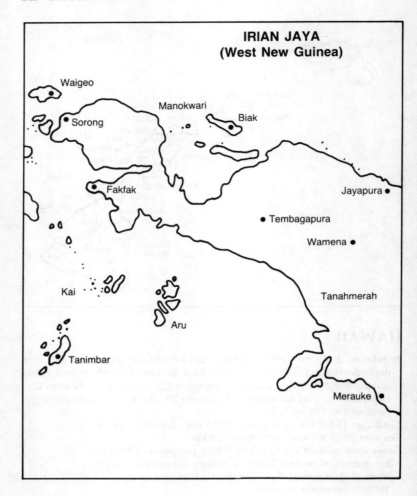

IRIAN JAYA

Population 1 424 800 (1983); Growth rate not available.
Land area 410 000 km²; land per person 0.29 km².
Population density 3.5 per km²
Gross domestic product not available.
Main sources of income Nutmeg, mace, copra, fish products, crocodile skins, copper, oil and other minerals, timber.

System of government

From sixteenth century (nominally) under the authority of Moluccan Sultans.

1828 proclaimed Dutch possession.

1962 Dutch handed over to Indonesia due to U.S.A. and U.N. pressure.

1969 declared a Province of Indonesia.

1973 renamed Irian Jaya.

Governing body

Effectively a military dictatorship under Indonesia.

Political parties Free Papua Movement (opposes present regime).

Head of State President of Indonesia.

Head of Government Governor Brigadier General Soctian.

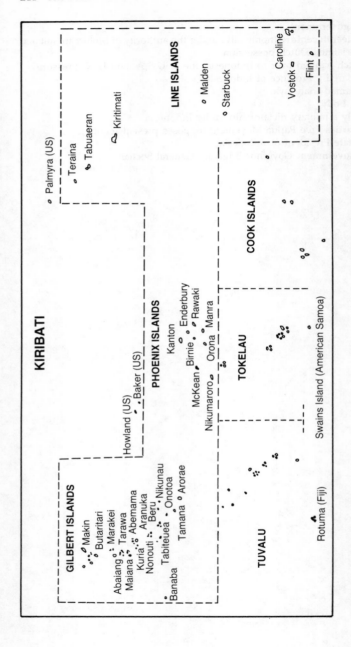

KIRIBATI

Population 63 300 (1986 est.); Growth rate 1.5%; Density 88 per km²
Land area 719 km²; per person 0.01 km²
Sea area 3 550 000 km²; per person 56 km²
Gross national product US$30 million (1983 est.); per person US$460 (World Bank)
Gross domestic product A$25 million (1982); per person A$421 (Asian Development Bank)
Aid A$17 million; per person A$287
Main sources of income Copra, remittances from I-Kiribati in Nauru and on overseas ships, aid from United Kingdom, Australia, and other sources. Phosphate gave most revenue until 1979 and interest on invested phosphate revenue is substantial.
System of government Independent councils in most cases for each island or major section of an island.
  1892 British protectorate.
  1915 Annexed by Britain together with Ellice Islands (Tuvalu) as Gilbert and Ellice Islands colony.
  1967 Legislative Assembly formed.
  1976 Ellice Islands separated and became Tuvalu again.
  1979 Independent Republic.
National governing body Maneaba Ni Maungatabu (Parliament) of 36 members elected by universal suffrage by citizens over 18 years of age.
Local Government 17 elected Island Councils and 2 elected Urban Councils.
Political parties None until 1985 when an opposition Christian Democratic Party was formed under Dr Harry Tong.
Head of State and Head of Government President Ieremia Tabai since independence in 1979.

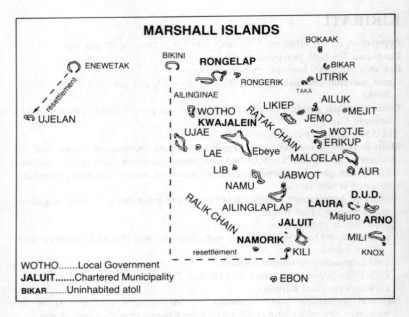

MARSHALL ISLANDS

WOTHO.......Local Government
JALUIT.......Chartered Municipality
BIKAR.........Uninhabited atoll

MARSHALL ISLANDS

Population 36 800 (1986 est.); Growth rate 2.7%; Density 204 per km²
Land area 180 km²; per person 0.005 km²
Sea area 2 131 000 km²; per person 58 km²
Gross national product US$46 million (1984 est.); per person US$1303 (Dev. Plan)
Aid US$19 million; per person US$531 (but U.S.A. military and other sources account for much more.)
Main sources of income U.S.A. military activity and U.S.A. aid.
System of government Traditionally chiefly rule of clusters of islands.
1886 German Protectorate established.
1914 Japan took the islands from Germany militarily.
1921 Japan acquired a League of Nations Mandate over the islands.
1944 U.S.A. took the islands from Japan militarily.
1947 U.S.A. acquired a United Nations Trusteeship over the islands.
1965 Congress of Micronesia established.
1979 Marshall Islands constitution ratified and government partially separated from U.S.A. Trust Territory administration.
1982 Draft 'Compact of Free Association' with U.S.A. vetoed by U.S.A. as it gave Marshall Islands the option of independence
1983 Revised 'Compact of Free Association' acceptable to U.S.A. passed by 60% vote in referendum. The Compact gives U.S.A. long-term effective control of major issues.
National governing bodies Nitijela (Parliament) of 33 elected members.
Local Government 25 Local (island) Councils and 3 Municipalities
Head of Government 1979–present President Amata Kabua.

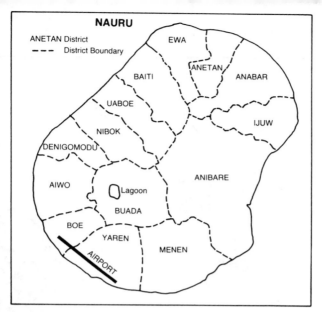

NAURU

Population 9100 (1986 est.); Growth rate 2.4%; Density 433 per km². (Non-indigenous population likely to decline with exhaustion of phosphate)

Land area 21 km²; per person 0.002 km²

Sea area 320 000 km²; per person 35 km²

Gross national product US$230 million (1978); US$47 million (1982); per person US$28 742 (1978), US$5 980 (1982) (UNDP 1985). Major fluctuations due to changing world phosphate prices and in volume of phosphate exports.

Aid Nil

Main sources of income Phosphate exports and income from invested revenue from phosphate.

System of government Until last century 12 clans.

1888 Incorporated with German Marshall Islands Protectorate.

1914 Australia took over militarily.

1919 League of Nations Mandate to Britain, Australia, and New Zealand, but administered by Australia.

1943 Japan took over militarily.

1945 Australia took over militarily.

1946 U.N. Trusteeship governed by Australia on behalf of Australia, New Zealand, and United Kingdom.

1968 Independent Republic.

National governing body Parliament of 18 elected representatives

Local Government Nauru Local Government Council (covers whole republic) of 9 elected members from 14 Districts

Political parties Nauru Party formed 1977 but not active. Most representatives are independents.

Head of State and Head of Government 1968–76 and 1978 to present, President Hammer de Roburt; 1976–78 President Bernard Dowiyogo; for a brief period during 1978, President Lagumot Harris; and a brief period in 1986, President Kenneth Adeang.

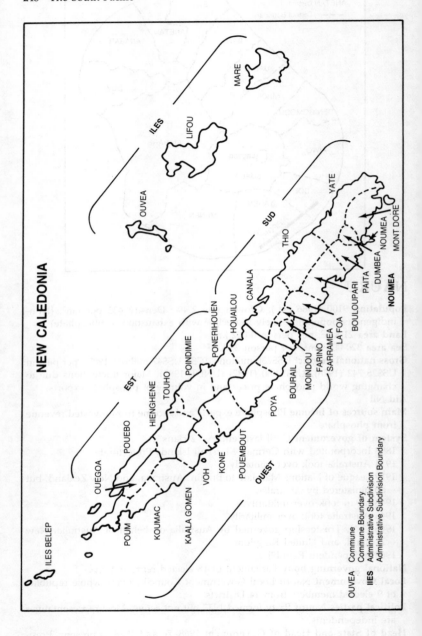

NEW CALEDONIA

ILES BELEP

POUM

OUEGOA

POUEBO

KOUMAC

HIENGHENE

TOUHO

KAALA GOMEN

VOH

KONE

POUEMBOUT

POYA

POINDIMIE

PONERIHOUEN

HOUAILOU

CANALA

BOURAIL

MOINDOU

FARINO

SARRAMEA

LA FOA

BOULOUPARI

PAITA

DUMBEA

NOUMEA

NOUMEA

MONT DORE

YATE

THIO

SUD

EST

OUEST

ILES BELEP

POUM

ILES

OUVEA

LIFOU

MARE

OUVEA Commune
         Commune Boundary
         Administrative Subdivision
         Administrative Subdivision Boundary

IIES

NEW CALEDONIA

Population 151 200 (1986 est.); Growth rate 1.2%; Density 8 per km². Ethnic breakdown in 1983, Melanesians 61 780 (42%); Europeans 53 974 (37%); Other islanders, mainly Wallisian and Tahitian 18 956 (13%); Indonesians, Vietnamese and others 10 758 (7½%)

Land area 19 103 km²; per person 0.126 km²

Sea area 1 740 000 km²; per person 11.5 km²

Gross national product US$1140 million (1983); per person US$7790 (World Bank)

Aid (Not available)

Main sources of income Nickel, French aid and military expenditure, tourism.

System of government Diverse language and cultural groups, largely autonomous.

1853 Annexed by France, administered by military governors.

1864 French penal settlement established.

1868 Forced resettlement and confinement of Melanesians began.

1878 Rebellion of Melanesian tribes repressed: leaders killed or deported.

1917 Second Melanesian rebellion: leaders killed or deported.

Since World War II local campaign for self-government and/or independence.

1953 Voting rights granted to Melanesians.

1958 Self-government with elected Parliament and Cabinet, followed by armed rebellion by European settlers and abolition of self-government. Various constitutional modifications since, but remains a Territory of France.

Territorial governing bodies (under the French Republic) Territorial Congress of 46 elected members (in which RPCR has the majority in 1986. More power was vested briefly in the 4 Regional Councils (established in 1985) three of which are controlled by FLNKS, and the fourth (Noumea) by the RPCR, but all significant powers were taken back by France in mid-1986. Represented in Paris by a Senator (electoral college vote) and two deputies (elected by universal suffrage).

Local Government 32 Communes.

Main political parties Front Libération National Kanak Socialiste (FLNKS) which is mainly Melanesian; Rassemblement pour la Calédonie (RPCR) which is the main French party; Front National which is also French, but extreme right wing; and other minor parties.

Head of State President of France.

Head of Government High Commissioner (appointed by France).

President of Territorial Congress 1986 Dick Ukeiwe (elected, RPCR).

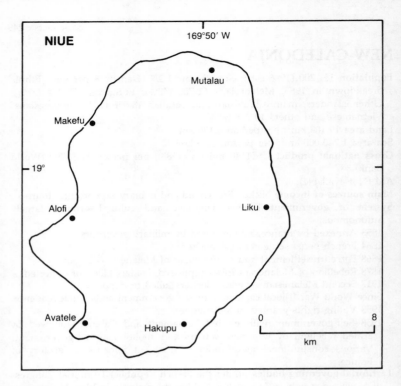

NIUE · 169°50' W · Mutalau · Makefu · 19° · Alofi · Liku · Avatele · Hakupu · 0 · 8 · km

NIUE

Population 2756 (1985); Growth rate (negative) 3.3%; Density 10.6 per km²

Land area 259 km²; per person 0.9 km²

Sea area 390 000 km²; per person 150 km²

Gross domestic product NZ$6.7 million (1984); per person NZ$2351

Aid NZ$6.5 million (1985); per person NZ$2281

Main sources of income Aid from New Zealand, remittances from Niueans abroad, postage stamps, handcraft, limes, honey, coconut cream, and fresh produce.

System of government Previously independent families and tribal groupings.
   1876 elected King.
   1900 British protectorate.
   1901 Annexed to New Zealand as part of Cook Islands.
   1904 Separate administration established.
   1966 Substantial local autonomy granted.
   1974 Self-government in free association with New Zealand.

National governing body Legislative Assembly of 20 elected members; 14 from village constituencies and 6 from a common national roll.

Local Government 14 Village Councils.

Political parties None.

Head of State Governor-General of New Zealand.

Head of Government Sir Robert R. Rex C.B.E., Leader of Government Business since 1966 and Premier since self-government in 1974.

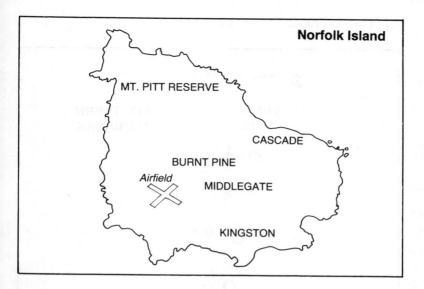

NORFOLK ISLAND

Population 1900 (1985 est.) plus 400 to 1200 visitors at any time; growth rate (residents) 1%; density about 78 per km² (including visitors). Immigration is controlled.

Land area 34.5 km², per person 0.018 km²

Gross domestic product A$4 million (1985 est.); per person A$2105

Aid Nil

Main sources of income Tourism, philatelic sales, customs duty.

Systems of government

Previously uninhabited, Norfolk was first settled in 1788 and governed as a British colony with naval, convict and free settlers.

Abandoned in 1814, resettled in 1825 as a penal colony for the worst criminals from Australia. It was abandoned again in 1856.

In 1856 it was resettled by the descendants of the *Bounty* mutineers and their Tahitian wives, with local self-government under the Governor of New South Wales.

1897, declared a Dependency of New South Wales. Although never annexed to Australia, in 1914 the United Kingdom government placed Norfolk 'under the authority' of the Australian Commonwealth Government.

1979, Legislative Assembly established and a gradual transfer of self-government powers initiated. Some powers remain with the Australian Commonwealth Government.

Citizenship Australian

Governing bodies Legislative Assembly (9 elected members) for local government;

A resident Administrator appointed by the Governor-General of Australia represents that government in matters of retained powers.

Head of State Governor-General of Australia.

Administrator Commodore J.A. Mathew CVO, MBE, RANEM

Head of Government elected Chief Minister of Norfolk Island, Hon, D.E. Buffet AM, MLA.

FARALLON de PAJAROS

MAUG
ASUMCION

**NORTHERN
MARIANAS**

AGRIMAN

PUGUAN

ALAMAGN

GUGUAM

SARIGAN

ANATAHAN •

FARALLON de MEDINILLA

SAIPAN

TINIAN

AGUIJAN

ROTA

NORTHERN MARIANAS

Population 20 400 (1986 est.): Growth rate 1.7%; Density 43 per km²
Land area 471 km²; per person 0.023 km²
Sea area 1 823 000 km²; per person 89 km²
Gross domestic product (Not available)
Aid (Not available)
Main sources of income Tourism, U.S.A. aid
System of government In ancient times, autonomous tribes.
  From 1565 Spanish possession.
  1898 sold to Germany after Spanish–American war.
  1914 Annexed by Japan and administered by military forces.
  1921 Japan governed under League of Nations Mandate.
  1944 Conquered by U.S.A., administered by U.S.A. Navy.
  1947 Incorporated in U.S.A. Trust Territory of the Pacific Islands.
  1975 Separated from U.S.A. Trust Territory of the Pacific Islands administration but remains part of Trust Territory.
  1978 Commonwealth of Northern Mariana Islands formed, in political union with the U.S.A.
Commonwealth governing bodies House of Representatives with 15 elected representatives; Senate with 9 elected Senators.
Local Government Municipalities with elected officials.
Political parties Democratic and Republican.
Head of National Government President of the U.S.A.
Head of Commonwealth Government 1978–1981 Governor Carlos S. Camacho; 1982–1986 Governor Pedro P. Tenorio.

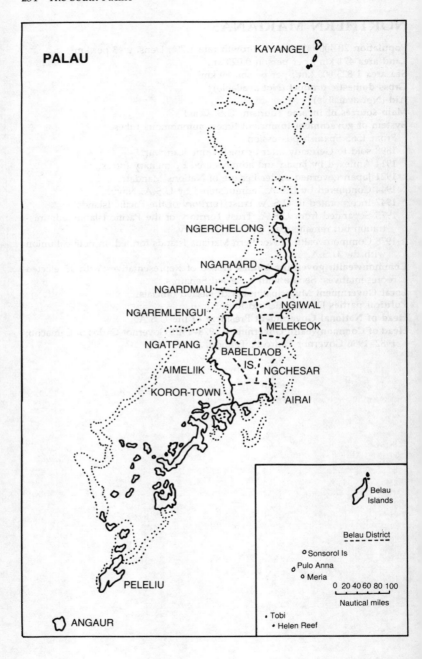

PALAU

KAYANGEL

NGERCHELONG

NGARAARD

NGARDMAU

NGIWAL

NGAREMLENGUI

MELEKEOK

NGATPANG

BABELDAOB
IS.

AIMELIIK

NGCHESAR

KOROR-TOWN

AIRAI

PELELIU

ANGAUR

Belau
Islands

Belau District
- - - - - - -

○ Sonsorol Is

○ Pulo Anna
○ Meria

0 20 40 60 80 100

Nautical miles

• Tobi
◆ Helen Reef

PALAU (OR BELAU)

Population 12 200 (1986 est.); (including 45 km² of uninhabitable rock islands).
  Density 24 per km²
Land area 494 km²; per person 0.04 km²
Sea area 629 000 km²; per person 52 km²
Gross domestic product US$32 million (1983); per person US$2623
Aid US$23 million (1984); per person US$1885
Main sources of income U.S.A. aid, fisheries, tourism.
System of government Traditionally two major confederations.
  1886 Formal Spanish annexation.
  1899 Sold to Germany with other Spanish possessions.
  1914 Japan conquers German Micronesian possessions.
  1921 Mandated to Japan under League of Nations Mandate.
  1944 U.S.A. conquers Japanese Micronesian possessions.
  1947–present Included in U.S.A. Trust Territory of the Pacific Islands (USTT)
    under United Nations.
  1981 Republic of Palau (Belau) Constitution adopted and government
    elected, still within USTT. U.S.A. control of major issues continues
    through 'Compact of Free Association'.
Territorial governing bodies Senate 14 elected members; House of Delegates
  16 elected members
Local Government 16 Municipalities (called 'state governments')
Political parties Liberals and Progressives main parties to 1978, Modekngai
  (espousing traditional Palauan values), Tia Belau (workers, students etc).
Head of Government 1981–85 President Haruo Remeliik (murdered); 1985
  to–present President Lazarus Salii.

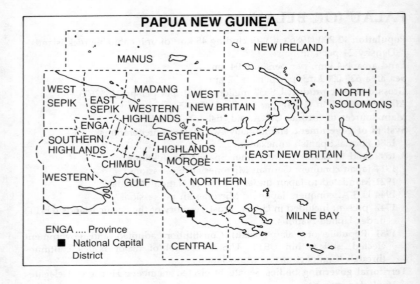

PAPUA NEW GUINEA

MANUS

WEST
SEPIK

EAST
SEPIK

ENGA

SOUTHERN
HIGHLANDS

WESTERN

GULF

CHIMBU

MADANG

WESTERN
HIGHLANDS

EASTERN
HIGHLANDS

MOROBE

NORTHERN

WEST
NEW BRITAIN

NEW IRELAND

NORTH
SOLOMONS

EAST NEW BRITAIN

MILNE BAY

CENTRAL

ENGA .... Province
■ National Capital
District

PAPUA NEW GUINEA

Population 3 412 000 (1986 est.); Growth rate 2.1%; Density 7.4 per km²
Land area 462 243 km²; per person 0.135 km²
Sea area 3 120 000 km²; per person 0.91 km²
Gross national product US$2510 million (1983); per person US$790 (World Bank)
Gross domestic product K1750 million (1982); per person K559 (Asian Development Bank)
Aid K202 million (1985 est.); per person K60
Main sources of income Copper, gold, coconut products, cocoa, coffee, palm oil, timber products, fish, aid mostly from Australia.
System of government Until last century isolated autonomous communities.
   1884 Protectorates declared by Britain in Papua, Germany in New Guinea.
   1905 British New Guinea became Papua, administered by Australia.
   1914 Australia conquers German territory and from 1921 administers under League of Nations Mandate.
   From World War II Papua and New Guinea administered together, although the latter as a United Nations Trust Territory.
   1964 House of Assembly established (64 members, enlarged to 94 in 1968 and to 100 in 1972).
   1973 Self-government instituted.
   1975 Independence, and joined the Commonwealth.
National governing body House of Assembly (Parliament) with 111 elected members.

Provincial Government 19 provinces and 1 National Capital District, each with its own elected Provincial Assembly, cabinet, premier and ministers.

Local Government Elected councils responsible for community affairs.

Political parties Pangu Pati, United Party, Peoples Progress Party, Melanesian Alliance, National Party People's Democratic Movement and other small parties.

Head of State Governor-General, 1975–77, Sir John Guise; 1977–1983, Sir Tore Lokoloko; 1983–present, Sir Kingsford Dibela.

Head of Government Prime Minister 1975–80, 1982–85, Rt. Hon. Michael Somare; 1980–82 Sir Julius Chan; 1985 to present Hon. Paias Wingti.

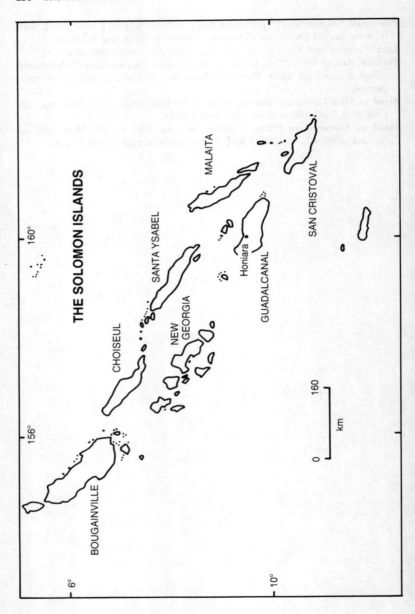

THE SOLOMON ISLANDS

BOUGAINVILLE

CHOISEUL

SANTA YSABEL

NEW GEORGIA

MALAITA

Honiara

GUADALCANAL

SAN CRISTOVAL

156°

160°

6°

10°

0   160

km

SOLOMON ISLANDS

Population 276 400 (1986 est.); Growth rate 3.3%; Density 10 per km^2
Land area 28 530 km^2; per person 0.10 km^2
Sea area 1 340 000 km^2; per person 5 km^2
Gross national product US$160 million (1983); per person US$640 (World Bank)
Gross domestic product SI$175 million (1983); per person SI$694 (Asian Development Bank)
Aid A$14 million (1980); per person A$137
Main sources of income Fish, timber, copra, aid.
System of government Autonomous communities.

1893 after abuses of labour trade Britain declared Protectorate over most islands. Others added in 1898, 1899, and 1900.
1921 Advisory Council instituted.
1942–43 Military occupation of most islands by Japan.
1960 Legislative Council and Executive Council formed.
1970 Governing Council replaces Legislative and Executive Councils.
1974 Legislative Assembly formed (24 members, increased to 38 in 1976).
1976 Self-government established with Chief Minister and 8 other Ministers.
July 1978 Independence as member of the Commonwealth.

National governing body Legislative Assembly of 38 elected members.
Provincial Government 7 elected Provincial Assemblies each with their own premier and ministers.
Political parties Between 1968 and 1976 early 'parties' were formed 'exclusively by members of the legislature after the results of elections were known. Their manifestos were casual, inconsistent and often not in line with the arguments their members presented in debates on policy matters.' (Ulufa'alu, 1983). 1973 saw the formation of the United Solomon Islands Party (USIPA) and the Peoples Progress Party (PPP), both of which later disintegrated. 1976 saw the formation of the first nation-wide party, the National Democratic Party (NADEPA — at first known as the Nationalists Party) supported by the main trade union. Between independence in 1978 and 1980 there emerged the Solomon Islands Peoples Alliance Party (PAP), formed by the merging of the PPP and the Rural Alliance and led by Solomon Mamaloni; and the Solomon Islands United Party (SIUP) led by Peter Kenilorea, and incorporating many former USIPA members. In 1985 Solomone Ano Sagofenua (SAS) party was formed by ex-civil servants and in October the same year the Nationalist Front. Throughout, the many independent members have formed an often powerful but unstable 'Independents Group.'
Head of Government Prime Minister 1978–81 and 1984–1986 Rt. Hon. Sir Peter Kenilorea; 1981–84 Hon. Solomon Mamaloni; 1986 — present Hon. Ezekiel Alebua
Head of State Governor-General since Independence, Sir Baddeley Devesi.

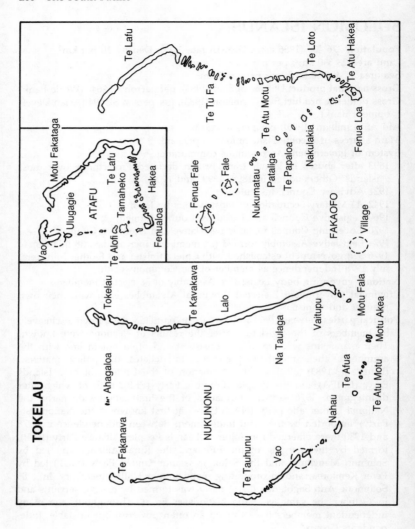

TOKELAU

Population 1600 (1986 est.); Growth rate zero; Density 160 per km^2
Land area 10 km^2; per person 0.006 km^2
Sea area 290 000 km^2; per person 181 km^2
Gross national product US$1.2 million (1982); per person US$760 (UNDP)
Aid NZ$3.8 million (1986 est); per person NZ$2375
Main sources of income Copra, remittances and aid from New Zealand.
System of government Autonomous atoll communities.
   1889 British Protectorate declared.
   1916 Incorporated into the Gilbert and Ellice Islands Colony.
   1925 New Zealand administered Tokelau for U.K. from Western Samoa as
   a territory of New Zealand.
   1948 Incorporated within the territorial boundaries of New Zealand. New
   Zealand Secretary of Foreign Affairs is the Administrator of Tokelau.
Governing bodies (Under New Zealand Government) Island Council (*Taupu-
lega*) for each island. Council members nominate candidates for the *Faipule*
(who is Chairman of the Island Council) and *Pulenuku* (Mayor of the village),
and all persons over 21 years of age may vote to elect persons to those
offices, every three years. The Faipule has executive, political and judicial
functions and is the chief representative of the Administrator (and the
Crown) on the island, and is the middleman between the Tokelau people
and the New Zealand Government.
Political parties None.
Head of State Governor-General of New Zealand
Head of Government New Zealand Secretary for Foreign Affairs as
Administrator.

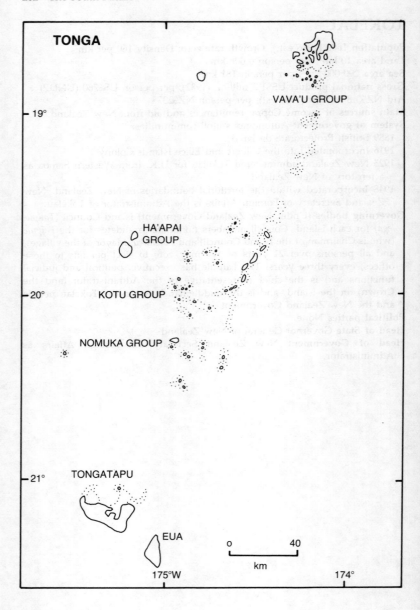

TONGA

Population 100 100 (1986 est.); Growth rate 1.1%; Density 143 per km²
Land area 699 km²; per person 0.007 km²
Sea area 700 000 km²; per person 7 km²
Gross national product US$83 million (1983); per person US$740 (World Bank)
Gross domestic product T$77 million (1983); per person T$912 (Asian Development Bank)
Aid A$13 million (1980); per person A$134
Main sources of income Copra, fruits, tourism, remittances from Tongans in New Zealand, Australia, and the U.S.A., and aid mainly from the same sources.
System of government
Until last century power concentrated on leading chieftainships.
In 1850s King George Tupou I emerged supreme.
1875 constitutional monarchy established.
1900 Friendship Treaty with United Kingdom gave Protectorate status.
1970 Complete independence restored.
Governing bodies
Privy Council is comprised of the King, the Cabinet, the Governor of Vava'u and the Governor of Ha'apai. The Privy Council is the highest executive authority.
Legislative Assembly is comprised of 7 appointees of the King, who are Ministers; 7 representatives of the nobles (who are elected by their 33 peers); and 7 representatives elected by popular vote every three years. All persons over 21 may vote. 4 of the 7 elected representatives are in business. The King appoints the Speaker from one of the nobles.
Political parties None.
Head of State HRH King Taufa'ahau Tupou IV since 1965.
Head of Government HRH Prince Fatafehi Tu'ipelehake since 1965 as Premier and since 1970 (with the change of designation at full independence) as Prime Minister.

TUVALU

○ NANUMEA

       ○ NIUTAO

    ○ NANUMANGA

           ◊ NUI

                  ɞ VAITUPU

                      °ᵒ NUKUFETAU

                      FUNAFUTI ᵒᵒᵒ

                           NUKULAELAE ◊

                      NULAKITA ₀

TUVALU

Population 8200 (1986 est.); Growth rate 1.7%; Density 315 per km²
Land area 26 km²; per person 0.003 km²
Sea area 900 000 km²; per person 110 km²
Gross national product US$5 million (1983); per person US$660
Gross domestic product A$3.7 million (1980); per person A$504
Aid A$4 million (1980); per person A$573
Main sources of income Copra, remittances from Tuvaluans in Nauru and on ships, aid, philatelic sales.
System of government
   Formerly separate chieftainships.
   1892 Gilbert and Ellice Islands Protectorate founded.
   1916 Status changed to Gilbert and Ellice Islands Colony.
   1 October 1975 Separation of Tuvalu from Gilbert Islands.
   1 October 1978 Independence as a member of the Commonwealth.
National governing body Parliament of 12 elected members.
Local government Elected Island Councils on each island.
Political parties None.
Head of State Governor-General since independence Hon. Penitala Teo.
Head of Government Prime Minister, 1978–81 Hon. Toaripi Lauti; 1981 to present Dr Tomasi Puapua.

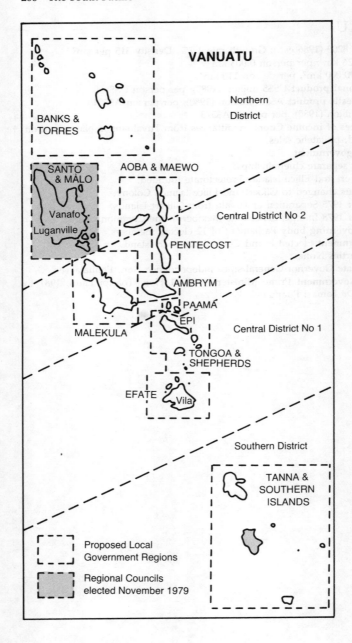

VANUATU

Northern District

BANKS & TORRES

SANTO & MALO

AOBA & MAEWO

Vanafo
Luganville

Central District No 2

PENTECOST

AMBRYM

PAAMA

EPI

Central District No 1

MALEKULA

TONGOA & SHEPHERDS

EFATE   Vila

Southern District

TANNA & SOUTHERN ISLANDS

Proposed Local Government Regions

Regional Councils elected November 1979

VANUATU

Population 138 000 (1986 est.); Growth rate 3.1%; Density 12 per km²
Land area 11 880 km²; per person 0.09 km²
Sea area 680 000 km²; per person 5 km²
Gross national product US$99 million (1982); per person US$810 (UNDP)
Gross domestic product 11 000 million Vatu, or roughly US$110 million; per person 79 710 vatu. But much of this money is generated by the expatriate sector, including the international finance centre. The estimated GDP for the Melanesian population (including an assessed US$100 per person for the value of subsistence production) is only 4000 million vatu, or about 29 000 vatu per person. This is less than US$300 per person and it is on this basis that Vanuatu qualifies for LDC (Least Developed Country) status with United Nations agencies. (These figures derive from National Planning provisional estimates.)
Aid 900 million vatu (1985 est.); per person 6522 vatu.
Main sources of income Copra, tourism, fish, beef, aid from Australia, France, U.K., New Zealand and other sources.
System of government Until last century independent tribal groups.
   1888 Britain and France established joint Naval Commission.
   1906 French–British Condominium.
   1974–75 Constitutional reforms and establishment of Representative Assembly.
   30 July 1980 Independence as a member of the Commonwealth.
National governing bodies Parliament of 39 elected members; National Council of Chiefs (Malfat Mauri) advises the government on matters of culture and tradition.
Local Government 11 Local Government Councils
Political parties Vanuaaku Pati which has been in power since Independence, and the UMP (Union of Moderate Parties) which is a combination of several small, mainly French-speaking groups, including Union des Communautés des Nouvelles Hebrides, Mouvement Autonomiste des Nouvelles Hebrides, and several other small parties. Nagriemel, once contending for a separate northern state, is now not active. Peoples Democratic Party formed 1986.
Head of State President Ati George Sokomanu since independence.
Head of Government Prime Minister Father Walter Lini since independence.

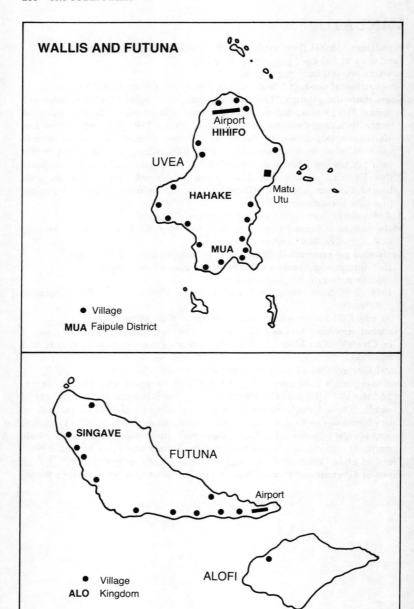

WALLIS AND FUTUNA

Population 13 600 (1986 est.); Growth rate 4.0%; Density 55 per km²
Land area 255 km²; per person 0.019 km²
Sea area 300 000 km²; per person 22 km²
Gross domestic product (Not available)
Aid (Not available)
Main sources of income Remittances from New Caledonia, aid from France.
System of government Last century struggles between rival chiefs for supremacy.
   1842 French Protectorate 'accepted in principle'.
   1877 French Protectorate formalised for Wallis, 1888 for Futuna.
   1913 Declared a Colony of France, but not ratified.
   1961 Overseas Territory of France following 1959 Referendum.
Governing bodies Territorial Assembly of 20, elected by universal suffrage, advises the French Administrator together with a Council consisting of the traditional King of Wallis, two Kings of Futuna, and 3 elected members. One Deputy (Benjamin Brial) to Paris elected by common roll election. One Senator (Sosefo Makape Papilio) elected by the General Assembly.
Head of State President of France.
Head of Government Administrator Robert Thil (French civil servant). King of Wallis: Singave Aio Lavelua; Conseilleur Basilio Tui; President of Territorial Assembly Manuele Lisiahi.

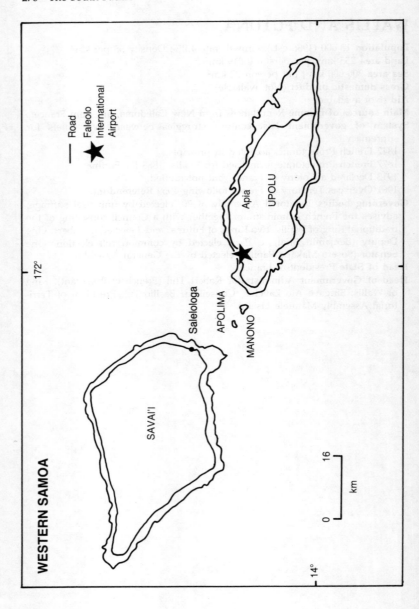

WESTERN SAMOA

SAVAI'I

Salelologa

APOLIMA

MANONO

UPOLU

Apia

Faleolo
International
Airport

—— Road
★ Faleolo
International
Airport

172°

14°

0   16
km

WESTERN SAMOA

Population 161 500 (1986 est.); Growth rate 0.7%; Density 55 per km²
Land area 2934 km²; per person 0.018 km²
Sea area 120 000 km²; per person 0.7 km²
Gross national product US$49 million (1982 est.); per person US$310 (UNDP)
Gross domestic product WS Tala 85 million (1983 est. in constant 1980 prices); per person WS Tala 529 (5th Development Plan).
Aid WS Tala 24 million (1986 est.) not including concessional loans; per person WS Tala 149.
Main sources of income Coconut oil, cocoa, remittances from Samoans in New Zealand and the U.S.A., aid from Australia, New Zealand, and other sources.
System of government Until last century ruled by chiefly families, often in transient unions.
   1889 Independent government under Malietoa Laupepa.
   1899 Annexed as Colony by Germany.
   1914 New Zealand took German Colony by military force.
   1920–46 Mandated Territory of New Zealand under League of Nations
   Since World War II a U.N. Trusteeship administered by New Zealand during preparation for self-government.
   Since 1962 Independent as a member of the Commonwealth.
National governing body Legislative Assembly (47 seats) made up of 45 *matai* (titled heads of families) and voted for by matai only plus 2 seats (formerly known as 'European' electorates) voted for by popular election.
Local Government No formal local government but an autonomous *Fono* (Council of Chiefs) governs local community affairs in each village.
Political parties Human Rights Protection Party (formed 1979); Christian Democrats (formed 1985) but in 1986 the Government was a Coalition of CDP and part of HRPP.
Prime Ministers
   1962–70 Hon. Fiame Mataafa Mulinu'u II
   1970–73 Hon. Tupua Tamasese Leolofi IV
   1973–76 Hon. Fiame Mataafa Mulinu'u II (died in office)
   1976 (until election) Hon. Tupua Tamasese Leolofi IV
   1976–82 Hon. Tupuola Taisi Tufuga Efi
   1982 Hon. Va'ai Koloni (deprived of office for electoral irregularities)
   1982 Hon. Tupuola Taisi Tufuga Efi (until end of 1982 when his budget was rejected)
   1982–Dec. 1985 Hon. Tofilau Eti Alesana
   Dec. 1985 to present Hon Va'ai Kolone
Head of State Malietoa Tanumafili II since independence.

Index

Taufinau, Cardinal, Pio, 93
Tax, 75, 93, 135
Teaching, 37
Technology, 7, 19, 21, 22, 55, 64
Telecommunications, 175
Television 31, 47
Te Rangi Hiroa (Sir Peter Buck),
   24
Tevi, Lorini, 15
Theologians, 29
Thermal heat, 21; wonderland,
   57
Third World, 167, 186, 201
Tika, 102
Timakata, Rev., Fred, 77
Timber, 185
Time, 26, 83
Tiurai, 103
Tobacco, 93
Tokelau, 5, 17, 152
Tolai of New Britain, 123
Tonga, 5, 12, 17, 143–5, 159;
   Tongan culture, 102, 196;
   economy, 139, 159, 203;
   ta'ovala, 28, 29
Tongatapu, 12, 145
Toorak, 31
Torres Strait, 4
Totalitarianism, 24
Tourism, 30–2, 54, 93–5, 100,
   103, 113, 134, 137
Tractors, 56
Trade, 19–20, 54, 184
Traditional child-rearing, 34–7;
   clothing, 99; custom, 63–81;
   design, 95; magic, 48; names,
   29; philosophy, 80–1;
   precedents, 29, 156; systems,
   111; technology, 56
Trade unions, 89, 155, 191
Travel industry, 99–100
Trust Territory of the Pacific
   Islands, 138
Truk, 6, 151

Tuamotu, 6
Tuna, 120
Turtles, 20
Tuvalu, 17, 63

Unemployment, 137, 207
Umbrella organisations, 171
United Kingdom, 15, 112, 146–7
United Nations, 156, 182; UN
   Development Advisory Team,
   172; UN Trust Territory, 143
United States of America, 12,
   15, 54, 121, 181–3, 187, 192,
   194, 197, 205–6
University, 171; degrees, 36;
   University of the South
   Pacific, 26, 63, 171, 175, 189,
   193, 203
Urban centres, 12, 36;
   proleteriat, 36, 39–40;
   urbanisation, 12, 84, 91, 137
U.S.S.R., 15, 47, 54, 167, 187–8,
   206
Utility, 56

Van Trease, 147
Vanilla, 123
Vanuatu, 4–6, 12, 17, 42, 46,
   135, 188
Vernacular, 44, 48–9, 68; song,
   68
Vietnam, 181, 188, 192;
   Vietnamese, 8, 10
Village 36, 80
Viti Levu, 12
Volunteers, 10, 92; Volunteer
   Service Association, 10, 205

Wage earning, 39, 91, 182
Wake Island, 152
Wallis and Futuna, 12, 46
War, 36, 108, 112; WWI, 125;
   WWII, 10, 75, 125–6, 145, 173
Wealth, 69

The author

Ron Crocombe is Professor of Pacific Studies and was from 1976 to 1985 Director of the Institute of Pacific Studies at the University of the South Pacific, which serves students from ten member countries in the South Pacific from its main campus in Suva, Fiji. Formerly Director of the New Guinea Research Unit of the Australian National University, he also held teaching appointments at the University of California and the University of Hawaii. Before that he worked for some years in government in the Cook Islands.

Professor Crocombe was born in New Zealand but has lived most of his life in various Pacific Islands, and has conducted research in most major island groups. His publications include a dozen books and monographs about the Pacific, and over a hundred articles in professional journals.

He is married to Marjorie Tuainekore Crocombe, a Cook Islander, who has written a number of children's books as well as some academic publications on Pacific history, is editor of the Pacific creative arts journal MANA, and President of the South Pacific Creative Arts Society. She is also Director of Extension Services for the University of the South Pacific.